Praise for *The Intel*.

"This guide book brings a practical clar: navigated, and that is crucial; but even mo. .... of herself. Her humour [and] candour[, …] and the playful, ever-present encouragement of her tone[,] model the very joy she is writing about."

—Philip Shepherd, author of *Radical Wholeness* and *New Self, New World*

"I have reached for Celeste's book many times when life was confusing, tiring, and, let's admit it, lacking deep Joy. Her list of 'Joy Corruptors,' such as doubt, and her instructions to 'Do the following,' followed by some 'Reasons for the feeling,' are like an ER for difficult emotions that threaten to spiral out of control. Celeste doesn't work small, and her first-person narratives are often funny, cringe-worthy, and universal. We have all suffered from "idiot compassion," but how lovely to find a fellow traveller who points the way towards safer, more Joyful and compassionate shores. In *The Intelligent Body*, Celeste throws the whole circus of her heart onto the page. A powerful and enriching book that offers deep, true wisdom for those seeking to live in a kinder and more open-hearted way. A brave and compassionate book."

—Shannon Leahy, Head Lighthouse Keeper, lighthousestorytelling.com

"When Celeste was a very young woman, she experienced a profound transformation of consciousness that put her into a state the saints and mystics from different traditions have called everything from 'divine mystical union' to *samādhi*. At the very heart of this experience was a state of pure, unadulterated joy. In this state, Celeste came to know that joy not only permeates our cells but it is also our true state of being. What's more, it is the birthright of each and every one of us. In *The Intelligent Body*, a born storyteller takes you on an adventurous, and humorous, exploration of the body's wisdom and what it has meant for her—and what it can mean for you—to live in joy."

—Teri Degler, author of *The Divine Feminine Fire: Creativity and Your Yearning to Express Your Self* and *The Fiery Muse: Creativity and the Spiritual Quest*

"Reading this book was refreshing; it felt as though we were sitting together on a park bench, chatting about our lives. Celeste gave me permission to feel more joy, every day. It's where I can choose to live. Enjoy."

—Elizabeth Verwey, Spoken Lives: Stories Women Share, spokenlives.com

"It reads like a park-bench conversation."

—Gary Newman

"As a yoga teacher, Celeste has this infectiously magical way of helping her students feel more joyful, heartful, and present. Now, years of her teachings on living in joy and wonder can be found in her inspiring new book, *The Intelligent Body*. In it, Celeste uses humour and candour to open up about her own personal story, showing readers how to thrive through all that life throws at us, all while becoming "joy contagions" of our own."

—Adria Vasil, bestselling author of The Ecoholic Series and Yoga House student

"Spiced with unexpected personal stories about her own road to acquiring and retaining joy, this book is both accessible and engaging. And for those readers who want to skip the story and get right down to how to access joy, Shirley's appendices offer the bare bones of how to do it successfully. An entertaining and riveting work that provides scholarship and years of experience without readers even realizing they're learning something of value."

—Carol Nash, PhD, Scholar in Residence, Faculty of Medicine, University of Toronto

"I have the pleasure of being one of Celeste's students, and I am absolutely amazed by her first book. It is truly grounding, inspirational, and informative. Celeste is tapped into the natural wisdom of our bodies and is able to explain how we can also live with deep and lasting joy—even in times of extreme sadness. She does this in a way that is accessible and uses her own life stories to paint pictures of her insightful ideas and messages. You will not regret reading this. I am a different person for having done so.

—Jill Kovacs, Yoga House student

The Intelligent Body

*Finding Joy through
Your Body's Wisdom*

CELESTE SHIRLEY

www.celesteshirley.com

ISBN: 978-1-7753137-0-0 (softcover)
ISBN: 978-1-7753137-1-7 (ePub)

Project management by Heidy Lawrance, WeMakeBooks.ca
Cover design, text design, and layout by Kim Monteforte, WeMakeBooks.ca
Edited by Andrea Lemieux
Cover photo by Peter Ghiang and Ben Agbeke, taken of the author in Lake Ontario at Hanlon's Point in the spring of 2018. It took only forty minutes for her legs to thaw out after the photo shoot.
Back cover author photo by Diana Quintana-James

Every reasonable effort has been made to trace ownership of copyright materials. Information enabling the author to rectify any reference or credit in future printings will be welcomed.

The five quotes in this book by Jiddu Krishnamurti are from chapter one of his work Education and the Significance of Life (http://www.jkrishnamurti.org/krishnamurti-teachings/view-text.php?tid=51&chid=66876). These quotes were reproduced with permission.

Permission to quote from the works of J. Krishnamurti or other works for which the copyright is held by the Krishnamurti Foundation of America or the Krishnamurti Foundation Trust Ltd has been given on the understanding that such permission does not indicate endorsement of the views expressed in this publication.

For more information about J. Krishnamurti (1895–1986), please see http://www.jkrishnamurti.org.

The information in this book is not intended as a substitute for medical or professional advice. It is strictly the opinion of the author. It is recommended that you consult with your professional healthcare provider if you have any acute physical, mental, or emotional health concerns.

Second Printing, 2019
Printed and bound in Canada

Celeste with her daughter, Sarah

Celeste on the day she entered constant joy

For my mom
Thank you for your continued support
in getting this book out there.

For my daughter, Sarah
The day you were born was the
best day of my life.

CONTENTS

Part One: Joy Is …

Part Two: Joy Isn't …

Part Three: Constant Joy

Appendices

FOREWORD

The body is suffused with intelligence. That is so dramatically the case that the title of this book, *The Intelligent Body*, could lend itself to a broad range of subjects. It could examine how the dance of cells within us continuously transforms the parts of the world we call food, air, and water into our flesh and blood. Or it could focus on the intelligence of the immune system, which on a microscopic level can tell the difference between self and other—detecting, learning, acting, and remembering in order to keep us healthy. Or at how our very genes interact with the environment to adjust who we are epigenetically.

When Celeste Shirley draws our attention to the intelligent body, though, she is illuminating a very different sort of subject. Speaking to a culture that tends to live in the head and considers that a normal state, she is urging us with a playful wisdom to embrace the one intelligence we have that is alive to the felt experience of the present. The body's intelligence is the foundation of the most crucial freedom we could enjoy—the freedom to be fully who we are in each moment. To realize that freedom in your moment-to-moment living is to suffuse your life with the joy of being. That joy isn't just a pleasant state to visit once in a while: it is the ground of your reality. Without it you live in a distracted, anxious, disconnected state of unreality—which is precisely where a separation from the body's intelligence leads.

The Intelligent Body is a guide book written by someone who's been there—a companion for the reader's journey back home to what the body knows. And what the body knows, beneath all the abstracting, second-guessing, categorizing white noise of the head, is a joy so simple that young children plunge effortlessly into it. That experience of being, I believe, is the nourishment we most deeply hunger for in our lives.

Celeste Shirley neither oversimplifies nor overcomplicates the journey that reunites us with the body's intelligence. She deeply understands the pitfalls along the way, as well as the forms of support that help smooth the way, and she points out both clearly. So this guide book brings a practical clarity to the landscape to be navigated, and that is crucial; but even more crucial is what Shirley offers of herself. Her humour, candour, and personal anecdotes— and the playful, ever-present encouragement of her tone—model the very joy she is writing about in a way that illuminates it more clearly than any mere account could achieve. As you feel that joy, you will find it carrying you through these pages, and more deeply into yourself.

Philip Shepherd
Author of *Radical Wholeness*
and *New Self, New World*

ACKNOWLEDGEMENTS

This book would still be in a file somewhere if it weren't for the encouragement and support from Dave Pyette, my friend, and closet organizer—he got me to "come out" as a writer. Mom and Dad, thanks for supporting my writing process and seeing the finished product before I could. Diana, thank you for your continued wisdom and for making me pee my pants laughing throughout the editing journey. Thank you to my editor, Andrea Lemieux, whose dear voice and attentive, straightforward care caused me to look behind and see if there was a shepherd in my field. Shannon Leahy, you crazy kid of a writing coach with jackboots on, thanks for kicking into gear my ability to write the pieces that hurt. Thank you also to Heidy Lawrance of WeMakeBooks for your guidance; I knew to make my book with you the instant I met you. And thank you to Kim Monteforte for your artistic talents in doing the design and layout.

Thank you to Richard Geer for his poetry, which appears within these pages, and for his insightful prodding into discovering how to write "right."

And to my dearest Sarah, thank you for the assignment of being your mother. Thank you for the ways your unique soul brought forth the lessons.

And thank you to all my students and clients who grace The Yoga House and who fart in class, laugh until they cry, and still come the day after they have been diagnosed with breast cancer.

Spirit Animals Who Assisted Me
in the Completion of this Book

TURTLE

I was doing yoga on the dock when you popped up. It was October in Georgian Bay and it should have been cold. An Indian summer was upon us and the day was splendid. You looked up at me, chin stretched, and I, like a doofus, said, "Oh, hi!" So of course you dove under and swirled below the shimmering ripples.

Our spirit animals teach us to care for our needs, to mother our qualities, and be true to our paths. They help us be at home anywhere. Years ago I would go to the forest in High Park with my friend Gennie and my journal in hand. She would instruct us to draw an oval—a turtle shell—and then write in it what we wanted to invite into our lives.

After I had penned every entry into your shell, Gennie instructed us to write outside it what we wanted to let go of. Your shell housed my dreams all those years, and you had come back to see how they were doing.

MONARCH BUTTERFLY

The morning you were on the beach as the wind tore along the shore of Georgian Bay, the rising mango sun lit up your flailing, flopping form. You looked like a sideways red sailboat. You were holding onto the branch on the sand with your white-knuckled legs. When I picked you up, I thought I could actually feel your "paws" squeeze around my index finger. I carried you out of the wind to the back side of the cabin. I put you in the flowerpot to nestle in nectar. I came back again and again to check on you, and you hadn't moved an inch. I knew I needed to do something. I brought you inside the cabin, and for no apparent reason, other than that my feet took me there, I brought you over to my honey pot. I pulled out a spoon and watched you stick your long straw-like tongue in and suck up the honey! It was like watching an elephant dip its trunk into a pond. I was so delighted that you had brought us over to the honey. Then you flew to the window! Your wing seemed fine again and I opened the patio door and watched you sail off.

Your imaginal cells had spurred the next passage I was writing, which happened to be about transition. Your ability to surrender your life completely from land-rover caterpillar into a new form complete with wings to fly is my mental model of courage in life. Whenever I feel as if I'm going to be annihilated, I think, if you can do it, I can. Thanks for that.

OTTER

You were on the dock right by me when I looked up from bathing in the bay. I was looking for shiny rocks in the sand as they glistened under the water in the low morning sun. Our childlike wonder met. I tried to stay calm, as if having you visit me was the most natural thing in the world. It was your first visit, so I didn't want to startle you. You reminded me to keep writing in the light way I was inspired to, and not to feel as though I needed to provide evidence. In Celtic wisdom, the otter catches the salmon of wisdom when the others, more earnest, fail.

PILEATED WOODPECKER

I finished my last chapter to the beat of your drumming beak. You were my shaman, coaxing my editing into committed prose. You clobbered the tree along my driveway the entire day I was writing. The fiery red of your crown and fierce, rapid beats reminded me to stay with my passion. I see your pileated, raven-sized species only when I am up in Northern Ontario. I was on the beach and you were by my car up on the hill. At the end of the day on October 31, my daughter's birthday, I went to see what you had done. It looked as if the City had been there with their wood chipper. What a pile! If my car had been three feet to the left, it would have been covered. When I looked you up in my book on animal wisdom, it said that your drumming has deeply mystical implications: If you cross someone's path, you bestow upon them a wonderful power that can be accessed for the shamanic healing of others.

I heard somewhere that scientists are studying your beak in the hopes of designing better helmets.

SAW-WHET OWL

For six weeks you were right outside my yoga studio's window. You sat silently with your feathers fluffed up like a nest around your tiny head. Each day, many times a day, I would look out at you in the pine tree and visit. Your silent presence, your half-open yellow eyes two feet from my face, were not inquisitive. You were not looking out. You were deeply nestled within. You were brooding eggs. You were there right up until the big storm. I finished the manuscript the day you must have left the pine tree to shelter from the winds. Thank you for your matriarchal wisdom as I finished the last page of my manuscript.

PREFACE

When I was in the first trimester of my pregnancy, I had nasty nausea. Because of my education, I knew that the discomfort was from the hormone relaxin, which was allowing my abdominal muscles and my ribcage to stretch to make room for the growing uterus. Relaxin is undiscriminating and will go beyond its job requirement by also loosening the muscles in the intestines, and you feel pretty gross. So I became a physicist. I decided I would move all my blood to my arms and legs and went running. (Doesn't everybody?) With the redistribution of blood, this would immediately move the relaxin out of my stomach. Instant relief. Plus it felt great to run.

If I hadn't had my schooling I would have felt—well—nasty, and I probably would have stayed home and eaten saltines. I have been schooling myself in the use of my mind's energy since my first experience of constant joy at the age of twenty-one. I know exactly when I am in a joyful state and when I am caught in the nasty delusion of separation—a state in which we can all find ourselves. I have spent most of my life being fascinated by how our minds operate. I can determine whether I am living from joy-based thinking or from the separated duality channel that only feels nausea and forgets to be interested in why it's happening. The duality channel creates effort, struggle, and anus mouth (that's the circular O-shape your mouth makes when you think fiercely).

Non-duality, or joy, fosters clear thinking and inspired action. In this book I include only as much "schooling" as I needed to keep me from believing non-joy thoughts. My intention is to relate my personal stories to help you stay in joy, while at the same time I know this alone won't work. We *all* would have stayed in joy a long, long time ago if happy stories could hold us there. We'd all be carrying around *Chicken Soup for the Soul* and warding off any discrepancies as we read a paragraph about puppies and rainbows to revive us. Such stories don't work. For that reason, I show how our minds make us all joyless and how to catch the joy corrupters.

There are no commandments or affirmations in the book. I left out the "Seven Steps for Successful Joy" so you can feel for yours. I ask that you be unscientific. Please take a break from searching for evidence of joy while reading. Please suspend your thinking mind. Your thinking mind is a weapon here. I have included an "invisible" metal detector in the inside cover of this book and ask that you leave your left brain and all its heavy metal concepts at the door. Trust me, it will go off if you don't do this.

This book came from my own experiences and clear "knowings." All the information in this book could be backed up with empirical data from epigenetics, physiology, chakra therapy, happiness psychology, cognitive-behavioural therapy, dialectical behaviour therapy, applied kinesiology, neuroplasticity, quantum physics, mystical truth claims, endocrinology, and ever so many more—and I didn't.

You can trust that I dove into all those modalities after living the discoveries within and transmitted them into this book so you wouldn't need to read about the amygdala—in your brain. I did all the heavy lifting so you can read the lighter integrated side. You owe me—and yourself—to get light joyful and read with a curious and open mind.

When Constant Joy Began:
The Wizard of Oz of Bodybuilding

When I stepped on stage, my sense of being alive and complete absorbed into one moment. I filled in. I became all I am and all that I am here to do. And I was doing it. It was the Wizard of Oz moment; I went from black and white to full colour. At the age of twenty-one I came to know what life was for. It was for this feeling. The joy I felt was full on cellular. I was connected to, and in absolute harmony with, the world around me.

Now, just to take you into the scene, when you step on stage at a bodybuilding competition, you are practically naked. In so many ways. You are scantily clad in a Band-Aid of a string bikini to bare your muscular thighs, and your body fat is seven per cent (!)—and lower if you are male. You are also one hungry mama. You haven't had carbs of any kind except broccoli since Thursday, and it's Saturday. In all likelihood you feel weak. You are having a really hard time remembering your postal code or holding onto any kind of thought as your brain is in red alert from the low glycogen levels that reduce any subcutaneous water your skin may hold. If you see someone eating a muffin, you feel that you may jump them. Sorry, focus.

This carb depletion gets you so lean you look as though your skin has been shrink-wrapped. You have absolutely tight skin with no fat under it, you are super tanned, and it's probably a good-hair day since you have spent quite a bit of time on your appearance for the judges and your family in the audience. You have not brushed your teeth with toothpaste in the last forty-eight hours as you cannot allow any sodium to enter your saliva glands in case you hold water. You have just pumped up your muscles by doing push-ups, squats, towel rows, and bicep curls backstage.

Let's just say you are pretty ready to peacock-present yourself after the months, or in my case years, of training that you have invested to be the most symmetrically muscular and lean woman you can be. So here I am in that moment. I step on stage and have not one mental iota of *presenting* myself. I am celebrating Self. I am celebrating life and all that it is. There is a picture of me smiling and leaning into the woman next to me. I am telling her, "You've got this!" I knew she would win. My feeling of joy went out everywhere. (She won.) I feel as though I'm at a carnival or in New Orleans caught up in the frolicking wave of abandoned street dancing. I am supposed to be concentrating on my dance routine, which I am about to do for the judges, to present the muscular physique I have been sculpting. I feel so happy I just want to go around and see everyone and appreciate how great they look. Yet they all look so serious. Oh, that's right, they are my competitors. Silly me. I feel so connected and a part of life that it is not possible to view any part of life as separate from me. I can't *compete*! Against what?

I go on stage and have a wonderful time moving felinely and lyrically with great prowess into poses. Front double biceps. Side chest pose. Rear double biceps. The feeling of oneness with life is so complete; there is no *me* presenting this body. I feel I am one with the audience, judges, and you, if you were alive somewhere. I do my routine and I quite honestly go to the moon. At exactly the same time, I feel just as I had before stepping on stage. I didn't feel elated—as if I'd had an epiphany or that I had been reborn at the top of the mountain and all *that* jazz. I felt quite run-of-the-mill, middle-path average, except I knew exactly what I *was* in that moment. I was everything. I also felt as if all that was happening was being orchestrated by an invisible harmonics engineer. Maybe it was Dr. Seuss himself, who was noted for saying "there is fun to be done."

Afterwards I'm quite ready to go home, but I stay as this *is* a competition and I am interested in the results. *My* results were in, and how I felt was telling me: You are complete. I didn't need to know anything past the moment I had posed on stage.

When I returned to university on Monday, my classmates and professors asked me how I did. I had to stop myself from claiming "I won." That March 16th day in 1985, I set a cellular template for the rest of my life on the stage of Northern Secondary High School's auditorium in Toronto. If you, the reader, trust what you read, you can believe that I felt the perfect semblance of enthusiasm, clarity, joy, passion, and calm that showed me what life is for: *to be exactly who we are in the way we need to and live this each moment—* through our actions and thoughts.

That's it. You can close the book now. This was a quickie book. And I truly wish you find it that easy to live in joy all the time. It *is* that simple. It's that we create complications and try to figure life out, and this only creates speed bumps. For that reason, there is a book—the book you are holding in your perfect hands will show you that, well … you are perfect. Perfect in all your aspects. If I told my classmates that I had come in seventh that day, the next question they would have asked would have been how many competitors there were (answer: fourteen). But that was not a question! To me, I had won. I did all that I set out to do and felt completely who I was on stage. That's all I needed. I told the truth to my friends, of course, the factual answer with the number seven defining my placement. I had produced the *realistic* answer to meet their question. If they had asked me how I felt about the competition, I could have answered with the truth, which is where the life is: I experienced all that I am and how to *be* it. The levity of the joy I felt changed me completely. All I had ever known about life and how to live in it was cancelled. I knew a fresh clarity that replaced how I had perceived life up until then. I felt an intelligence that now was *who* I was.

*"To understand life is to understand
ourselves, and that is both the beginning
and the end of education."*

~ JIDDU KRISHNAMURTI (1895–1986), INDIAN
PHILOSOPHER, SPEAKER, AND WRITER

INTRODUCTION

*"The teacher who is indeed wise does not bid you
to enter the house of his wisdom but rather leads
you to the threshold of your mind."*

~ KAHLIL GIBRAN (1883–1931), LEBANESE POET

To live in joy is to live exactly as yourself. You feel alive and free no matter what happens in your life. The experience of constant joy is so completely *who* you are that how you feel doesn't fluctuate. You say what you have to say, you feel what you feel, and you do what is important to you. This allows for steady living. What you feel and what you do are congruent. You can rely on yourself.

The first time I experienced constant joy was after the body-building competition, and it lasted for three months. From that moment on, everything that happened in my life felt like a bonus. Each moment of life was another *experience*. That I could keep having *more* experiences was a dizzying privilege. I had a constant feeling of perfection in whatever was happening. Life became a vivid display of non-stop perfect moments. All my faculties were enhanced. I couldn't *use* any of my senses. They were all being utilized exactly as needed: I didn't need to watch or read with my eyes, I saw what was essential. I knew that everything was here. There was nothing to *do*. Life was already complete. I was complete.

The assertion "I could die now" would have expressed how I felt, and the bonus was that I could keep living knowing *this* without the drama of needing to croak. I knew that this was the only way we are ever to feel. The "this" was later revealed to me.

Four years later, I read about my experience in a book, *The Myth of Freedom and the Way of Meditation*, by Chögyam Trungpa, one of North America's Buddhist teachers. When I read his description of non-duality I practically stood up and cheered as someone understood what I had experienced and was describing it precisely. It was after reading this book that I understood the experience of constant joy to be a state of consciousness referred to as "non-duality." I was twenty-five years old when I discovered this description of my uninterrupted joy. That book became a part of my wardrobe. It was always on my person. It became so worn and tattered that it fell into pieces. I would carry around a ten-page piece in a pocket and read it daily, wherever I was, in line at Loblaws, waiting for my nephew to wake up from a nap in the car, everywhere I could get a glimpse. I felt this absolute resolve that if I could understand the state, then I would be a candidate to invite it back into my being. It seemed that if I could practise the disciplines of meditation and contemplation presented in the book, I might re-evoke the state.

Yet at the back of my mind, this felt like a lot of effort. Since I had not been "practising" any discipline when constant joy had taken over, why would I need to start now? That year I experienced it again when I gave birth to my daughter, Sarah. (Just to be ever so clear, childbirth lacks joy-filled sensations.) I recognized the pattern. It occurred when I brought myself to an edge and went further in my life. I sensed that if I stayed intentional and followed through with the goals in my heart, especially the biggies, I would experience joy constantly.

I experienced constant joy eight more times, which now equated to ten times. The first time at twenty-one lasted for three months(!), some of the times were for minutes, other times were for hours, and once, following a drunken evening in cottage country, for four days! Another time I was walking along Bloor Street in downtown Toronto, and, voilà, I randomly returned to non-duality for five blocks.

The confounding thing was that I was practising Ashtanga yoga only one of the times that I found myself in the "state" of non-duality, so that didn't explain the other nine times. How could they qualify? I was certain I had to earn this lofty state since it was described as a level of supra-consciousness. Who was I to randomly enter it? Was I a random "non-dualist" and didn't need to practise? That seemed arrogant to me, and I am terrified of being a big shot. Who did I think I was? Some kind of exception to the rules? And then it occurred to me: There are no rules in non-duality. There were no rules when I was *in it*, and there cannot be rules prescribing what I need to do to experience it again. I realized you don't *enter* constant joy, it happens. It takes over and becomes you. It initializes instantly and feels anything but miraculous. It feels seamless and normal. It's not a big deal at all. I don't want to present this experience of constant joy as something that you aren't already. *It is who you are.*

Let me back up. Living joy constantly is you—the you who is here in this moment. Non-stop joy is the innocent, curious you before all the careful conditioned thinking thinned you out and wore you out. That vibrancy living in you can be *uninterrupted*, no matter what is happening and no matter what you are feeling. Honest.

I don't want to *tell* you how to reach this experience as this would be a disservice and just wrong. Since you *are* pure joy, then I don't technically need to point out *how* to be it. If I outline what constant joy is, and you see it as a state of a highly functioning mind or, even worse, a spiritual aspiration, then I have misrepresented joy. My aspiration is that you will know how it feels to be you, which is what joy feels like. *Simply, the experience of constant joy is to be exactly who you are no matter what is happening around you.* That is what this book is about: ways to feel who you are.

Most people don't think constant joy is possible. There is one reason for this: *the need to feel in control.* We keep trying to control how we feel. We are so resistant to our feelings and how they could *interfere* with our day that we don't even trust them. What we don't know is that the intelligence in the emotion unlocks our cellular genius. This genius reveals a dynamic stamina for adaptation that far supersedes trying to stay focused.

How can I *teach* you how to reach an experience of constant joy? I can't. It's not possible. Joy cannot be taught. Joy is *not* accessed through intentional thinking. This is *not* a remedial project. Joy is to live in harmony with the intelligence that blinks your eyes and beats your heart. Joy is within you. Since it is currently beating your heart, how do you touch down into this voluntary intelligence? *Through the body's wisdom of feelings.* The intelligence of felt feelings and their accompanying inner promptings direct a life of joy.

I will outline the qualities of joy and how to keep it alive. Alongside this dissection you will see the ways that we mess joy up and how to stop that. When you can't feel joy, you are *viewing* a moment in your life as good or bad. If you were late while standing and waiting for the bus and thought (or said out loud because you're menopausal), "Where's the bus?" with vehemence, which is a pretty way of saying pissed off, then joy got corrupted. If you're late waiting for the bus and think, "When I get there it will be closer to lunchtime." Then you are in joy.

I am so delighted you are here because I sense that by reading this book you will enhance who you are. You will understand what is important to you and feel the potent promptings that are your natural inspiration. Natural inspiration comes from feeling. I will reveal how you can trust your feelings. Trusting how you feel is messy, yet massively revealing and helps you see how capable you are of experiencing life directly. The best part is that drama will leave your building. You will feel how to be with "what is" happening and lack the consciousness to call it difficult, even if it is—and you can prove it. Instead, you will experience effortful moments directly. That's how joy works: You experience all of life's moments directly and don't need to notice the harsh, impossible moments because they help guide your actions as they are happening. Real life examples will follow. Now let us begin your real life.

"There is an efficiency inspired by love which goes far beyond and is much greater than the efficiency of ambition; and without love, which brings an integrated understanding of life, efficiency breeds ruthlessness."

~ JIDDU KRISHNAMURTI (1895–1986),
INDIAN PHILOSOPHER,
SPEAKER, AND WRITER

PART ONE

Joy is ...

"Keep knocking, and the joy inside
will eventually open a window
and look out to see who's there."

~ RUMI (1207–1273), PERSIAN POET,
PHILOSOPHER, THEOLOGIAN,
AND SUFI MYSTIC

CHAPTER ONE

Joy Is Not Happiness

The *Oxford Dictionary* describes "joy" as "a feeling of great pleasure and happiness." Yet to constantly live in joy, you are not always happy.

Happiness is pending; that is, because it is a feeling, it wavers. It wanes after the shine of a new purchase has worn off, or when you are concerned about your relationship. Happiness is based on *how* you feel. If you feel good, you feel happy. If you experience great loss, happiness gets cancelled by the feeling of sadness. This is *not* the case with joy. Joy never wanes; no matter how you feel, joy is always there.

> Joy is a mind that experiences life free of emotional tampering.

Joy is referred to in Tibetan Buddhism as "non-duality," which is the ability to live with what is happening in your day without separating yourself from it. A non-dual existence means you are, as Jesus said, of this world, not in this world. Thank you, Jesus. You feel a part of life. Instead of categorizing your life's circumstances as pleasurable or difficult, a mind in non-duality simply experiences; each moment in your life is an experience.

When in joy, you don't need to understand what is happening in your life. Trying to understand or analyze what is happening separates you from your experiences. Joy is the free mind that doesn't need to analyze or use mental tactics to be free. You can set your analyst and therapist free. Unless you like them.

A mind in joy is *not* a sacred practice of intentional mindfulness. It is not practised with protocol. You do not have to sit in lotus position. In our Western culture, just as yoga has become an industry, mindfulness is the new stress management and mental flossing. Joy is *not* a practice. Joy is yoking with each moment of your life.

Joy is a non-virtuous way of living. No religion, moral code, or mental tool manages your behaviour or directs you. In non-duality, or joy, you feel alive in each moment, exactly as it occurs.

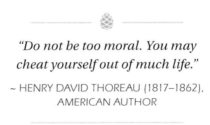

"Do not be too moral. You may cheat yourself out of much life."

~ HENRY DAVID THOREAU (1817–1862),
AMERICAN AUTHOR

Joy Is Permanent

Joy, or non-duality, is permanent. Joy is our baseline. Why? Because joy is not dependent on thoughts. Joy does not derive from thoughts. It does not derive from joy-filled thoughts. It's there all the time.

Just as oxygen is in your lungs, even when your nose is stuffy, joy is always there, even if you have a painful experience.

Joy has a vibrational tone that permeates your cells so completely that you simply cannot experience pain as being wasteful. You cannot experience disappointment or feel discouraged. You are simply not able to experience great life changes or slight annoyances without being broadened and informed by them. This means you get upgraded to a larger version of you.

This larger you is you with experience badges on your heart. You are a boy-/girl-/trans-scout who is bruised and still selling cookies. Often you don't even need time to grieve, or process what has happened to you. By being "in" your life as it is, you process the experience.

When big changes occur, you can work with them and make necessary adaptations. You are more flexible and feel informed by what is happening. At exactly the same time, you *may need to step out of life to grieve if the circumstances are extremely difficult.* There are simply no foundational codes of conduct that you need to live by. You simply live. If you need to grieve, you grieve, and this doesn't interfere with your day. Instead, the slowing down and tenderizing effect you get from feeling grief allows for a softer, less grating experience of your day.

In fact, life assists the adaptations you need that allow you to experience exactly what you need. It's as if the whole world is conspiring to work in favour of your highest growth. Which is *exactly* what it's doing.

This way of living is so unimaginable to us. It sounds suspicious to our thinking minds. (Which you were supposed to leave with the [heavy] metal detector.) Constant joy? How can we feel joy always? We can't comprehend that we could constantly feel joy when life is so erratic. How can life be experienced joyfully when great, painful events occur? The answer to this logical question is simple. In joy you simply can't have a view that these painful events are "bad."

Joy includes all emotions, painful or exhilarating. Although joy is believed to be happiness, it is actually all emotions dropped into it. Joy has the melting-pot capacity to infiltrate into and utilize all emotions' powerful messages. For this reason, joy is fearless.

Our task as humans interested in how to live joyfully all the time is to notice how we feel and allow the emotions to roil through us rather than define us. We recognize that the feelings are showing us what is important. We feel the emotions' ability to usher us towards true action or non-action. They are useful. Joy constantly reveals what we need, want, feel, and know.

*"Know what you want and all the universe
conspires to help you achieve it."*

~ PAULO COELHO,
BRAZILIAN NOVELIST

Joy Is Our Cellular Metabolic Intelligence

I am six years old in grade one and sitting on the cool marble floor with a classmate. We have been assigned a problem to solve in pairs. There isn't enough space in our classroom for the pairs to spread out. To solve this, our teacher has sent the two of us out into the hallway to discuss the problem.

It takes some time for our lovely teacher, Miss Evans, to go around to each pair individually in the classroom to find out what they've discovered. Eventually, she comes out to us. I have no recollection of what the problem was. I only remember how it felt to realize the solution.

When Miss Evans comes out to us, I start to inflate into a delighted Thumper the rabbit from the movie *Bambi*. I swear my right foot was slapping the ground in sheer cheerleader excitement. I start to tell her the solution we had discovered. As I am about to describe how we know it's the right solution, I pause. I am filling with a sense of such wonder, awe, and expanding consciousness that I am feeling a huge love. I cannot believe how perfect what I know is. As I start to describe the solution, I realize that I didn't know what I was about to say before. Ever! Yes, what I was about to describe, revealed an awareness of something I had not known fifteen minutes earlier. This was incredible! Can this be true?

As I describe the solution and tell my lovely teacher (she is beaming as if her whole role as "teacher" is being realized), she is delighted to see my fascination with life. I tell her I had never known this until now, and that this had happened *last week* too! I continue to expand and feel lit up from the inside until I meet a climactic realization that connected me into an eternal sense of oneness— at the ripe age of six—that I know something I never knew before this, and it's going to keep on happening for my entire life!

In our physical development, at six years old we are on the cusp of solidifying how our thinking minds will govern our behaviour. *You can think of the non-thinking aspect of your soul as your innocent self who only knows how to experience.* It knows only how to feel and act. At about six it begins to fuse with the conditioning we receive as we grow. We learn codes of conduct, proper behaviour, phonics, how to hold a pencil, how to ride a bike, manners, how to hold a fork, how to tie our shoes, and not to tickle our sister while she's drinking milk. All of these learned skills and manners fill and develop our thinking minds.

According to Swiss psychologist Jean Piaget's stages of cognitive development, the ages from two to seven are termed "preoperational." During this time, young children become intuitive, perceptually driven, and egocentric. The mind starts to develop the sense of a separate self. This separate self creates preferences and *chooses* how it will act. Before this stage, we never thought about how we were to behave. Instead, we were guided by what felt good or what satisfied a need.

By the ages of five to seven, this thinking mind starts to govern our actions. We learn what constitutes appropriate behaviour. We learn what will be rewarded and what will bring punishment or be disagreeable. Some of us experience the more painful version: We learn what will be considered appropriate behaviour as love and care are withheld. Each learned experience develops grooves in the mind. These pathways become well traversed and, eventually, memorized.

This is the most powerful and pivotal time in the development of our minds. Our earliest influences determine whether we will carefully repeat successful responses or feel free to explore and discover our world. If we keep up the memorized safe responses, we often self-monitor for much of our lives and use guilt tactics to keep ourselves in check. We may forget what we really want to do.

In that moment out in the hallway, my swelling sense of oneness with life connected the thinking mind to its true purpose—to experience each moment of life as if it were a brand new occurrence. I felt the purpose of my life in every cell of my being. Our non-thinking minds are our sense of wonder. The joy-filled mind that acts in ways that express who we are.

I recalled this grade-one moment only a year ago, when I was writing this book. The experience was identical to the feeling I had of entering constant joy at twenty-one. Joy filled my being in that hallway. What I couldn't register at the time was that I was feeling exactly how life is to be lived.

"Living has yet to be generally recognized as one of the arts."

~ KARL DE SCHWEINITZ (1887–1975),
SOCIAL WELFARE ADMINISTRATOR,
EDUCATOR, AND HISTORIAN

CHAPTER TWO

Joy is Trust

Broke and Prosperous

In July 1998, I bought my first house. A small starter, semidetached, in the east end of Toronto in an up-and-coming area of the Upper Beaches. It was a whopping 900 square feet. At the time it was one of the only areas of Toronto that had a house I could afford.

Buying this house took every penny I had. I used all of my savings, including all retirement savings plans. I was committed. As a single, self-employed mom, I needed to prove that I could pull this off. It took every angle of financial "savvy" (swanky word for bolstering numbers) to work out a way to purchase the property. On July 30, I closed the deal.

I took a month to move in and unpack. My nine-year-old daughter, Sarah, was staying at her father's during summer vacation, and I spent this time, between teaching sessions, to set up our home. The day after I moved in, Sarah came to see her new room, home, and 'hood. We went to Monarch Park right by our house. Monarch is a huge park with a recreational centre and outdoor pool. It takes up an entire city block. We climbed on the swing, she on my lap, and rocked back and forth. We were there until my hips went numb.

The sun was shining and it was one of those super splendid days Chicago sings about in *Saturday in the Park*. As we looked out over the playground and rolling hills, a palpable magic was in the air. I felt so happy and proud, having invested in myself this way and provided a home for Sarah and me in such a gorgeous neighbourhood.

I drove to this neighbourhood for a month before signing for the purchase of the property. I sat and meditated in this park. I watched the activity, the families, and the dog walkers. I did yoga on the grass. Not in the dog area (poop joke!). I parked my car in front of the house I was going to purchase, sometimes for half an hour at different times of the day, watching the activity. I made my business calls and did my paperwork in the front seat.

Fortunately, no one called the police. I watched the people going in and out of their small semis. I introduced myself to the homeowners and told them I may be moving into number forty-seven. They were warm, outgoing, and friendly. The five houses around me were all single-parent families, with children Sarah's age! It was a perfect fit. I felt safe and assured that this was the neighbourhood for us.

Now, swaying on the swing with Sarah curled on my lap, we were like a happy pine cone. I felt as if we were nestled into and merging with the tree of life itself. We were one with the day and the sparkling park life around us. All barriers were removed.

As we swung back and forth, a small, muscular man dressed up in a colourful body suit stepped before us. That's the only way I can describe what he was wearing. It was some kind of stretchy yet stylish suit that a circus performer would wear. A large square climbing jungle gym sat in front of the swing set. He stood in front of it, standing like a mountain, arms stretched down his sides, chin lifted and face alert, as if he were greeting the queen. He turned to us and did a tiny, humble bow. He had on makeup: sparkly eye shadow, lipstick. and eyeliner. Swear to God.

He then ceremoniously jumped up onto the bars and started

to perform Cirque du Soleil–like manoeuvres. He was good! After a particular movement, he would turn his eyes towards us and give a coy smile, brighten his look with a flash, and then continue. His eyes were playful and penetrating.

He was not a park freak. I got the impression that he was a brave soul on his way home from performing at a kids' party and took a break at the park. Then he saw us and decided to give us a fabulous show. That's what I told myself. For it was so magical that I couldn't really believe what was happening!

At the same time it was right in sync with how wondrous I was feeling. Sarah, of course, was her usual wondrous self. She kept looking at him and at times up at me from my lap as if to say, "Cool." He "performed" his talented gymnastics for quite a while. There was no one in our immediate vicinity at the time. I remember wondering if this was actually happening. Was this really occurring? Was he *real*? I felt a hiccup of disbelief. I actually did a check-in with myself to see if I was really here and that he was really there. He was. Sarah was. This was real.

At the end of his "performance," he jumped in front of us, just as ceremoniously, with a curtsy. This five-foot-five man was done. We clapped. He left as quietly as he had entered the playground, closing the gate as he disappeared. There was this naturalness to the whole event, as if this was what was to occur at Monarch Park on this particular Saturday afternoon.

I was in awe, yet at the same time it felt natural. As if life was supposed to be this enchanting and charmed! (Which, of course, upon writing this passage I realized it *is*.) I felt filled with an enthusiasm as if the reward of buying this house, moving here, and basking in the new neighbourhood park was the perfect celebration. Yes, my body, my being, felt celebratory.

Next, a woman in her seventies parked herself on the swing beside us. She arrived a few minutes after the circus performer. Was there a schedule? Sarah and I were still hanging out on the swing, toes pointed, swirling snake designs in the sand. We continued chatting and turned to include her. She leaned into us, swinging and twisting side to side.

The woman lived in a local retirement home. We talked about how wonderful it is to swing, and how great it is for the spirit. And hips. We decided that every retirement home needed a swing set and that it may reduce hip replacements in the future. We decided we needed to call Reuters with this information. It was news.

We felt happy and alive on that swing in the park. After sharing stories, and solving world peace, we swung for a time in silence. We swayed under the dappled sunlight of those giant hundred-year-old oaks that formed a canopy over us and encompassed our increasing joy. Sarah snuggled into my lap as the woman swayed side to side beside us.

She was a small woman with dyed chestnut-brown hair and a hip, grandmotherly way about her. Her eyes were warm, bright, and curious. After a period of silence as we absorbed the beauty of the day, she got up and we said our goodbyes.

She said, "I know I don't know you, but I wish you the most magical and beautiful life." I felt she was speaking The Truth. She was like some Jesus figure walking up to us in the park and telling us what life would be like from now on. I knew it was true.

The shine of her remark embedded itself into me like a seed of germinating intelligence: *Live magically.* Yes, from here on in, live with abandonment and trust. I was so grateful. With that she was gone. *She* was definitely real.

Sarah went back to her dad's the next day. I continued to unpack boxes and dig and plant in the garden. I ran on the beach every day. It was a nineteen-minute run through the winding streets from my home until my heel hit the boardwalk of The Beaches of east Toronto. I was alive and enjoying the quiet summer months as many of my clients were away, allowing me time to unpack our stuff.

I would often go for a run, come back soaked with sweat, and head right for the garden fresh with ideas. I looked like Pig-Pen from the *Peanuts* comic strip. I got lost in the creation of the garden. I remember the exuberance I felt from investing in myself. I was the Energizer Bunny with a shovel.

One day I opened a letter from my bank and found a returned cheque stamped NSF. It was for a fairly small amount. Then, over the next two days, I received four phone calls from others whose cheques from me had bounced. I was stunned and confused. I couldn't figure out how this was possible. I had been meticulous about my running account balance because I had written the largest cheques in the history of my cheque-writing life!

Making the down payment for my house was the biggest financial transaction I had ever made. I wrote that dollar figure out *very* carefully in my chequebook. I couldn't figure out how this overdraft had happened. I contacted all the affected people and sent them another cheque or delivered the funds. I apologized. Everyone was gracious and understanding. I had just enough money to pay them. There was nothing left. Not a nickel. I didn't even go out for a cup of coffee. Especially at Starbucks.

Realizing I was temporarily absolutely fund-less, or what most would call "broke," I decided I would turn it into an adventure and line up free activities. I didn't feel broke. It was just the *fact* of the situation. I organized biking trips with friends in the country. They would drive, so I didn't need to pay for gas. I couldn't even buy gas at the time.

I ate simple, inexpensive veggies and any protein I still had in the cupboard. People would call me up to take me out for lunch, as if they were aware that I needed a meal. It was humorously amazing to see how life was supporting me! I felt truly embraced, humbled—and unconcerned; however, the feeling of being unconcerned was a choice. I initially felt worried about the unexplained overdraft, yet I knew I had enough for the mortgage and bills from then on, and that this was only temporary.

I recognized that day when I opened the envelope from the bank that the NSF cheque was simply a fact. I could feel the alarm rise in my body like a gasp. At exactly the same moment, I recognized it as a test: Was I going to let it take me down, or was I going to keep living with the same zeal?

I vividly remember realizing that my choice would determine if I would continue to feel the same wonderment or let the "fact" dampen my summer.

Sarah was away at her dad's for the rest of the month, and I continued excitedly to unpack and plant a huge garden, complete with the help of the construction crew that was building townhouses ten houses down.

This crew delivered two huge boulders that I added to the landscape. They loaned me their industrial-strength wheelbarrow and insisted on taking the soil I was digging out of my garden and dumping it as landfill in their construction site. I felt like Cinderella commandeering the birds in the forest. Men at my disposal, with hard hats and shovels, does it get any better? I ask you (women)! I was certifiably happy and temporarily penniless.

Six weeks after receiving the NSF cheque from the bank, I received another NSF cheque! I thought, "Dear God!" The cheque was the identical stationery as my own cheques. Only this cheque was *to me*!

It was from Sally, a longstanding client. I knew there must have been some random error, and I could simply have Sally give me a new cheque the next day when I saw her for her session. The amount of this cheque was significant. It would mean that I would have absolutely no financial worries as I had already covered all my bills and hadn't spent any more money. It would mean I would go from being in the red to green, green pastures. In my mind, I had never left the pasture.

One of the best moments during the delivery of the giant boulders was when the men came with their Bobcat carrying the first boulder. This boulder was the size of half a Smart car! The foreman driving the Bobcat said, "Where do you want it, Celeste?" I put my hands on my hips and said, looking from one part of the property to another, "Let's see ... how about ... well, no, that won't work. ... How about over here, no, I mean over there." It was ever so fun.

Learn to Trust in "Easy"

"Is there anything more dangerous than getting up in the morning and having nothing to worry about, no problems to solve ...? That state can be a threat to your health. If untreated, it incites an unconscious yearning for any old dumb trouble that might rouse some excitement."[1]

ROB BREZSNY, AMERICAN
ASTROLOGER AND AUTHOR

I discovered that when I am living in constant joy, when everything is moving in an accelerated manner, I don't know how to trust it. For example, when life is going well, I feel as if I can't handle it. It feels as though the hard wiring in me can handle things only when I need to *do something*, but cowers when I need to receive and trust that everything will unfold without my needing to do a thing.

When I can't trust that I can trust, my whole posture contracts like a drying sponge. I remember teaching a dance exercise class in a corporate setting and getting right into a groove riff. One of the participants at the front of the class yelled out her excitement, "You go girl!" The class was grooving with the energy and rhythm

---

[1]Rob Brezsny, *Pronoia Is the Antidote for Paranoia: How the Whole World Is Conspiring to Shower You with Blessings* (Berkeley, CA: North Atlantic Books, 2009), 77.

going down. This woman was someone I highly respected, and considered to be so fit, successful, and everything I'm not that I was instantly terrified. My insecurities flared, "Oh, who am *I* to be so dancerly and leading *her*. I immediately separated from life. My ego self-deflated any sense of dance ability I had. I felt frozen.

What a terrible feeling! There I was with everyone with me, and I stumbled because they knew this was a stunning moment where anything could happen. Why?

Why do we believe that when life is going well it will inevitably end? (Or is it just me?) Why is there this insidious visceral vibration that is poised for struggle and just waiting for it to show up?

What is this home-wrecker that says, "Oh yeah, you may *think* your life is going well, but just don't get too comfortable, proud, or used to it. You can't really live this way! For that would just be way too easy." For example, you may need to have something fixed, and you walk right past someone who could fix it because you don't want to bother them. Meanwhile, out in the real world, they would have been delighted to help.

The other day my friend Renée was on her way to an appointment when she got a flat tire on her bike. The friend she was meeting is a time-snob and always punctual. At that moment, her cellphone rang; it was her friend calling to say she would be twenty minutes late. Renée laughed and said, "Perfect, me too." Then Renée noticed that her mind was telling her she could find an easy way to fix this. So all she did was look up.

She saw a young man on the sidewalk across the street with ten bikes in front of him. It was a pop-up bike-repair depot. He was using a tire pump and pumping up a tire. Renée laughed out loud. Then she thought, "Oh, I can't just go over and pay him to pump up my tire, I really better go to a gas station." Renée called her sister to get the location of a gas station close by (no Googling back then), and although the bike pump was right across the street, she did the Toronto "big city" thing and didn't *bother* him, and like a good, decent girl, she hauled her bike over to the not-so-handy gas station.

After pumping up her tire, she rode on to the restaurant to meet her punctual friend. When she arrived, the tire was flat, yet again. She groaned as she realized that she would have to walk her bike over to the local bike store, which she did after her lunch with her friend. When she walked into the bike store she told the guy that the tire must need a new inner tube because it had gone flat after she had pumped it up. The bike guy asked, "Did you fill it up at a gas station, or did you use a bicycle pump?"

She didn't know how this could be so important and decided to humour him. Rather annoyed, she said, "Gas station."

He smiled and said, "You need to use a bicycle pump because it has the right gauge setting for the tire. Gas-station pumps won't work. They always go flat again."

Renée looked at him. "Of course," she thought.

It is rather confounding that we often walk past lovely angels, complete with bicycle pumps, and go to the inappropriate, not-as-convenient gas stations in life. It is *not* ironic. Ironic is defined as coincidental or unexpected, as in, "It was ironic that I was seated next to my ex-husband at the dinner."

It is confounding, confusing—and usually quite normal—to live in this arrested, imprisoned manner where we believe that life just *can't* be *this* easy. But just to save time, it is that easy. Life is that easy. It is natural to experience ease and connection in life with what is important to you.

*"The world is full of magical things patiently
waiting for our wits to grow sharper."*

~ BERTRAND RUSSELL (1872–1979),
BRITISH PHILOSOPHER

True Use of Your Mind

This ease you experience in constant joy can occur only if you use your mind effectively. A mind in constant joy uses its energy in two ways only: (1) To be aware—not think and "figure it all out," and (2) To live in inquiry—ask questions. Questions open us up to receiving. Receiving allows us to experience ease. Receiving will feel weird. You won't trust it. You may for a minute, maybe even for six months. Then, when you need to stick with what you know you need to do, trust will leave your building.

This is a powerful moment. When trust wanes, we are being tested to see if we can *keep on trusting*. If we have the stamina of mind to stay open to receiving, everything would go so very well, even if we hadn't planned it.

> "As God and Satan were walking down the street one day, the Lord bent down and picked something up. He gazed at it glowing radiantly in his hand. Satan, curious, asked, 'What's that?' 'This,' answered the Lord, 'is Truth.' 'Here,' replied Satan as he reached for it, ' let me have that—I'll organize it for you.'"[2]

It is so hard to trust in *easy*. We question and poke at "easy" to see if it will flinch. Then we believe it will fail, since, let's face it, everything has an expiry date, and there are no exceptions.

When your "easy channel" starts to reach its internal expiry date and you no longer know how to allow your life to go so well,

[2]Rick Fields with Peggy Taylor, Rex Wyler, and Rick Ingrasci, *Chop Wood, Carry Water: A Guide to Finding Spiritual Fulfillment in Everyday Life* (New York: New Age Communications, Inc., 1984), 283. Used by permission of Tarcher, an imprint of Penguin Publishing Group, a division of Penguin Random House LLC. All rights reserved.

then you need to start trusting—*again*. A mind in joy is a purely present mind. It doesn't get all "efforted"; it actually doesn't know how. If we *could* keep experiencing an aware, present mind, our lives would flow effortlessly. Yes, effortlessly. There will be bumps, grinds, and extremely bad-hair days. There will be people who mindfuck. There will be tumours, bunions, and the city sending us newly revised taxes. Life will still be there. Yet, when in joy, you will trust again. The flow will continue. The flow you feel inside will experience life's events, flinching, yet not actually fluctuating because of it.

We keep forgetting that these moments in our lives, when doubt enters our day, are a test to see if we will go off course. The doubt isn't really *real*. It's actually a *provision*. It is an interruption to see if we will keep trusting ourselves to do what we know we need to do.

Once again, we *must* "keep trusting." It's super-redundant to keep living in joy. You keep on doubting the doubt. Until eventually, when you feel doubt, you kind of appreciate it because you know you're growing. Then it's not so bad.

Doubt becomes that annoying boy or girl who teased and bullied you when you were a kid, and now you know it was because they were jealous of you or liked you.

Doubt, being the opposite of trust, is convincing when we don't know what to do. Doubt wants to start something. Anything. Especially self-sabotaging thoughts to kick over your furniture. If doubt does not disturb *you*, it will settle for a fight with someone else. You will project the doubt onto some innocent bystander, such as your partner since they're usually the handiest, causing a misunderstanding. Doubt will sabotage you, creating despair, disappointment, depression, anxiety, lack of focus, or a sense of failure. You may even try to distract yourself and go to a movie, surf the internet, shop, eat popcorn, clean the closet (if you do, please come to my house), or really go for it and affect your mind with drugs, alcohol, or meaningless sex. (Not that sex is meaningless.)

Doubt makes us become super busy. You may offset doing something for eight years because you feel you need to stay at your job. The doubt keeps you small, wavering, and you turn into a dull … I have to stop! This is just too hard to write. The doubt says, "Who do you think you are?"

That's where I come in. It's intervention time. The doubt-squabble is over. You can keep up the fight; you can rumble around in there and keep knocking over your furniture and *not* do what is really meaningful. *Or* … you can catch the doubting thoughts as they occur. When I feel I need to put the laundry away (or reply to that email) just when I have set aside time to write, I know I am doubting myself. Why would I suddenly become June Cleaver? My closet was actually super orderly when I finished this book. A bonus of energy is bestowed upon us when we do what is most important. Somehow—mystically—we get everything else done that needs doing. Ain't doubt grand?

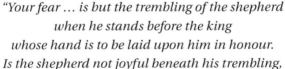

"Your fear … is but the trembling of the shepherd
when he stands before the king
whose hand is to be laid upon him in honour.
Is the shepherd not joyful beneath his trembling,
that he shall wear the mark of the king?
Yet is he not more mindful of his trembling?"

~ KAHLIL GIBRAN, FROM "THE PROPHET"

Doubt feels like an interruption. When you feel interrupted by doubt, let the doubt *really* interrupt you. Feel the interruption as a stuck growth spurt. You are being tested to see if you believe your doubting thoughts. These are the doubt-thoughts I had about finishing this book:

- I can't write, I'm more a teacher.
- I have been writing this book for over thirty years, and I still haven't finished it.
- I can't afford the time and financial investment to publish.
- When I read what I've written, I feel psyched, but I always do, and yet I don't stay with it.

I want you to know that you are safe when you doubt yourself. You are safe even when you don't know what to do. You can stay in this uncomfortable doubt escrow, in this spacious, undefined, not-knowing-how-ness and be absolutely as alive as when you were busy figuring out "The Way."

Trusting that your life can be easy, unfold positively, and be good for you will take a large amount of receiving. To actually trust, to actually *not* doubt, you will feel uncertain. Let the fear put you in pause and let the doubt provide a real (truck)stop that allows you to pull over and feel for the true way. This pausing will release the crazy, confused, anxious, depleting, and congested energy you feel.

You will release. Clarity, the "how," or the recognition that you don't know what to do will surface. Actually, you get to use all your mind-energy to continue doing what you set out to do or complete. And isn't it just so handy to have all this released mind-energy? This is, hands down, the very best part of feeling doubt: All the mind's energy that is released when you feel your doubt shows you what you need to do to continue or stay with what you started. Ain't doubt grand?

And finally, it is worth keeping in mind that joy may feel brazen and greedy. When you feel joy, you may feel selfish and as though you need to stop being so free and join the others in the suffering and effort channels. Yes, it's strange to know that when you feel joy you may feel that you need to keep joy down to a dull roar and feign being concerned like the rest of the gang. So to keep joy alive, I share with you the following email from my writing coach, Shannon, who knows all about the need to do joy when doubt enters your building. She tells us to remember to tell our stories.

One-Minute Story Tip: How to Banish Your Black Parrot's Black Heart

Let's play a game. Look at your left shoulder. Go on. I'm not looking at you. See it? Sitting on your shoulder is a giant Black Parrot. Cupid and his arrows are harmless against this guy. Chocolate bribes, champagne, and rose bouquets? Nope. The Black Parrot is like Terminator. He won't quit until your Work is (gulp) terminated.

Every time you doubt, procrastinate, give up, or get down (I mean, it *is* February but for only *one more sleep!*), your Black Parrot squawks in murderous glee.

Every storyteller/change-maker/daredevil/Cupid-lover/ St. Paddy's-Day-celebrator has a Black Parrot perched and poohing on their shoulder. But writers who write and storytellers who story know one thing: The Black Parrot needs a good staking (à la Dracula) before we can sit down and summon our Work.

When the Black Parrot shows up and starts whispering nasty things about you and your creations, and starts breaking your sweet, sweet heart –

Celebrate. The only time your Black Parrot pays attention is when you're growing, learning, and falling from the nest. Your Black Parrot will *never* tell you to get off the couch, put down the fork (drop the bonbon), or hold your tongue. Black Parrot squawking? Good. You are *definitely* bringing Light into the world. Yay!

Accept. You probably have an idea, a dream, or a memory you believe matters. Let's say it out loud: You matter, your stories matter, and you + your stories help other people. *What is to give light must endure burning.* Good. The bigger the Parrot, the bigger the Work, the brighter the fire. Burn, baby, burn.

Move. Did you know it's easier to navigate a moving car than a parked car? Most people live at the starting line, on "get ready," but they never *Go.* When you do your Work, you're in the race, on the field, in the arena. You're not up in the stands or out in the parking lot. You're moving so fast the Black Parrot falls off your shoulder and limps off the field. (But he'll be back.)

Here's to staking the Black Parrot, hugging Cupid, and smooching St. Paddy, sweet storyteller!

~ Shannon Leahy, Toronto writer and storyteller

CHAPTER THREE

Joy Is a Choice

Joy Is Kept Alive by Actions

There is a rightness that we know is the way for us. In life, when we need to make a choice, we can feel a certainty that is not based on our need for a certain outcome. We know what we want. Choosing is unnecessary.

No one else knows like we know. No one can determine how to meet our needs like we can. This "rightness," this way, feels true. There is a free-willed recognition of what to do or not do.

Changing through Self-realization

In joy, reaching a goal is an experience of self-realization. We choose to keep joy alive. By feeling joy we naturally progress towards goals that are so meaningful to us. The goal is a need.

This is *very* different from how we set goals when we are results-oriented. Focusing on a goal means the goal is outside us. External goals mean we *try* to reach them. Trying does not occur when you are in joy.

> If I ask a client to do an exercise or stretch between classes at home, and if they say, "I'll try." I know they won't. When I see the client take in what I say and ask me how many times to do it, then I know there's a chance. The word "try," in all my years of teaching, is a marker for "they won't."

In joy, we move towards goals we need. When the goal is a need, we change. We are *in* the process of change and interested in how this will occur. Being interested, we are motivated. Without motives. It's rather fabulous.

TRUE CHANGE

When we don't *need* our lives to be different, we can change. Our new choices cause an alchemical reordering that calibrates a courage. In English that means our bodies and our brains become brave. This is alchemical as we are energetic beings directed by neurotransmitters in the brain. We are moving into the change we need—naturally. The cellular mechanisms of brain and blood rerouting create a strength and vigour that mental determination cannot.

When my daughter was young, I sent her to the Waldorf School. "Waldorf education," also known as "Steiner education," is based on the educational philosophy of Rudolf Steiner, the founder of "anthroposophy." Its pedagogy emphasizes the role of imagination in learning, striving to holistically integrate the intellectual, practical, and artistic development of pupils.

"Reading is not taught until second grade. Waldorf educators believe that in the early years children should be read to, be told fairy tales to stimulate imagination and be allowed to play. This encourages oral skills before reading skills commence. In the

Waldorf School writing is taught before reading and the alphabet is explored as a tool to communicate with others through pictures. This way writing evolves out of art and children's doodles instead of reproduction of written content."[1]

By being read to and learning the alphabet first, children learn through their imaginations and creativity. When the child's brain develops through creativity, they develop skills by an intelligent order. Skills arise from imaginative knowledge. Sarah would often write what she wanted to say rather than explain what she had learned from a book or what the teacher had said. This Waldorf education, which emphasizes creativity and expression, fostered the development of her inner "knowings." Sarah often blew my mind with her insights. She would laugh at me when I would run to get my journal to write them down!

One day we were driving along a main city street and Sarah looked up at a billboard advertising a major fitness-club chain. The motto exclaimed, "Be yourself, only better!" Sarah lost it! "How can you be better if you're yourself?" she scoffed. We nodded in grumpy commiseration.

Needs Are Beautiful

A need is beautiful. A need is more than a longing. We don't need the need. We feel an interest and care to experience the need, not a push to get it.

A need to experience intimacy is beautiful, for example. It is not desperate or lonely. A need to have someone in your life to go out with or have sex with is more a want. Wants are trying to get something. They create mental tension, timelines, plastic surgery, and urgency. When you want someone in your life, you look for them,

---

[1] Wikipedia, "Anthroposophy" (n.d.), https://en.wikipedia.org/wiki/Anthroposophy.

or wish they were here. You feel separate when you are wanting.

Needs are different. Needs do not create wants. In joy, needs are self-expression. A need to feel intimate with someone shows that you want to share what you are with someone. Your desire to feel intimate with another shows how the love in you wants to go out for a spin and pick up a great passenger and drive around to the museums, cafés, and art galleries and tell them you are writing a book, or that your dog sneezes weirdly. You delight in life and express who you are and find that you attract others who do the same.

Each day is an opportunity to meet all the candidates. You're newly honoured recognition that you want to be intimate with someone elects a ministry in you. You feel a strong sense of yourself that acts like a neon wickedly bright pheromone that sends massive waves out onto the sidewalk in front of you. Those who can "see" you nearly trip and pretend there was a crack in the sidewalk. You glow because you feel so much more like yourself, and this is how you celebrate your need. Feeling a need is always gorgeous. You feel so much more like yourself because you feel what you need. You have stopped pretending it doesn't matter that you don't share your life with someone. You have become super honest with yourself. You are living as you, rather than a tough-guy imposter who says, "I like living alone, I can do what I want when I want to." "I don't want to have a 'live-in.'" "I like that I don't have to have inane conversations." And other such resentments. No, you are done with being angry and fed up, and you are now walking in the beautiful world with a beautiful need. You will meet the world and what it has in it for you. You are now an honest you with a need. That is so sexy you will be dripping with humility, care, warmth, beauty, and candour. (Look! The next person just tripped on the sidewalk going past you!) I also think you'll be funny.

The need to share is beautiful. Even if you are introverted and socially challenged, the need to share life with someone will shift how you feel in the world, and you will be more attentive to others that you are attracted to—and them to you as you feel this beautiful expression of the need.

Needs are always, always beautiful. They are not needy. Oh, and if it seems as though all those "candidates" are married, trans, bi, gay, or simply not a "good idea," then feel how good it was to feel the spiking flirt of attraction. It is a test run to feel how the sweetness feels when you want someone. The need to feel intimacy is opening you up.

Realizing Goals Means Temptations Visit Us

As we become more of who we are, we feel whole. We feel more capable. We can rely on ourselves. We become more of who we are by sharing our lives with others and by reaching and actualizing the big juicy thoughts that make us smile and at the same time make us feel scared about doing them. We become more of who we are, not *better* (remember not to say that around Sarah!) when we reach the massively meaningful goals inside us. When we become more of who we are, the old ways that we lived by have no real power. These old habits appear in their true form: as temptations. If we didn't experience these old habits as temptations, our goals would carry no power. The presence of a temptation to *not* do what you know you need to do means you are advancing. Yay you!

THE POWER OF TEMPTATIONS

Temptations are tricky. They arise when we change. Temptations arise when we need to do something for ourselves. We can walk the dog. We can do the dishes. These are easy; they have an outwardly recognized result. If we don't walk the dog, well, everyone knows. If we don't exercise, no one really knows except us.

Yet the reason we don't exercise is that we give in to the temptation to not exercise. Temptations are not associated just with chocolate cake. Temptations are more than the desire to skip exercising and pull the covers over our heads.

- Temptations are a testament that we are headed in the right direction. They show us that we are growing.
- Temptations are when we feel we can't continue to exercise or that we won't keep it up.
- Temptations are the convincing belief that we can't say what we need to say to someone.
- Temptations are the convincing belief that we can't say no when we need to.
- Temptations are self-sabotaging thoughts, such as thinking we can't finish what we started.
- Temptations are uncomfortable. They reveal the place in us that does not yet believe.
- Temptations show us that we don't know how.

> **Not knowing how is our biggest evolutionary moment.**
> **Not knowing how is the most loving interruption**
> **to your growth that you can experience.**

Feeling as though you can't, or doubting that you can, shows how much your choice can change you. The doubt feeling also shows you how much you really want to change.

Feel the discomfort there.

Pause.

Nothing bad will happen.

Again, stay in the pull of temptation to give in.

Hang out there to create a mental space. This mental space allows for a "meme," or a new way to enter your consciousness. A meme is a spool of wool from which a tapestry of thinking is woven. A meme is an accepted ideology; the status quo is believing. When we grow and evolve, we move out of self-restricting memes.

Soon you will be ever so interested in temptations, and it will be like a bright-red flag that you are growing.

When we feel the temptation, we put on the brakes. We pause. It could take everything we've got. Feel the suction of the pull. Make a bad joke about it if you want that red wine, or if your goal is to get rid of sugar in your diet, say to a friend in a cookie monster voice, "Cookie wants weekend cookie!"

My drug is red licorice—the healthy kind from the health food store that uses organic maple syrup and has no food colouring. See how I can make it look fabulous right off the top? I have no off switch once that bag is open. Abandonment takes over and I think I am so liberated when I eat that sticky stuff. And even as I'm doing it, I know I'll feel like poop when I'm done. Yet, there I am, with the ripped cellophane, hand reaching in until I reach and there's nothing there! Damn. My binge is a blur of rapid fire "I want this!" If you try to tell me I'll feel like poop in the morning, I won't respect you. So what to do?

Pause. Once, again.

I know! It's not even sexy.

After you pause, remember who you are.

Who are you?

I'm so glad you asked. For *that* is sexy.

You are pure consciousness. You are *not* disciplined or undisciplined. You are *not* on a slippery slope in this tricky moment. You are simply you, all ruffled by temptation.

And you are a perfect, whole human. Perfect in your sticky tempted moment.

Not feeling it? I know, it can be hard. Feel the pure you. The you before you became inundated with habits that gulp red licorice and drink red wine. So I'll help.

You are pure consciousness—mind-energy that is right here in this moment with the pull of temptation. If you feel the pull and stay right here (with me if you wish; I'll support you), you will make the mental gap that is necessary to keep from going for the wine glass or drive to the licorice store. That mental gap is in the gaping space where you don't know *how* to *not* move towards the culprit of food or drink. You stay in that gap until it grows in time from a pothole in your road to a chasm preventing you from crossing the street. You stay there all pulled at and shaky. Right there, standing in time and space on that side of the road, where you are about to repeat the old habit.

You stay put, again and tomorrow. If you are able to stay and feel tempted, angry, as if it's unfair, as if you want just a little red wine for God's sake because you've been such a good person all day and why can't you have what you want—then you become more of you. You stay all alive in the pulling temptation and upgrade and grow into a fuller you.

Once you've done this a few times, there is no more suctioning pull of temptation. It is so over. You are you free of the habit. This is how you get into joy: Feel the pull of temptation and stay with what you *really* want to do.

Keep What You Know Alive

When we do *not* feel joy, we do not feel like ourselves. We will not be able to sense what we need. When we are overwhelmed and confused like this, we *try* to keep going. Effort happens when we try. Effort happens when we force ourselves to follow through with something that we don't know how to do, or that is not meaningful to us.

The effortful moment, or how we push ourselves to get things done, is so important to understand for the purpose of creating a life that is who we are, that we need to *feel it* in our bodies.

Can effort be so easily recognized that you feel it in your psyche as a strong poke? Like realizing you left your wallet in the store? Can you feel how *trying* to do something pulls on your mind's attention? Like realizing you forgot to hold the door for someone right behind you.

We need to recognize the feeling of effort that nags at us so we can see that it is a nuisance. Instead of *trying* to get things done, can we completely engage with what we are doing? *We need to reveal the moment when we start to push ourselves to get things done.*

When we start to "effort" or "should" ourselves, we feel an inner shove that reminds us what we need to do. That's it really, it is simply a reminder. The reason it feels so pushy is that *we delay taking action by making up a story.* The "story" is the run-on in our minds about *how* we must take action. For example, the story could be a perception of what is required to take action, such as money, the right education, or understanding from our partner. Now we have created requirements. And this makes us rather busy.

Requirements won't motivate us. Motivation happens when it is our story, not the story about how we are *supposed* to do it. When we let the heavy story convince us that we cannot do what we want, we cancel all the enthusiasm, passion, and clarity that was motivating us just a moment ago. We are all born with a passionate enthusiasm. When we feel this we must do what we believe. It will feel false to live any other way.

When I was pregnant, I knew I had to raise my daughter on my own. I knew it would not be a happy or healthy journey to do it with Sarah's father. Alongside this feeling was the crippling belief that I must be crazy to leave him. I pressured myself into believing I had to "make it work." I couldn't raise a baby on my own! Opposing this was the real knowing that I wanted to live *my* life and build on the consulting practice I was already creating. I didn't want to just *cope*! Coping was the way I felt when I considered doing the "right" thing, which was to stay. (I also felt I had to stay because we had just bought a condo together.)

In retrospect, it was not *me* who was afraid of leaving him, it was what it would *mean* if I left. It was not meaningful to *me*, but to people around me. I thought I had to work it out with him because I was afraid I could not possibly make enough money to raise Sarah on my own and be a full-on mom. And I knew I couldn't stay.

I felt insecure knowing this during my pregnancy. I was doubt stricken and scared to stick with my resolve. I felt guilty for getting pregnant. That was the self-restricting story. I felt as if I was wrong somehow for getting "knocked up," and I felt too scared to do what I needed to do.

I was still learning to trust myself. Although it appeared I was living with disciplined focus, I was semi-terrified most of the time, yet determined that I would not do something that didn't feel true.

I started to notice this when someone would give me advice. I started to notice how I *felt* when they gave me advice. For example, many people advised that I must "get a job." My mom was certain that if I got "settled" in this way and received a steady paycheque, I would get what I needed in the form of security, a dental plan, sick days, and other benefits.

My mom's advice was a form of distraction. It would have been easy to submit to its attractive pull of financial security. I listened to her, and not one cell in my body felt alive. Instead, I sensed her fear, and I felt her concern. Concern is commonly intended as care. When she suggested a number of institutions I could work for and seek job interviews with, I felt how much she wanted to help. At the same time, I felt how much I wanted to *live my life*. Which meant do what I love, and teach about the body, and continue to study it. For me there was no other way. It did not feel safe to make this decision, I only knew I had to. The true *had* to, not the nasty *have* to. For my mom, her story was to seek security, and that meant a man, and if not a man, a job.

A dear friend asked me if I thought my mom doubted I could do it on my own. I didn't. I knew my mom was afraid. She couldn't understand the way I lived. She just couldn't handle the choices I was making. And how could she? I didn't share my passions with my mom. I thought she wouldn't hear them. I was careful about expressing how motivated I was to run my own business when I was with her. I felt she wouldn't be able to hear how inspired I was as she had often cut me off in the past when I would talk about my teaching gigs. I eventually stopped telling her. It hurt too much to hear her cutting words.

Eventually, I didn't trust the passions inside me and the drive I felt to follow through with my inspired teachings. This caused many slowdowns in my life, where I would doubt what I knew.

My mom's concerns started to affect me, and I began looking for a position in my field. For me it was truly intolerable to get a J-O-B. Yet I tried to align with her thinking and managed to last a few months working as a trainer and administrator for a personal-training company. Ever so perfectly, eight months into the job, eight months into faking my life, I jolted back to the real me without even a phone booth for a quick change. Which is good since there aren't so many anymore. (For the younger readers: A phone booth is a tall Plexiglas structure with a large phone unit attached to its back wall. You enter a swingy door to make a call. It's usually unoccupied.) I quit and walked out of the building. I leaned back against the warm brick wall. I lifted my chin to the sky, shaking and wondering what the hell I was doing to have walked out like that, and I felt myself fill in again. *I was back!*

I was a single mom, an "unemployed" single Mom. My daughter was eighteen months old.

I felt like a crazy person. "*What* am I doing?" Which was a fair question. But the best part was, it wasn't the usual interrogation: "Who do I think I am?" This was a huge improvement. I felt crazy and alive all at once. There was no franticness. I was shaking because I felt so free.

This decision (re-)launched my career. Over the next few days, I reported to all the clients that I would be leaving the company. They said they were coming with me. I was not surprised, yet I was really nervous. I didn't know what to say. Each client responded in the same way: They had signed on with me and it was me they were going to work with, and they would tell the company.

This was my first test at believing in myself. It's hard to *not* believe in yourself. It's even harder to uphold when everyone else does. They wanted me. *Me.* Yikes! This would take some getting used to.

When they told me this, I actually felt a part of my body cower and contract, as though I was in *big* trouble. I thought that after they called the company I would meet my manager in some dark, narrow alley, in the rain, where he was Harrison Ford in *Raiders of the Lost Ark*, and I would be the sheik with the measly machete.

Yet it never happened. I was never pulled over by the police or stopped on the sidewalk in public. This getting away with it felt awful too. I literally would have turned myself in if there were a holding cell to do this. Guilt and shame have created a lot of disturbance in my life. (I'm often creating or believing there's a prison out there somewhere.) I have felt myself cower whenever the spotlight was on me. I get this feeling of disturbing turbulence that tries to muddle up my thinking and convince me that I don't really know what I'm talking about. This occurs when life gets better. It creates self-doubt and my clarity disassembles. It's frustratingly rapid. It's a self-sabotaging setpoint I feel. If I go past it, I get nervous and feel I better settle down and not be so big.

When in undisturbed joy, there is no disturbance. I get huge and take up a large amount of space. I only feel a continuum of being who I am with no endpoint where it crashes. There is incredible clarity and an ongoing faith. The faith is kept alive by actions. I don't *feel* the faith. My actions reveal it; I realize that living my life as the real me supports my evolution and progress. The constant feeling of joy, which always occurs when I feel like me, highlights self-critical thoughts, revealing how they cause disturbances.

It can be really hard to keep alive what you know. It can be really hard to keep alive what you know long enough to live it. To act and do what you know you need to do, stay in the seed of the inspiration. If you feel doubt, and you will, know you are going further. Feel the doubt and know it is temptation to keep you small. Then kick the fuck out of it. Technically speaking.

It was clear. I had to teach people about the body, and I had to do it the way I was learning it, rather than teach in a clinic or organization following their protocol. I knew that working in any organization would dampen my spirit. My excitement and respect for the body was contagious, and it was my contribution to society. It was time to keep building on this and see where it could take me.

The nervousness I felt, the lack of certainty, is the common denominator we feel as we create and carve out our lives.

> When you live your life, you don't even need to "carve it out." Your life happens by living it.

When we feel the most uprooted, the most frightened—I mean immobilized with fear—and that we must be crazy to be doing this, then we are onto something!

Some people sail through such events. I want to be those people. It is so ironic that a culture that conditions us to believe we must be in control to be free is really imprisoning us. And we don't question it. Our society teaches us to self-manage, self-regulate, conform, get a good mortgage rate, and buy RRSPs. We believe we must be in control to feel free. Yet striving for false security dismisses our imagination. The belief is: If we are prepared we will be free to live. But whose lives are we representing?

This is all based on an economy of fear that conditions us to grasp at means of security and replicate them. By buying into this epidemic, we support the illusion and delusion that we are doing the Right Thing. Enter the realm of fear-based thinking.

Fearful thinking keeps us cautious. We watch our imagination sink into the rubble of our no-risk choices. It takes imagination and vision to know what we know. Knowing what we know is feeling what is true for us. Once we fill in again and be who we are, the vision will unfold step by (sloppy) step. Swear to God.

"The following of authority is the denial of intelligence. It may help us temporarily to cover up our problems; but to avoid a problem is only to intensify it, and in the process, self-knowledge and freedom are abandoned."

~ JIDDU KRISHNAMURTI (1895–1986),
INDIAN PHILOSOPHER, SPEAKER, AND WRITER

In Joy, Change Is Direct

In joy, we change naturally. The letting go part of change is often effortful; in joy it is effortless. The change may be uncomfortable, but we know it is necessary. Clearly, the discomfort during change is our resistance to a new way of seeing things.

When we choose to stay in joy, change doesn't grate at us. We know instantly, as the discomfort is occurring, that it is useful.

If we feel ourselves resisting change, we know we still don't feel "ready." We are being tempted to cling to what we know. That's why we feel the mental pressure of a temptation. And it is precisely that temptation that is pushing us up to choose (know) what we really want to do.

I knew I wanted to inspire people to exercise and live an alive, spontaneous, playful, and truthful life. I knew I needed to teach the way I was discovering how to work with the body. I sought a series of contracts teaching exercise classes and wellness workshops in organizations, and I held in-home private personal-training sessions, worked as a waitress, and put treadmills together at a friend's sports store while I finished my university degree.

"Your pain is the breaking of the shell that encloses your understanding. Even as the stone of the fruit must break, that its heart may stand in the sun, so must you know pain. And could you keep your heart in wonder at the daily miracles of your life, your pain would not seem less wondrous than your joy."

~ KAHLIL GIBRAN, "ON PAIN"

After I had Sarah, I continued to build my clientele and my fitness consulting business in Toronto, until one day I could no longer schedule in my part-time jobs. I didn't need to; my full-time job was now my business.

I am not sharing my story to motivate you. We are all accustomed to motivational numbers from great speakers with large shiny white teeth to humble, beautiful monks with difficult-to-pronounce names.

True inspiration is an inside job. Feeling the spark of someone else's inspirational story may only be that. A spark. It may light up that part of you that says, "Yeah! Let's do it!" Then, when you go home, park your car, and get out, you see the lawn and the weeding and the side shed that needs a new handle, and you lose it. The inspiration that is. Real, honest, radical (it only seems radical because it is so unusual and that feels weird) inspiration emanates from a prompting bigger than motives. True inspiration lifts you into action. It is much like helium, and it *does* you.

> Inspiration is so deeply entrenched in your cells that
> it is the voluntary respiratory muscles that undulate
> your lungs with each breath. You are not really *doing*
> it—the inspired feeling—it is your inner terrain and
> expands out into the actions in your life.

We are not getting motivated and then trying to "keep it up." That would imply that we are repeating an affirmation to stay focused. No, inspiration is deeper than this. Inspiration is the alive you under the (thinking) mind. Inspiration is you engaged in your life rather than trying to make it better. Life gets better being in it.

If this doesn't sound familiar, to be living with inspiration, then you are doing battle with life. This equates to suffering. We are extremely talented sufferers. I create suffering when I engage in thinking about what I'm doing in my life. This is when we create those silly *stories*, such as, "I can't possibly raise a baby on my own." When I don't *think* about what's happening, I stop being a storyteller of "reasons why I can't." I connect directly with life as it is. This frees me up to choose (know) in each moment rather than think about what is best.

You are not figuring out *how* to live, but knowing what you love, and this tunes you into what is meaningful to you. You always feel what matters when you are in joy, and this evokes your next move.

Birthing a Buddha

Right after I had Sarah, we lived in Forest Hill in a nice, affordable basement apartment with a gorgeous backyard surrounded by old trees. As I continued to expand my client base and the organizations I taught for, I had one person on my executive board. Her name was Sarah. She was two years old and counting. When I made a decision about how many contracts I would take, or how many clients I would work with, if it felt monumental, that is, if it required more time than I was willing to take away from Sarah, then I would ask her. I never made a business decision that I did not feel clear about without asking Sarah.

I did this because it felt right. Not because I felt I must be a full-time mom because I was the only caregiver, not because all the books told me that the personality develops in the first seven years of life, or the care and direction for the child during this time is critical. I felt all these were important, but my incentive was not fear-based. I did it because I wanted to be with her.

I will never forget the time I got a call from one of the biggest corporate fitness businesses in the city offering me a rather attractive contract. At the time I was running my business full time; teaching classes; and facilitating private sessions for the City of Toronto, T.D. Waterhouse, and other centres around the city. Many companies would call me for classes, but rarely for contracts, which of course spelled *consistent income*. It was the words of the director of the company that got my attention.

I respected Jan, she had built her business up over the years, and I watched her grow from small business contracts to large corporations such as Imperial Oil. She said to me, "Celeste, you can't afford to turn this down" in a woman-to-woman kind of way. I knew she was trying to be supportive and remind me that I needed consistent work. I knew she felt this because I was a single mom. I could hear it in her voice. More fear-based finagling tried to enter my zone.

I pondered it for a few days. I thought about my "situation." My single-mom situation, which could get me believing that I needed to provide future opportunities for Sarah, such as college, private schooling if the public school system didn't work, piano lessons, funeral insurance, and dental plans. This kept me pretty busy.

I was teaching each day from 6 a.m. until noon by design so I would have the rest of the day and evening to be with Sarah. I was practically the only single mom at the parks. I loved that I had created that luxury. Which to me was a necessity. Every day from noon until the streetlights came on, I played with Sarah.

The only reason I would have taken the contract would have been to "get ahead." We had enough to pay the bills and any other necessities. We lived a simple, playful, spontaneous, creative life. I could tell you of every free event that went on for children on the weekends. Yet I still felt that I *should* consider this opportunity.

For that reason, I went to my sole executor. I said to Sarah (she was three), "Hey, sweetie, I've got an opportunity to work more, which would mean we would have more money. That means we would be able to buy more. We could buy more things, such as toys, maybe videos. It would also mean that I would see you less. We could make up a wish list of whose house you would like to go to or who you would like to take care of you when I'm working, and then see if they can do it. What do you think?"

Sarah had been looking at me intently during this whole speech with that "taking it all in" sponge look that toddlers do, and then she calmly looked down at the toy bricks she was building and said, "Stay home, Mommy." She continued playing.

The meeting had adjourned. I had been agonizing for three days.

I did not take the contract. When I called Jan back, she sounded tightly unimpressed, as if I had resigned to some inner quibbling. It was clear in her tone that if I turned down this offer she would not be sending one my way again. It was hard not to feel like a bad girl.

That year my business made more than the contract offered. Staying home paid big dividends—with more time to build my clientele. By staying with my vision, I was able to really *be* there with Sarah.

I always remember the support my clients offered when I called last minute to cancel a private session because Sarah was sick. I could have had children's Tylenol home delivered. I found that people, my clients, were so endlessly supportive that I felt humbled. I felt embarrassed that I had done all this worrying when I could have just trusted myself and made the whole process a lot easier, even fun. What a concept.

Designing my business as a single mom rather than trying to fit my life around the needs of my clients showed me how very compassionate and supportive humans are. Suddenly my version, my story of being alone and needing to be strong, was being eroded by the support that doing it my way was revealing.

I wanted to be Sarah's mom. I wanted to *be* there as her mom. This clarity was not a moral decision; it was what I wanted to do.

I wanted to share the natural world with her through play. I wanted to share with her all that I had discovered. Full-time daycare was not an option. I wanted Sarah in daycare only enough for me to earn a good income to do the things we wanted to do and live in a beautiful environment. I wanted Sarah to have the loving community and social skills that the daycare provided, and this was delightful. It was not a decision, it was a free-willed, inspired, sexy choice.

Sarah was right—stay home. I felt she was telling me to stay home in myself, in my heart and my vision, and not sell out. These little Buddhas that we birth, who teach us and remind us of the true path, need more executive airtime.

Takeaways

1. *Be* **your truth.** When you follow your own story, you create true outcomes. True outcomes resemble who you are.
2. **Forget concepts.** When you feel afraid of what you know you need to do, you create concepts of how to live. Forget ideals that

do not represent your own and create your meaningful values as you go.

3. **Negative feelings destroy your enthusiasm and passion.** Your negative, distracted feelings chomp away at your enthusiasm. You know what you want, but you don't feel as though you can do it, so you create feelings that support this belief. In my life, I thought I couldn't raise a child on my own, so I had all kinds of support from society and statistics that showed that it would be a daunting task, because I was fearful that it would be.

4. **Practise noticing.** The way you *don't* create this kind of discord is to stay with the desire and notice the discrepancies you bump up against and see what they are really revealing in you. My concept that I had to *get ahead* caused me to doubt what I really wanted to do.

5. **Notice your fearful thinking.** My fear was of raising a child on my own, just the statement itself reveals the impoverished mind that was speaking. Raising a child on my own ultimately was not possible; a community would inevitably grow around us when I had a child.

My fear was based on the belief that I had to live my life on my own, and the pressure I put on myself to do a good job. This made it difficult to connect with others and share the responsibilities. My fear was that I was not good enough and that I must be more. This stirred up a disempowering pressure to fulfill the responsibilities that would be involved.

For most of us, we believe it takes effort, hard work, and determination to succeed. We never imagine that we could know what we want, trust this knowing, and let it direct us.

It's obvious that raising a child will be loaded with challenges, and that's one perspective. Choosing to raise a child creatively is another. Welcome support that makes sense to you. In this way you can experience more guidance, advice, and opportunities that help you along. The guidance and support that you attract is the support that is *good* for you. It serves your evolution into becoming more of who you are. You start to fill out when this happens. You start to feel who you really are. It connects you to *your* story.

How to Really Love a Child

"Be there. Say yes as often as possible. Let them bang on pots and pans. If they're crabby, put them in water. If they're unlovable, love yourself. Realize how important it is to be a child. Go to a movie theatre in your pajamas. Read books out loud with joy. Invent pleasures together. Remember how really small they are. Giggle a lot. Surprise them. Say no when necessary. Teach feelings. Heal your own inner child. Learn about parenting. Hug trees together. Make loving safe. Bake a cake and eat it with no hands. Go find elephants and kiss them. Plan to build a rocketship. Imagine yourself magic. Make lots of forts with blankets. Let your angel fly. Reveal your own dreams. Search out the positive. Keep the gleam in your eye. Mail letters to God. Encourage silly. Plant licorice in your garden. Open up. Stop yelling. Express your love. A lot. Speak kindly. Paint their tennis shoes. Handle with caring. Children are miraculous."

~ SARK, MOTIVATIONAL
SPEAKER AND AUTHOR

From Basement to Mansion: From Poverty Consciousness to Prosperous Living

As a single mom since Sarah's birth, I made sure she and I lived in a communal way so that we felt part of a family. I was committed to discovering a way to live in any kind of inspired co-creative, resource-sharing environment. I did not want Sarah and me to live in an isolated apartment where Sarah learned the world according to mom. I wanted her to have lots of interaction with different people, cultures, music, art, and languages.

This decision allowed me to have affordable housing in what would be considered an exorbitantly priced, affluent, beautiful neighbourhood. I rented a large house in the wealthy area of Forest Hill, next to the Casa Loma stables in Toronto. I had students from Hong Kong living with me, a friend who was a journalist who travelled internationally stayed with me, and other friends would live with us for short stints.

Sarah met many people as she grew and was in contact with many cultures. One day, when she was three, I had my repairman, Mario, come to fix the washing machine. Sarah took one look at his large toolbox and said, "Are you moving in?"

Our home was a hub of activity, with making art, having friends over for play dates, and consciousness-raising meetings through Parents Without Partners. This exposure to many cultures, personalities, and artistic expressions offered myriad connections as we grew together. This home education was stable and diverse.

I saw that as she grew, Sarah had an extended soul family who loved and cared for her. Our home thrived on a currency of sharing, encouragement, diversity, expression, and emotional sanctuary.

In retrospect, I realize that I was able to make these choices because I knew what I *didn't* want. I would not live in a way that was a desperate consciousness, which I refer to as "poverty consciousness." I knew that I was going to have a sense of soul family and community in my life. I knew that it would have been easy to isolate myself.

As a single mom, finishing my degree and running my business full time, I was certifiably exhausted. My sense of humour would wither with the demands of my daily schedule. My mind was almost always on what I had to do next. To remedy this intensity that I lived, I made sure I felt supported and reminded myself again and again to play and share time with others.

I also exercised every day. I never missed. I scheduled all other activities around it, even if it meant missing a social engagement. (Who am I kidding, it *usually* meant missing social time—yet the exercise was more enlivening for me than casual conversation.) This was one way that I connected to myself and nature.

This living arrangement made for one happy home! I found on the days when I was exhausted that Sarah would be engaged in her blocks or Barbies for extended periods, or play in Jason's room, our student from Hong Kong. I could finish my paperwork. It was as if she was intuitively giving me what I needed.

As a single mother, I knew I would need to live frugally to make ends meet. (I can't use the word "frugal" without thinking of how my mother used it; she would explain, rather defensively I might add, that she was not being "cheap.") Yet I didn't want to live in housing that didn't offer us a beautiful home. It was easy to fall into the trap that I would need to apply for subsidized housing and live on the fringes of society in an apartment. Yet I truly felt that we could live an inspired life and I kept finding ways to do this.

Let me clarify how this moved me from the poverty consciousness of "I can't afford good housing" to an inspired life. Inspired consciousness meant *feeling* how I wanted to live. It felt good to reach out to the landlady of this large three-bedroom home in Forest Hill. It was almost affordable for me. After finding out the rent, I offered the landlady, Irene, $300 less as I sensed that the cost of the monster oil furnace would be very high in the winter months.

And it was. However, she agreed to the reduced rent, and that easily covered this cost.

Also, when I moved in, it came complete with a young woman who was working in the film industry and who was just finishing a movie. She was a friend of Irene's son, and she asked if she could stay until they were done filming. She stayed for six more fun-filled weeks (and she and Sarah were inseparable), and then she moved back to Vancouver. This gave me time to put out the word for more housemates. Within a week I had a student from Japan and a student from Hong Kong living with me. They were truly the sweetest guys. Jason loved to do dishes. He and Sarah were practically inseparable. Literally. She would hang onto his thigh as he ambled along with his new wooden Sarah leg. If ever I couldn't find Sarah, I always knew she was in his room. One night, my spidey mom sense felt she wasn't in bed. Sure enough, she had gone into his room to get candy and watch TV. Sarah was teaching him English while she kept building her vocabulary.

The way of joy sees opportunities, and when those opportunities don't seem possible, we find ways for them to be possible. After I asked Irene for the reduced rent, I wondered what would happen. Would she agree? If she didn't, it would show me I was making sure I hadn't overextended myself, which felt good.

I was learning to listen to these "knowings" that would ask the big questions that my needs revealed. I truly felt the house was for us. It felt unrealistic because I was paying way less rent than I was for a basement apartment. Yet there was this (irrational) knowing that it was the best decision. So I asked.

Joy asks for what it wants. After you ask for what you want, you have no designs. It actually leaves your mind. That's why you can be in the moment, each moment. You know what you want, you ask and you're done with it.

Two weeks after moving into this large, gorgeous Victorian house, with the rent from my students I was paying much less than

I had been for the basement apartment! Now I lived in a wonderful community, complete with "Jason" dishwasher.

Knowing Does Not Require Choosing

When we know something is true for us, we do not need to choose. Choices arise from this knowing. Nothing is considered difficult. We will still feel the effort, but we will lack the view that deems it difficult.

Regardless of how complicated a next step in your life is, it is never *complicating*. A hard-to-take step may feel really hard to do, *and* it will not add layers of confusion. When you are in joy, you live your life simply and clearly, even when it's hard to. Your action is known as you need to do it. There is a steadiness that you live. It can be painful. It's that in joy pain directs you.

Joy Is Imaginative

- Imagination is the ability to feel what is *not* here yet.
- Imagination is the seed of new actions. It is the petri dish for new ideas that we never, ever thought of before.
- Imagination and vision can rise from us *even* when we feel discouraged, frightened, and uncertain. That's when we really need to dig deep to feel for what we know! There was nothing in me that believed I could raise Sarah on my own.
- Imagination activates only where there is trust.
- Imagination breeds courage.

Fear will never imagine. How can you feel the ability to think new creative thoughts when you are muddled and feel stuck? How can you feel imaginative when the appeal to take the safe route is what's clearly attractive or what the world is telling you to do? Like a paycheque and sick days? Honestly, there is no "how" to this.

The only truth is you simply *have* to! Not the mean *have to* as in you *should*. This is the true *have to* that is willing to do what you know you need to do (or not do!).

In every mess we experience is an opportunity for us to shift. When we cool down enough to be imaginative and feel open to what we can experience next that is *not* fearful, we meet the fear. Then we name what is scaring us and can take action, or recognize what we need to do to stay true to ourselves.

We become courageous. This kind of courage needs to be arduously developed. We misplaced it after age four. To be courageous, keep going into the unknown space that is fear. The courage will show up in your actions. Courage-filled actions are bravery.

Joy Is Creative

Let's begin by exploring creativity or the creative impulse. As humans, our evolution depends on creativity. A creative person is a free thinker, spontaneous and inventive, and has initiative. Spontaneity is the ability to act in that very moment, rather than premeditate, calculate, or plan our next move.

When we probe into what being in the moment is, we find it to be "timeless." We have no identification with the *idea* of time. There is no deadline.

The idea of no tension in the mind's awareness is important here. With no pull on the movement of the mind, the mind's energy is simply present. Freedom to choose allows the energy of the mind to flow freely. The flow through such a mind will be undefined. Reference points are lost.

Our minds flow with clarity and insights. We have *new* thoughts. A new, fresh thought is the mind directed by *you*. If the fresh thought is influenced by negative emotions, we try to focus to complete a task.

Right after I had Sarah, I was influenced by my mom's fears that I needed to get a job to be secure. *My mind wasn't directing me.*

Then, when I could feel that it was too suffocating to stay in the job, I couldn't feel alive. I would have had to let go of the knowing that I wanted to run my own business. I would have had to force myself to focus on staying in the job.

Forged Focus Cancels Joy

When we try to focus, and stay with a task when we are not inspired, we become insensitive. We get out of touch with ourselves. We won't feel inner promptings of intelligence. (Cue the scary music.) In this way, driving focus causes us to tighten mentally and makes everything crustier. We also look crusty, and develop anus mouth. (Anus mouth is that puckered tight *O* our mouths make when we focus with severe mental intensity. Please don't do this.)

Let's look at what it means to *not force yourself to focus*. When I was thirteen years old I started exercising daily with weights. My inspiration was spawned by the desire to become a stronger swimmer and develop a bum so my Levi's would fill out. (To this day I still exercise six days a week. The bum is good.) I loved the feeling of going into the weight room among all those crazy, dedicated gym rats with their pumped up biceps. They taught me everything they knew. I loved the meditation of isolating, sculpting, and lengthening each muscle group. Michael Angelo at the bench press sculpting a rib cage and pec muscles.

Exercise did me, I didn't do exercise. I was psyched to work the body this way, discovering its prowess, sensuality, strength, and abilities to go beyond last week's experience. Every day I went to the Barrie Y, got the buzz for the weight room, and pumped iron alongside those muscle heads. The token girl. I simply never missed. It never occurred to me to prioritize another responsibility and bump this one. To this day, I still get an odd look on my face when someone says they schedule their workout first thing in the morning to "get it over with." Get *what* over with?

And still to this day I marvel at how mine and all of our *bodies* put up with our sheer, supreme, privileged neglect and work for us. Most of us would have quit and left the job site years ago if they were treated like we treat our bodies. I digress.

If I wasn't *inspired* to exercise daily (that would be awful, like losing my favourite volunteer position) and spiralled down to thinking I *must* exercise daily, I was creating a requirement. Now I must follow it. Enter the realm of space-time causation. The better way is if my body starts to feel the results from exercising daily, then I don't want to miss a day. Even when I'm exhausted, even when I'm distracted, even when there's popcorn, a good movie, and my young daughter is waiting to watch it with me. How do you run when your gorgeous daughter is there with popcorn? You get really phenomenal. You amaze yourself with your discipline. You make sure that you get the exercise in first, before it gets to popcorn hour.

For we all know that as the days unfold, there are more and more popcorn opportunities, so we better make ourselves the number one focus. It's the same when you commit to exercising daily. You see the popcorn, you see your sweet daughter sitting there with the movie, and you feel the enticing pull and say, "Tomorrow night, sweetie, I missed my run this morning and I really want to get out there." You own your enthusiasm and show yourself (not to mention your impressionable daughter) that you love yourself and take care of your body.

When I did this (and I really wanted to watch that movie!), I was ten minutes into my run and turned around to find my daughter running towards me with a big grin. She doesn't even run! Or didn't until that day.

What was most amazing was not that she joined me and caused me to feel even happier about my decision, but that she knew which direction I was going in. I ran east because the sun was setting. I've never run that late in the day, so I had never gone that way, ever. She ran in *that* direction. It was truly a miraculous moment. When

I asked her how she knew where to run, she gave her usual shrug and said she *asked*. Sarah has a strong connection to what she feels is Life, some call it God. When she wants to know something, she asks. I marvelled that I was so highly rewarded on that cold evening when I couldn't access the feeling to go out and run. Simply choosing to keep up my commitment allowed for the most magical run I have ever known—at sunset with a most wonderful being.

When I can't find the juice to do something and pull it up to do it anyway, the rewards are bigger. It's like working on a statutory holiday. You feel isolated and wonder if you made the best decision. Then you feel sneaky and opportunistic being paid double time to do what is taking the usual amount of work. I find that when I exercise when I can't feel it in me to do it, someone at the yoga studio or on the beach during my run says something that rocks my world, and it's exactly what I needed to hear.

Please join me.

CHAPTER FOUR

Joy Is a Constant

Joy is a constant in your life. It is the baseline and default that is you. You can never separate from *who* you are. Not feeling it? I know, it can be tricky to feel joyful when we create complicated lives. Let me help.

Joy is always beating, just like your heart. You don't tell the involuntary cardiac muscles in the ventricles to pump. They pump. Your body is alive; that's not complicated. It only knows how to be alive. The only disruption to how alive your body feels is stress. Yet even in the most stressful situations, during the fight-or-flight response, the nervous system doesn't turn off. It always meets the stress.

It is the same with joy. Joy meets all experiences. When we feel joy, we stay connected to each moment in our day. I call this ability to meet what happens "directly experiencing." We become interested and curious. When we are in joy we lack the judging consciousness that separates us from what is happening and looking at it with disdain, frustration, or any form of resentment. Even if what we are experiencing infuriates us. How? I'm so glad you asked.

By living with an open mind that experiences the world with Wonder. A mind in wonder is the antidote to feeling stressed, and thereby separated from the world. A wonder-filled mind is curious as it opens to truth and beauty, magic and flow, moment by moment. (Quick disclaimer to help you keep believing that you can live in joy: A mind in wonder is not ridiculously agreeing to life like an overly compassionate idiot and losing your sense of logical comprehension.)

A mind in wonder is the antidote to feeling stressed, and thereby separated from the world.

On a flight to Costa Rica, I watched a documentary about a world-famous magician who travelled the globe. She performed her spectacular magic in Los Angeles, for tribes in Africa, and in the outback of Australia. When asked how her audiences responded to her tricks, she replied, "I am amazed at the difference between a person from three to one hundred in a developed country and one in a tribal outback. The child or elderly person in an African tribe exclaims, 'You can do that!' A child or older person in a developed country always has the same reaction, 'How did you do that?'" The power of an innocent and inquiring mind is its capacity for wonder and truth seeking. Asking *how* to do something is a thinking mind.

A wonder-filled mind creates a more adaptable body. The body craves more movement because you feel better. When you feel supple, you want to check out what your body can do.

"Wonderment is the first of all passions."

~ RENÉ DESCARTES (1596–1650),
FRENCH PHILOSOPHER AND SCIENTIST

One early morning when I was in Thailand studying Thai massage, I was running through the side streets. In Chiang Mai, as in many of the Thai cities, the streets are more like alleyways and paths. They are busy with stray chickens, dogs, and cats. There are no recognizable street signs that separate intersections, alleys, sidewalks, or lanes.

The reason I was running was clear. I felt exhilarated from the most incredible two-hour Thai massage I had been given the night before, and my leg muscles felt blown open. I normally have a lot of tension in my legs. After this massage, where my practitioner walked on my legs(!), I nearly passed out from the pain, and then, after the toxins had been released, I felt the rush of blood flow in my legs. That night I felt ecstatic and walked with incredible zeal through the streets of Chiang Mai. My body felt like a Raggedy Ann doll in front of a fan.

I was running that morning to feel my new legs. They had felt so light and swingy that I couldn't wait to take them for a test drive. As I was running along a street, crossing one of these strange, unmarked intersections, a motorcycle hit me. The driver was slowing down but couldn't stop in time as I ran across the narrow street-path in front of him. As his bike hit me, I felt no alarm in my body. I didn't feel the usual adrenaline that this kind of trauma would cause. Instead, I felt clear.

It was simple. There was a motorcycle, it was coming towards me, and I would move *with it*. My body memory recalled my aikido training, and I felt this intelligence in my bloodstream: Work with the force, then there is no counterforce. It was a spontaneous gift that my modest aikido training filled my plasma. I moved and *danced* with the motorcycle and rider. I held on to the handlebars as if he were my partner, rotated to face him, and skipped my knees up and together. I was hopscotching into the insult of the impact. When he managed to stop, I was happily facing him and hopped down. He apologized profusely (I think it was in Thai) and was ready to help me home. I smiled and said it wasn't his fault, explaining with my hands, touching my knee and smiling meekly that I was fine, thanked him, and kept on running. I still felt amazing, even more energized from the adrenaline.

When I got back to the guesthouse, my husband looked at the tire marks on my shin, "What happened?" I just waved my hand and said, "I got hit by a motorcycle" as I went into the shower giggling. I couldn't feel any insult to my body. My body was in such harmony with all the activity going on around it. For that reason, life became an interesting orchestra of events to dance with.

When the body feels relaxed and energized, it works with "what is." Stress is no longer impactful; it is another form of life. A mind in joy works directly with life in all its forms. There is a natural cellular willingness that alerts us to necessary actions. Stress is met as if it is the moment before it, which may have been pleasurable. Without a perception of each moment, the mind in joy meets all experiences with equal interest.

How to Live Joy

At this time in our evolution, we humans have an assignment. Our task is to learn on a cellular level how to live in joy. How do you know your cells, your plasma, your blood are circulating joy? You could measure your blood levels for oxytocin (the cuddle hormone) or serotonin (the happy hormone). Yet we know this is unnecessary.

We know when we feel joyful. There is no mistaking this feeling. You can forget what you had for lunch; you won't forget how someone made you feel. You won't forget how a date felt; if it is joyful it leaves a large, bright imprint.

Have you ever met someone who went to see a movie and said it was just awful? And then later that day you meet someone else who saw the same movie and was delighted with the script and recommended it highly?

When you are in joy, you are the second person. Not because they *liked* the movie. You are the lighter second person because you related to what you liked about it; you noticed where the talent was. You are the second person because you appreciate and tune into where the life is. If you were the second person and really didn't like the movie, you would have reported that you left and went for a burger, and "Damn was it good."

"I've learned that you can tell a lot about a person by the way he/she handles these three things: a rainy day, lost luggage, and tangled Christmas tree lights."

~ ATTRIBUTED TO MAYA ANGELOU (1928–2014),
AMERICAN POET AND CIVIL RIGHTS ACTIVIST

So … our task as an evolutionary human interested in feeling how to live in joy as a constant (not just on a good-movie day) means we hone how joy feels in us and choose that feeling. Joy is a choice. Choosing joy creates joy permanence. That's obvious! Why would I write something so very obvious?

We need to make joy more obvious in our lives. Up until now we have considered joy a luxury we earn. We need to discover and continue to discover where the joy is and choose that thought, event, person(s), environment, project, activity, and expression. We choose joy again and again. This is not only for our own good, it is also for our evolution. We evolve when there is peace or a present mind. We cannot evolve when we don't feel joy. That is so over.

CHAPTER FIVE

Joy Is Greater Physical Ability

Joy exists as a physical cellular intelligence in our cells. I discover this every day. When my arm reaches overhead to side bend with a soaring helium feeling, without my *doing* it, I feel fabulous. These spontaneous bursts of energy are how enthusiasm feels when we move without doing a rep of an exercise. This is inspired movement. The inspiration moves you. It's how your arms would raise if you found out you just won the lottery. (Congenitally blind people will shoot their arms overhead in elation if they found out they were lotto winners. The Victory arm movement is universal. It is not learned.) The Victory sign is joy on a cellular level.

Nietzsche said, "Put no trust in any thought that is not born whilst moving freely about." Bravo, buddy! My exact sentiments. We must move our bodies to feel joy. We must move our bodies to feel inspired. Please, please move your bum and hips in ways that feel amazing. Stop making bums of steel. Your bums need joy. When the bums-of-steel-athletes come to my yoga class, it's ugly. Their downward dog looks like they're vomiting. Please make a healthy, joyful body and move with clever joy. Movement keeps joy alive.

When you move, your mind moves with you and excavates a lot of the nasty footnotes in there. Inspired thoughts, solutions, resolutions, and compassionate feelings return. Try being frustrated as you drive home in gridlock from a game of volleyball on the beach, still sweating and with sand between your toes. It just doesn't happen. Gridlocked nasty people giving the finger forgot to exercise. You can't. You just can't rob your body of movement each day. It's mean. If twenty-four hours go by and you didn't raise your arms over your head—or your version of a big stretch, over time you could lose lung capacity. When you're in your lovely old, old years, you may die because you couldn't cough well. I don't usually like to pull out the big bad guns to threaten that you could die from pneumonia because you couldn't cough adequately when you're seventy-four. It's that, for some reason, we keep believing that the better our lifestyle gets the less wood we need to chop and the more gas fireplaces we can buy for our home. We are getting lazy on convenience.

Joy chops wood. Joy breathes deeply in yoga because it feels good. This deep breath keeps the alveoli in your lungs, which are moist grape sacks, swelling and stretching. The amount of oxygen you take in will expand your lung capacity. Your big breath means you can breathe less often and your respiration rate goes down, heart rate goes down, and you feel more alive. Instantly.

Joy takes you out for an early walk, long before you go to work, because joy knows you feel so good afterwards, even if you didn't sleep well. Joy knows that you always feel good after you move and that it will replace the extra hour of sleep you surrendered. And besides, you can feel self-righteous, and that's always fun.

Ugly exercisers are the joyless people you see slogging through the hills and pushing themselves at the side of the road. And I'm sorry about that as I used to be one of them. Now I have replaced hard-core results with the admirable way moving spontaneously makes me feel. Sarah used to tease me about my exercise time. I schedule ninety minutes a day to exercise. That doesn't include parking or showering. It's the time I spend on the booty *moi*. I know it's a lot! Yet ninety minutes a day for a physical vehicle that works for me twenty-four seven seems fair. We have struck a deal and I say it's non-negotiable. Nothing can bargain me out of my exercise. Even if the dishwasher breaks and the massive puddle is now towelled up and under control. I still go to the gym or beach if that's where I was headed. The dishwasher will still be there when I get back. I may not even call the repair guy until after my exercise just in case I let his urgent appeal to let him come right away coerce me.

No, exercise, movement, dance, or whatever gets your booty swishing is so relevant. Be relevant. Make your body relevant and let joy move it.

How much courage is needed
to play forever,
as the ravines play,
as the river plays.

BORIS PASTERNAK (1890–1960),
RUSSIAN POET, FROM "BACCHANALIA"

Oh yes, Sarah used to tease me because I would roll out my yoga mat, get the room nice before starting my practice—maybe play tunes or light incense, get on the mat, and start. She would be going upstairs as she saw me do this. Five minutes later, she may go by the front door and see me putting on my running shoes. "I thought you were doing your yoga?" "Me too," I'd say. "Apparently we're going running." Let your body tell you how to move. Be super good friends with your body and this will allow for clear communication. Like all relationships, you must listen to each other.

Eventually you will have a built-in interest that constantly listens to your body. Learn how to move. Learn the ways to move effectively and with care so you don't need to worry about going too far or bothering your knees. This can be done inexpensively or for free.

Just please, please move. Don't miss. Okay? Five days a week, minimum. And finally, just to be a wise guy, I have never heard someone regret that they exercised. Can you imagine? You see Jim at the office and he looks pretty glum. You ask him, "What's wrong?" He pauses and you wonder if you pried too far. He finally replies after a long sigh, "I got up early today and went for a run. And … well, I did it yesterday too. With others. I snuck out. There's a running group that leaves from the Running Room. I just … well, I couldn't stop myself. And I know I'm going again tomorrow." Ridiculous, right? Yet we are so filled with reasons why we can't exercise that there's no room in there for inspiration to enter. There is only one reason we don't exercise. Well … five actually:

1. We don't know how to value ourselves enough.
2. It's inconvenient.
3. We're afraid of injuring ourselves.
4. We're afraid that we won't keep it up and can't afford to feel discouraged if we don't, like last time.
5. We don't have enough time.

Yet all of these reasons are really the first one: We don't know how to value ourselves enough to exercise. We do the tasks we need to do in our day first. We are responsible. We help our children with their homework and miss time for ourselves. We are playing out the reliable, I'm-not-selfish script. Yet it is mean to not take care of yourself. Eventually this will affect your child. We just can't miss moving our bodies every day and taking care of them with fun, playful, spontaneous movement of some kind.

Because I often couldn't afford or get childcare, I included Sarah in my exercise time. During her first four years, she was my passenger in the baby jogger; the weights I "airplaned" over my body for bench presses and resistance curls; and my "backpack" for long walks on the beach, complete with cross country-skiing-like strides and lunges and merciless squats. She was also my personal trainer. One day as I was pushing her in the baby jogger up a hill, steeper than one wants to envision, at the ripe age of four she kept saying, "Faster Mommy! Faster Mommy!" I got childcare after that.

Also, to be a dedicated joyful body, you need to be joyfully self-ish. You need to put you and that bod of yours first. This means *you* before you make dinner, *you* before you run a last-minute errand, and *you* when on an all-inclusive in Cuba with the family and they're waiting for you to come to the breakfast buffet. Yes, oh Yes! You turn to your soon-to-be bewildered family and say you're going to do your exercises. You may feel like a selfish weirdo for only about a year. Give it all the seasons. Selfish people are happy. Selfish bodies feel amazing. Joy is selfish. Not for long though, as all the bodies around you soon feel the joy contagion, and you act like a pied piper accidently cajoling others into moving their buns. (You've got to own it!)

The body itself, our physical cells, have no ideas about what they *can* do. Thinking can never represent our physical potential. This is why movement is paramount when it comes to living joy. Joy doesn't *think*. Joy acts. A joyful body knows that thought limits our abilities because our full capacity cannot be known. If we simply move our bodies with play, frolic, trust, and the accompa- nying abandonment (while breathing well), we can experience a new range of motion in a joint. Please note: The range of motion will come from educating yourself with sensitive awareness of what movements work for you.

Someone says, "Take me to your leader!" You say, "You're looking at it. My body is the leader."

On its own, the body is not bothered by difficulty or being stretched far. The body will move with whatever leadership our minds give us. If we lose our minds, in the good way, and just be our cells, the body operates according to sensations. We directly experience *being* the body. I am happy to report that when you do something you have never, ever, even on a good day done before, you feel amazing and nothing blows—only the limit to what you thought you could do. By feeling the sensations in the body, you will not go too far. This is the joy of experiencing a new capacity that you have never felt before. You renew life in and around you.

This is yoking with your body and becoming one with your body, which is what the word "yoga" means. When you are one with your body, you move it with precision and playfulness. There is little time for discriminate thinking. Instead, you are "done" by the movement, in my case, the yoga.

What does it mean to be done by the yoga? Imagine a fire hose filling with water. Imagine a child chasing a runaway ball. Just imagine the falling, playing, and dropping into your life so completely that you think of nothing else. This is oneness with the body. This is to *be* your body rather than have a relationship to it.

Instead, you can be stimulated by how you live in your body. Meaning, when I do what is really, really important to me, such as exercising and moving, I feel the energy (code for incentive) to keep moving fluently and exercising in new and ingenious ways.

I discover new walking paths, and I find an art installation of red canoes on the North Don River Trail. I try balancing on a log I find on the beach—I don't plan to work on balance that day—I just see a large beckoning log. I am not following a requirement that I adhere to, it's just that I *do* it. I don't need new gyms, new programs to follow that are stimulating and provocative. The next new experience is inspired by the moment. This morning I started running slowly on the boardwalk when a little three-year-old guy broke away from his mom's hand and ran beside me. "You are soooo fast!" I enthused. I'm sure his mother will find us soon.

I love the look on a client's face when I bring their leg near their ear and they realize that they are not tight, they just needed someone to show them how to get their hip to release and how to pull their shoulder forward to get their leg back. A lot of what looks like Cirque du Soleil medieval torture in yoga is actually all about leverage, form, relaxing, and trusting. Honest.

You will become a person who knows the mind might have limits, and you will drop the mind and happily work with the body and see what happens. The joy you feel when you play your body this way will silence the mind. It will invite change. Changing enlivens your body. It is the result of this no-mind state. You will become a joy contagion and contaminate all the bodies around you with your inspired body.

One day I was working at a client's home doing a private exercise session. I had sprained my ankle the night before and it was quite swollen. Driving my standard car was a real test, and when I arrived at Susan's home I was still limping. Susan loves to use the session to share her personal issues and drink tea. Most activities are painful for Susan because she has severe scoliosis of the spine and finds most movement limiting. When we actually do exercise, I perform very gentle stretches on her using Thai massage and energy work on her muscles. On this occasion, at the end of the session when I was putting on my coat to leave, Susan asked me about a yoga pose. I was so excited that she wanted to know that I stood on my "bad" ankle and demonstrated the stork stand (tree pose). Then I turned and limped out to my car. However, when I was demonstrating the pose on my bad ankle, there was absolutely no pain because I was truly delighted that she wanted to know.

When the action is inspired, it is effortless. Even if the action is difficult, it doesn't register as difficult.

A Joyful Body Wants to See What It Can Do

The body is constantly guiding us in life. Where we feel stiffness is a kind of congestion in the tissues that keeps us from experiencing free, abandoned movement. (This may sound less than inspiring—it could take about ten years to feel the intelligence of your body. Isadora Duncan, one of our first modern dancers and choreographers, knew this back in the early 1900s. Later, Malcolm Gladwell confirmed that it takes a decade to develop any level of mastery over a skill.) When you geekishly observe the tension and want to know what it's about, you develop this ability to feel what the tight place in your body is telling you. It's like knowing your partner. You know when your partner is frustrated. You can tell in their body language and the tone of their voice, or whether they make eye contact.

It is the same with our bodies. If we feel the tension with a Sherlock Holmes curiosity, messages arise. They may not be known as you are stretching or practising a yoga pose that opens a tight neck. The message in the tension can show up hours after yoga, when you feel clear to say something to someone at work that creates effective teamwork. The opening in your neck during yoga helped you cess out what you needed to say.

One day when I was conducting a phone support session with a client at her workplace, she complained about her manager being a royal pain in the neck! I started to laugh. "Gloria, do you think that's why your upper back is jammed and you can't move your head?" She got it, her body got it, and she could feel the tension in her neck while I asked her this.

We objectify the body when we set goals for it. We lose the magic that is in an inspired body that wants to play, move out stiffness, and learn skills. We lose the beauty in our bodies' ability to move when we compartmentalize our bodies into components.

Often we think of our bodies in parts: buttocks, thighs, biceps, abs, and Achilles tendon. When we think of toning or stretching a part of our bodies rather than *living* that part, exercise becomes a task. This is not inspiring. An inspired body thrives, feels vital, and wants to move, be on a team, play, get outside and jump in that chalk hopscotch on the sidewalk. An inspired body takes itself to the gym or the basketball court. An inspired body organizes times to meet people for walks, runs, and hikes.

People think about their bodies. They think about body fat, tightness, soreness, symptoms, aches, arthritis, ability, and skill. Where's the love? Where's the "let's see what my body can do today?"

I don't know how we can live in joy without an inspired body. I just don't know if it's possible. Is it? I think of all the times in my life when I was in massive joy and I *know* my body felt amazing. Can we feel joyful when we deny the body of movement or high-energy food?

In all my years of experience with thousands of bodies in workshops, classes, in-home and clinic rehab, conferences, and private sessions, I have always seen folks feel amazing after an exercise, yoga, or dance session. Our bodies never wish we didn't exercise. We need to play our bodies to feel joy.

Interlude: Love is …

When my daughter, Sarah, was older, she would go to her father's for a month in the summer. I was used to having Sarah full time. Every summer friends would ask me, "Do you miss her?" "No!" I would laugh. Sarah and I were together all the time, in close proximity in our house, and we spent much of our time together out in nature. I knew Sarah really well, and she knew me. I always felt her in my heart. I loved my time with my friends and myself when Sarah was away.

Love is not needy, or fragile. Love thrives whether the beloved is here or not. When Sarah wasn't with me to share something funny that a squirrel just did, I didn't miss her. Having these wishes to share life with her felt like a celebration of our love and what we do together.

When Darwin wrote *The Descent of Man*, he mentioned "survival of the fittest" twice and the word "love" ninety-five times. In our society we have a perspective on love. Love is considered an emotion. It's an emotion that has so much charge to it that we may have reduced its meaning to a concept. When love is an emotion, it becomes a feeling to seek, share, and experience. Just as time is a concept to help organize our lives, seeing love as an emotion often conceptualizes our way of being in the world and treating others.

Love can be seen as being tolerant or understanding. Yet this is not love. "Many good and bad feeling are mistaken for love, [including] caring for, forgiveness of, tolerance of, infatuation with, dependence on, feeling close to, being friendly with, going to, accepting from, sacrificing to, being excited by, understanding of, and countless others."[1]

Yet true love is a reciprocal experience. When we love, it rewards us. Our experience of humanness is expanded. When we love someone, the beloved becomes all that they are. As do we. To love someone is to be all that you are.

"The resting place of my soul is a beautiful grove where my knowledge of you lives."

~ KAHLIL GIBRAN, FROM
LETTERS TO MARY HASKELL

Love is more than a sense of connection. It's when we meet ourselves. When we love another, we may believe we are extending

---

[1] Thomas Patrick Malone and Patrick Thomas Malone, *The Art of Intimacy* (New York: Simon & Schuster, 1987), 10.

out to them with a feeling or gesture. True love is *more* than an expression; it is within us. It connects us to what *is* us. Love inhabits our blood stream, it *is* the cells of our bodies, and it permeates our very being.

The statement "Love conquers all" is true. When we experience love, not feel it, it becomes our very biology or the vibrational hum inside us. This hum is a matrix that creates an inner harmony and enhanced communication between the systems of our bodies: endocrine, circulatory, lymphatic, muscular, skeletal, and more. When we experience love, our immune systems are enhanced for six minutes; our voices have a deeper resonance; our eyes dilate, creating a crisper picture; we become more alkaline; our heart rate lowers; and we have greater flexibility. Love cultivates creativity, teamwork, progress as we know it, and sensitivity, and thereby a greater sense of ourselves. When we are more sensitive, we experience what life has to offer.

A research team that randomly assigned a group of people to learn ways to create more micro-moments of love in their daily lives found that the function of the vagus nerve, which connects the brain to the heart, showed lasting improvement. This discovery shows how micro-moments of love can serve as nutrients for your health.[2]

When we truly love, we love someone for who they are. We connect to them and have no expectations. We love them in their messiness and their tenderness. We may not be able to say the reasons we love them for love is vaster than any thought. Love is the vibrational experience of being in non-duality or joy.

[2]Barbara Fredrickson, 10 Things You Might Not Know about Love (January 24, 2013), https://www.cnn.com/2013/01/24/health/love-psychology-book.

"Your love lifts my soul from the body to the sky
… I want your sun to reach my raindrops,
So your heat can raise my soul upward like a cloud."

~ RUMI (1207–1273), PERSIAN POET,
PHILOSOPHER, THEOLOGIAN,
AND SUFI MYSTIC

PART TWO

Joy isn't ...

*"Unravel the ravish;
mingle in the magnitude of the mess."*

~ CELESTE SHIRLEY

CHAPTER SIX

Living with Expectations

Expectations are when we have a view of how our life is *supposed* to look. I notice, for example, that I expect someone to follow through with what they say they will do. To me, that's basic respect. Yet today's fast-paced living and Rubik's Cube windows of scheduled time show me that many people rush to make last-minute plans, and as a result they don't do what they said they would. I see "basic respect" as an expectation. I expect people to behave or act a certain way, which makes me a fantastic candidate for disappointment.

Expectations cancel joy. Expectations set us up for disappointment. They birth feelings of discouragement, anger, depression, anxiety, and resentment. Expectations diminish our intelligence by creating confusion.

We are confused when we expect. If I expect you to be on time for a lunch date and you are thirty minutes late, I'll be the ugly one in the restaurant. If I don't have expectations, I'll be the person in the restaurant eating great food until you arrive, writing another blog, meeting a great man, finding out about raw chaga mushrooms that are good for my immune system from the server who is a granola raw foodist/vegan, or cleaning my ears with the (free!) Q-tips I discovered in the fabulous restroom, which I am having a hard time leaving.

I am not confused about what I want to do with this extra time I have. (Yay, extra time!) When you live in joy, you are sooo in the moment that you are annoying. Simply nothing, nothing gets to you. You experience all moments directly, and no occurrence causes negative emotions that stick.

Because I have no expectations, I am not confused. I will state and clarify agreements, boundaries, and ways that work. Stating and creating boundaries is the opposite of expectations. When you arrive at the restaurant, I will clarify how much time I have to meet with you.

Why do we develop expectations in the first place? We are convinced (been brainwashed actually) that if we didn't have expectations and ideals, we would be aimless, or, God forbid, radical, free-willed humans. We believe we need A Plan. Our brains—which think—don't know how to be free willed. To be free willed is to be in the unknown. When in the unknown we're vulnerable. Our brains will register vulnerability as risky. When we are scared, we scramble to design The Plan. We are terrified of our own unruliness. Aimlessness is unnerving to the mind. It means we are not in control …

*"… when the earth is quaking
and the compass is lost."*

~ RICHARD GEER, POET AND ASTROLOGER,
FROM THE POEM "THE HAND"

When in pure joy, we experience pure consciousness. Pure consciousness does not think. Pure consciousness senses what to do in each instant. You can sense what to do as you are not on the defensive or calculating. You stop Googling.

When you see that you are having expectations, you are in a fabulous position to drop them.

How Do You Know You Are Having Expectations?

It's ridiculously fundamental. When you are experiencing anything that is *not* joy or pure presence of mind, you are having expectations. Or you are carrying forward a concern that is clouding that moment. When we are scared, rather than being interested in what is happening, worry and concern thoughts arise. For example, if I expect to feel good after yoga, I will be concerned if my knee hurts.

If I don't expect my yoga to cause me to feel better, then I will be interested in the sensation in my knee and how to best move it during practice and the rest of the day. I may realize that my ligament is out of alignment and work on certain poses to help the alignment. If this is the fourth time it has hurt after yoga, then I may schedule time with my physio to check it. The discomfort shows me what's working in my body and what parts need attention. This is good to know.

Joy is an inside job, not a feeling that is based on limber knees. A mind in joy cannot assemble an expectation with its own energy. You can only directly experience what is happening. When you are in joy, you can only taste a taste, hear a sound, see a view. You experience only how it makes you feel. At the same time, how you feel does not define you, it opens you to the experience and dilates your moment in life.

A mind in *duality*, or out of joy, is different. If you like what you are tasting, hearing, or seeing, no expectation develops. If you *don't* like what you're tasting, hearing, or seeing, you develop a view of it that is a judgement that then becomes an expectation. Expectations and judgements hang out together. They are codependent.

Expectations Cause Discouragement

When life's events do not turn out as we planned, we often feel discouraged. Discouragement fosters regret. We feel regret when what we expect to happen doesn't occur. Regret is a form of petulant non-acceptance. Regret is expectations solidified. Expectations destroy the moment; we get busy wishing and comparing. We actually corrupt and deploy the energy of the mind that is creative and imaginative.

CHAPTER SEVEN

Living with Judgements

"I prefer to see life as an undulating force—which is more an Oriental process of perception. I disagree with Western thought, with its mind/body split, its good/evil split. You have to cultivate a dialogue with life that's less judgemental, yet has a greater attention span."[1]

~ JONI MITCHELL, CANADIAN SINGER-SONGWRITER

Expectations complicate our lives. By having expectations and wishing life to be different than it is, we birth judgements. Judgements are when we rate *how* life is going. We become a critique. That is a lousy way to taste life.

When we judge, we are separate from others and from life. Judgements separate us from what is happening. A pure mind in joy is not interested in rating life this way. Actually, a mind in joy cannot

---

[1] Joni Mitchell, interview by Timothy White, *Joni Mitchell*, March 17, 1988, http://jonimitchell.com/library/print.cfm?id=390.

feel a judgement; it can only directly experience life. Judgements distort connections with others. When we think of someone in a certain way, we create a view of them. Even if we truly love and appreciate them, the judgement view will reduce the connection.

Have you ever noticed how convincing a judgement thought is? How very helpful it is to think of someone in a certain way and then act from that perspective. It offers a sense of certainty. It gives us a sense of direction. We confuse judging with a kind of mastery to take the best course of action and reduce risk. We are not trusting, we are discerning.

So why don't we live free of judgement when it is actually more enlivening?

We start to judge when we don't like what's happening. It is a form of self-preservation. By judging how *they* are, we can stop feeling how we are separating from them. Separating always feels uncomfortable. The more we separate from someone because we don't like what they're doing, the less discomfort we feel temporarily. Focusing on how someone behaves distracts us from our own discomfort.

If we are able to be in the discomfort rather than judge someone or what is happening, we can be alive in the discomfort. What does it mean to feel awkward *and* feel alive? It feels unsettling and provokes anxiety. Isn't that just so attractive? To be alive in the discomfort will not sound like a good move. It's ugly and is not a confidence builder. Yes, feeling out of control, not knowing how or exactly what to do will feel like the very best time to judge. Yet you can't.

You simply do not want to judge when you feel uncomfortable. You can't because you will miss out on what that moment is showing you about yourself. (Stay tuned for how this is true.) We open to the reason we feel uncomfortable or angry and know ourselves more. Opening to the judgement and milking it to see what's really going on allows us to be compassionate towards the other person and our own discomfort. This softer view will foster a clarity to take the best action.

So what do you do when you feel judged? You get really intelligent. You dig down below the sticky grit of judgement where you feel you are not allowed to be you. It's tricky to spatula yourself from the awful feeling. Yet you must pause and keep feeling for your true self. You are in there.

You will not feel like *you* when you are judging. Even slightly. There is no real slightly judging. Or slightly being pregnant. Judging births tighter, less inspired thinking, and any tiny or convenient judgement will reduce your joy.

When you feel like yourself again you will fill in with a warmth. The muscles of your eyes will release and your pupils will dilate. You will see a crisper picture of life.

When I think I'm *not* allowed to do something, I know I am judging myself. A learned conditioned-thinking program is taking over. The program tells me what I *am allowed* to do. This inner critic developed when I was young. As a child, if I didn't do something the way it was expected, my mom could be critical. I was often nervous about making sure I did a good job and on time. To this day, when I see someone taking their time when doing something, I think, "What a slacker! What are they doing?" If it doesn't seem as though they are really going to work at what they're doing, a deep-seated template in my mind has a hard time being with them. At the same time I know, because I'm not comfortable with how they operate, I'm critiquing how they act and anticipating how they will act. I can even feel when I'm doing this, and it feels terrible. I feel guilty for and helpless from watching them this way. I feel ungenerous and I know I'm separating from them. Sometimes I feel that I can't operate the way I do around them and feel I must slow down. In those moments where I separate, I don't know how to be who I am or

> When I think I'm not allowed to do something, I know I am judging myself.

how to operate alongside them. I'm not respecting myself.

It used to be so tricky to catch the fact that I was having a hard time being with that person. I had to dig deep to *be* there. I didn't know how to feel free to be me, which is to move at high speed, usually in a blur, without having a view of them. I was used to noticing how people behave because I was used to being watched.

I knew I had to be free of a view of them to be who I was. This was the only way to return to myself and feel alive again. It took arduous practice to catch myself judging someone and thinking about *them*. (Today it doesn't take discipline; it is natural for me to recognize when I am judging. Then I choose to return back to what it feels like to be who I am and how I operate.)

After I catch myself judging, I pause and come back into what it feels like to be me, which always feels enlivening. When I judge, my head feels tight, and I feel slightly, or extremely, contracted in my posture. When I feel this, I know I have to do a personal intervention to bring me back.

Judging Judy: Stopping the Judgemental Thoughts

I used to find myself judging my mom for judging! One day when she was speaking, all I could hear were the disapproving accusations she was making about her friend Judy. I would get to the point where I couldn't believe the way she was speaking, and I would have such a hard time listening to her.

When I realized I was judging, I knew I needed to make a correction in my thinking. So I would pause. (When you make the correction, you actually change how you feel and are able to stop thinking about the other person. You simply listen.)

As my mom would be talking about Judy, I thought, "How can you say that?" My mom told me that Judy was going to therapy for the sexual molestations she experienced when she was a young child. When my mom finished outlining the details, she became agitated. She felt that Judy's going to therapy was a waste of time and "just unnecessary" at her age.

I realized I was thinking the same thing about my mom. "How can you say that, Mom?" Then I thought, okay just *be* with Mom. Everything in my physiology started to shift, soften, and relax. A stillness was pervading the tight feeling and opening up my contracted posture. My brain stopped. I could feel my neck and shoulders relax and my chest area expand back and my shoulders drop. I opened up to her and was *with* her again instead of watching and thinking, "Why are you so critical?" And I will never forget this: My mom stopped talking. She looked up to the right and completely changed the direction of what she was saying. In my comic mind, her head boomeranged around and back.

Then she said, "Maybe that's just what Judy has to do." She completely changed her demeanor. She looked deep into my eyes. We had a moment of crystalline, potent silence. I felt a deep shift in the air. Angels sang.

I felt fabulous. I chose joy instead of judgement. I milked the judgemental feeling. I didn't separate from her like I usually do. This time I was really able to catch myself judging, and this didn't feel like I was *with* her. As soon as I milked the judgemental feeling, the air completely reset, her story shifted, and she simply spoke of Judy's choice with more interest. She humbly expressed that she didn't understand her actions. She shrugged her shoulders, eyebrows raised, as if to say, "Well it's up to her."

*"If you are irritated by every rub,
how will you be polished?"*

~ RUMI (1207–1273), PERSIAN POET, PHILOSOPHER,
THEOLOGIAN, AND SUFI MYSTIC

When I judge others in my life, I know I am out of joy. I can never, ever feel a judgemental thought when in pure joy. Ever. In the months I have been in joy continuously, a judgemental thought could not assemble in my mind. I experienced each occurrence in my life only directly. When I am in duality and I look at the ways I judge others in my life, I see that I think I know that they are not doing enough to be what they could be. As if I would know! This mirrors the desperate, separated aspect of myself that feels that I must be really, really good.

By noticing when I have a judgemental feeling and milking it, I see how the judgement highlights how I feel about myself. The value of my perfectionistic, self-incriminating inner critic is its impeccable ability to detect when anyone is minimizing themselves. If I hear a client, student, friend, or even a soul on the subway say something negative about their aging body, big bad bum, or any other body shaming, I feel as though I'm going to jump them. After I jump them, I want to hug the shit out of them to make them stop. (Clinically speaking.)

I did this in Thailand with my husband, André. We were riding on our bikes back to our guesthouse. We had just completed our Thai massage certification exam at the Old Medicine Hospital in Chiang Mai. The practical exam was held in a large room where we were examined in pairs working on Thai massage mats. It took each of us up to two hours to complete. After I finished my exam, I spent hours at the side of the room passionately speaking with a guy from Australia while André was still taking his exam.

After André finished he started to come towards us. I looked over to see if he wanted to go. He could see we were deeply engaged and waved his hand indicating that we continue. Mr. Australia and I continued conversing for a very long time, and then I looked over at André again and asked him with my eyes if he wanted to go. He nodded, and I finished my exchange and said goodbye to Mr. Australia, and André and I jumped on our bikes.

Halfway home in Chiang Mai traffic, which resembles a Rubik's Cube, André looked back at me, "Do you like that guy?" I thought I would melt on the spot! I forced him with my bike to pull over onto the sidewalk and jumped him. Once I tackled him onto the grass and was sitting on his pinned-down waist, I said, "No, I love you! *And* I loved talking to him, and I love being with you, you bonehead!"

If we could just show our vulnerability like André did, then we could tackle the fear out of each other when we felt it. Generally, we keep acting like a bunch of tough guys. We don't share how scared we are. How could we? No one showed us. You don't say to your wife, "Do you like that young thing?" I was so touched by André's vulnerability that I loved him even more in that moment. I felt closer to him. He was only slightly injured by my tackle.

Self-criticism Gets Useful

When I have a self-critical thought, I now know I am pushing myself to do something right.

I'm not free to create a fantastic outcome that represents my creative ability. I'm not free to be who I am and trust myself.

I developed this inner critic from the way my mom chastised me when I was young. She unknowingly shamed my body and my ambitious mind. If I went past what she considered a particular amount of fun or got "carried away," she would say, "That's enough" or "Leave your father alone." I developed an innate What-Is-Allowed Ceiling, which to this day says, "That's enough, Celeste. You are clearly bothering people with your unbridled enthusiasm and you need to get off the stage."

It can be really scary to say what I know without believing a firing squad in the form of my wee mother won't show up. This commonly experienced phenomenon of shining too bright is referred to as "imposter syndrome." My insecurity of shining too brightly plays out alongside not feeling good enough. Together they create speed bumps.

When I fly with what I know, the teaching soars through to the audience. I feel all that I am in that moment. I see the group commune into a great knowing. They nod and touch down into greater self-understanding. The class leaves brighter, lifted, lighter, more themselves. When I teach what I know, I shine and take the group with me. We lift each other higher. We become all that we are.

Judgement of self or another can't even arise from a lifted mind. This expanded awareness (of this lifted consciousness) is when we are completely who we are. We feel unified and whole. All the ways that we are and all facets of life meet, converge, and create a confluence of "invisible rainbows folded into light."[2] In English, this means that you can trust life. You can trust that if you are *living* in each moment, it is workable and weaving a larger next moment. You don't need to settle down; you can be your big self.

So next time someone tells you to settle down, shine, open, press your shoulders back and say it anyway.

"When I am unhappy, dear Mary, I read your letters. When the mist overwhelms the 'I' in me, I take two or three letters out of the little box and reread them. They remind me of my true self. They make me overlook all that is not high and beautiful in life. Each and every one of us, dear Mary, must have a resting place somewhere."

~ KAHLIL GIBRAN, FROM THE LOVE LETTERS
OF KAHLIL GIBRAN AND MARY HASKELL

---

[2] Drew Dellinger, "Hymn to the Sacred Body of the Universe," in *Love Letter to the Milky Way: A Book of Poems* (Ashland, OR: White Cloud Press, 2011), 11.

To know what you know, to stay true to your way of living, requires support. Find your tribe. Be with folks who hear you. Be with lovely people who listen. Be with people who see you and where you become more of what you are.

Make Sure You Feel a Part of a Tribe

I have done this for years. I have a coven of friends who know how tender I feel in the world and how deeply I experience life. At times I can feel like open prey in the world marketplace. I can call on one of these souls and unleash the sobs, the disbelief, the feeling that I must be living wrongly. It helps me realize that my knowing that "life is perfect and can be lived magically and with an accelerated ease" is not insane. Even if the world is telling me to "get real," or "that's just the way it is," or "you can't have it all," and other such "don't get too excited" warnings. I can call them up and touch back into who I am and live with self-agency. I stop feeling as though I need to play small, stop loving with such abandonment, or stop feeling that I better settle down.

When you live in joy, you will be living a misplaced sanity that is different from the mainstream. You may feel like a different species. Living joyfully you will do what is important to you and may have a hard time relating to others. Hone the unique aspects of yourself.

Make sure you spend time with people who respect how you live and care about what you are experiencing. I often find after I leave a conversation I feel so affected by the general mood of apathy that I wonder if anyone even heard me. I feel as though no one saw *me*. I feel invalidated! Take care of those hard feelings after you feel deflated by an environment or the people in it. Have a cavalry you can call. Develop a team that's on your side. Call the buggers. Anytime you

There is no such thing as "too sensitive." The way you experience the world helps you feel what you need.

need it. Practise until it feels weird to hold pain, like an outfielder running with the football and saying, "I don't have anything!"

Strive to have nothing. Carry forward nothing, no stories, no "what he dids" and absoloootely no shames. Be good to you. So good that feeling a painful hurt becomes the gift it is—a place where the discomfort directs you.

Life after Judgement Day

When not judging, we live the free mind of non-duality and know instant by instant what to do. We are locked into each moment like a child chasing a butterfly. In the next moment she is on her knees looking at an ant. (I *know* because my daughter had a bug catcher. If we weren't on the teeter-totter, we were collecting bugs and looking at caterpillars through the magnified bottom of the bug catcher.) Children are so fit, alive, and active because they live in joy. The first passion of joy is wonderment. They are wonderment experts. They experience life directly and see how it occurs.

When you experience directly, you are unable to judge. A judgement cannot arise from you as no seeds of liking or disliking can create a view. No ideas of good, bad, colourful, bland, exciting, dull, or even mean people bother your creative mind.

Why does not judging allow you to live with more intimacy, joy, and a sense of interconnection? I'm so glad you asked. When you experience life directly, it's like removing a film that has clouded your view. Now you really sense and feel what you need. In joy, you feel safe. When you remove the judgement film, you recognize that –

- you no longer believe you need to protect yourself from life and that it will hurt and affect you;
- you know there will be hurtful moments alongside the beauty in life; and
- you know the hurting is opening you up.

Now, or soon, this difficult experience will deliver a potent and vibrant experience of life. You will sense a truth that courses through your body. This truth is like answers to prayers. The answers can be subtle "knowings" of what to do, recognition that it doesn't matter what the cost is, or a realization that you cannot continue in the same way. These truths are promptings that afford you true action. You get real. You become super you. Soon it is impossible to feel any occurrence in your life as bad, worrisome, or unfair. What a relief. Really.

Let's pause and have a beauty moment. You can actually relax in life, even when life is falling apart. One time when I was supporting my daughter who was going through an emotional breakdown, I looked up at the tree we were under in the ravine. My face lit up. There was a family of baby squirrels piling on top of each other. She was talking, and I looked at her and said, "Sweetie?" as I didn't want her to think I wasn't listening. She knew I was going to point to something. I was so captivated by the beauty that I couldn't ignore the frolic of the squirrels, and her face lit up when she looked at them. Beauty is all around us and can open us up at all times.

If you are here and openly reading this, even if you have just recovered from a whippingly wicked divorce or your child is ill, missing, or depressed, then you know you're hurting will tenderize you and open you to feel the next supportive experience that will occur. For when you are *here*, you experience everything.

When you *don't* judge, you experience the support in your life. Each moment of our existence has an element of support. When you are not judging your experience, the support can enter.

The Self-care of Non-judgement

If I *must* follow a rule or requirement, be with or experience someone who is mean or cruel, or listen to painful news, then I find a way to express *how* the occurrence is affecting me. I find a way to say what I feel.

Expressing how life affects and touches you is provocative. Find a mentor or emotional sanctuary where you can air your frustrations or explore and imagine how you would do what's important to you if you had a choice. Go crazy with this. Let all your monster thoughts come out to play. Be ridiculously, radically playful with wild solutions and let them randomly run around the front lawn of your imagination like a bunch of five-year-olds.

Self-expression is the flip side of judgement.

This kind of experimental exploration helps you stay interested in life, inspired, and imaginative, and not become a dull automaton lying in a puddle of deflated dreams. It helps you invent better ways. Even if you can't apply those ways, it helps you see what you think to reveal your talents, abilities, and imaginative knowledge.

This helps you to grow and cultivate ideas you have and see who you are and how you love to live in the world. This will amp up the imaginative part of your mind. Sussing out the imaginative knowledge is a way to stay fresh in a hard world when you need to feel the organizing, tender inner truth.

No Forgiveness

The root of "forgive" is the Latin word *perdonare*, meaning "to give completely, without reservation." (That *perdonare* is also the source of our English word "pardon.") *Per* was replaced with "for," a prefix that in this case means "thoroughly," and *donare* with *giefan* ("to give"). The result, *forgiefan*, appeared in Old English, meaning "to give up, allow."

When I read this original meaning of forgiveness, I felt relieved. I admit, I'm a linguistic snob and have a bristling response to the way forgiveness is commonly used. When we use forgiveness to "pardon someone" or "tolerate" them, we are positioning ourselves in a firm stand of "power over."

Power over someone is how we separate from them. Power over someone is when we focus on what they have done or what happened. We let the difficult occurrence cause hard feelings. If the hard feelings continue to escalate, we try to command the situation through force. It is to judge. In this way of using forgiveness, we are pardoning another's actions. Not a powerful or fun place to plant ourselves, and certainly lacking in levity. How can self-growth arise from such a forceful stand? Are we really in touch with what we're feeling and thinking?

How can we forgive another? Don't we need to give our power away to forgive them? Would we really do that? We can't really forgive *them*. They didn't take our power away. We did. We give our power away when we view what someone has done, rather than what we feel (and what you need). We are thinking about them. Them. We are not thinking about ourselves. We need to forgive ourselves.

The original meaning of to forgive cited above portrays what true forgiveness offers. When we forgive someone, in the true sense, we *give for*—give and offer up ourselves. We find ourselves when we feel how the difficult occurrence affected us.

In my life I feel a generous enthusiasm to help others. At times I can go far with this enthusiasm and feel inspired to offer more than is best for me. In Buddhism this unabashed overly generous behaviour is referred to as "idiot compassion." A compassionate idiot gives and offers more than is healthy.

In 2000 I took my Ashtanga yoga certification with a world-renowned yogi, David Swenson. There were thirty teachers from around the globe clustered together to learn the poses of this flowing yoga. In our large room there were teachers from Japan, the States, Alaska, and many from Canada. They were all qualified practitioners of Ashtanga yoga. Except me. I was a newbie and didn't even know the basic routine. I respected these yoga teachers and was highly impressionable (code for candidate to be an idiot).

I began my training and finished the course with the group in ten days. By the end of our gruelling days of training, lunches together, adjusting each other, and sharing clothing and tears, we had bonded. Many friendships were established. One woman, who was a teacher, lived close to me and we would travel on the subway to and from the course. Her name was Amelia. I liked Amelia's down-to-earth style and relaxed approach to this powerful yoga practice. She taught in-home private sessions to her clientele.

At the end of our certification, I committed to practising Ashtanga yoga six days a week. Amelia suggested I hire her for private sessions. We started seeing each other once a week. She would teach me the series of poses. After six months, we had become close friends.

A few months later, Amelia said she was going to buy a large investment property and needed to get a mortgage. She was living in an apartment at the time. She asked me how I had managed to get my mortgage. She was a single mom and self-employed, just like me.

I made some helpful suggestions and she came back saying none of them had panned out. She asked me if I had any equity in my property. Before she could even ask the next question, I said, "What a great idea!"

Enter the idiot compassion contestant, moi. I remortgaged all, yes, *all* the equity in my wee house and gave it to Amelia. I felt fantastic doing it. Until I didn't. Just before we closed the deal, which took a lot of legal fees to transfer the funds, I asked her for a signed agreement. Her response: "Well that would kind of go against the whole reason we're not using an institution in the first place, right, Celeste?" I felt embarrassed and somewhat guilty—like a bad girl (my usual shamed response). Shame caused me to doubt the scary red flag flailing in front of me.

For the next year and a half, payments were made to my bank account on time every month. Then there wasn't one. I called

Amelia. She had many reasons why, and most of them were bizarre. She apologized and deposited the money into my account. Then a few months later, the same thing happened. This went on for a while longer, until the payments stopped completely. After months of going to her yoga studio to address this and all attempts on my part to get my fucking money back, I hired an assassin, I mean lawyer. Robert White was said to be the best in his field. I discovered Amelia was selling her house. He put a lien on her property. He said it didn't look good, at all. It turns out that dear Amelia had already been through many States and had been up to this kind of fraudulent behaviour for quite some time. He said there was a very slim chance I would get any of my money back. There were many liens in line ahead of mine for larger amounts. Gotta love those yoga teachers.

I was, as my mother would say, livid. I couldn't believe it. I was worried beyond repair. I told no one except the good people in my life with whom I could share such news without being chastised and my sanity questioned. I was already doing that quite adequately myself.

Sleeping became an option. Joy was not in my building as much. I used every skill that I had to come back to feeling joy and feeling alive. I wasn't very successful. Until I let myself lose it.

One day I called my neighbour, Norm, in the semidetached house I lived in and told him I was practising for a play and that it would be loud and nasty. I let him know not to worry and that I wasn't being attacked.

I went to the full-length mirror. I looked at an imaginary image of Amelia. I screamed my rage at her. I let out every morsel of hate I felt. This was real hate. It was rage, it was disbelief, it was "who the fuck does that!" As I raged, I saw the "me" leave. I saw a hollow, piercing face complete with darting eyes and constricted throat. I looked soulless. I raged until I was done. Immediately I felt free and energized.

The phone rang. I looked at the display and it was my friend Terry. Four weeks earlier he had called me to get together. He was feeling depressed after seventeen weeks of interferon treatment. Terry had contracted hepatitis C when he was young. Now in his sixties, the symptoms were overwhelming and he decided to treat it. His doctor made it clear that the interferon treatments had only a fifty per cent success rate. Terry had completed the treatments months earlier and was only just starting to feel a little better. He was really depressed. We got together and went for a gentle run on the beach. I ran circles around him and teased him to catch up. He told me all about the treatments. "When do you get tested to find out the results?" I asked.

"In two weeks, August 11th."

"What day is that?"

"A Thursday."

I knew I would be teaching that day and couldn't go with him, and he didn't seem to want me to. "Hey, Terr, would you be okay if I asked all my friends to be with you in spirit on that day and we can hold that your cells are in harmony?"

He looked a little perkier. "Sure, why not, it can't hurt."

"Great."

On August 11 at eight o'clock in the morning, I asked the client I was working with, Merle, if we could hold in our consciousness for Terry that his body was back in harmony and free of hepatitis C. We both made a silent wish for him.

Then he called. I knew he would have the results. I clicked the phone open. "Celeste …"

I started screaming, "Yes! Yes! Terry, that's great!" I could tell by his voice that the test was negative. He was free of hepatitis C.

He laughed. "Yeah, okay, I guess I don't need to tell you." I was so elated that I forgot the reason I was yelling *before* Terry called. Norm must have thought the play had a happy ending.

Back to my beloved yoga-teacher witch, Amelia. Each day, with utter sarcasm and fetid frustration, I would send love to the awful Amelia. I would bless the bitch. I would consider how crazy pained she must be to take money from people with no remorse, while adjusting people's downward dogs. She was running a yoga studio in central Toronto.

After I got *that* over with, I would do a blessing of the whole situation. I asked that the truest outcome for both of us would occur. I asked that the situation bring forth the highest learning for everyone (oh yes, and that Amelia would fall down a very large pothole into an abyss where there was a lot of fire). I would feel the charge of what I felt about her. I thought she was cruel. I felt trampled on. As I let all the hard feelings surface, I saw that I felt as though I had prostituted my energy. The money I had loaned her could be taken. I realized I needed to value myself more. This was a theme in my life: (1) not feeling enough, (2) giving myself away energetically, and (3) feeling I needed to give so much, in this case to share all that I had. The lessons were clear each day as I felt the anger and fear. Each time I felt the anger and thought of her as a whore, I knew it was the feeling of prostituting my energy away that was the cause.

"Much of your pain is self-chosen. It is the bitter potion by which the physician within you heals your sick self. Therefore trust the physician, and drink his remedy in silence and tranquility: For his hand, though heavy and hard is guided by the tender hand of the Unseen."

~ KAHLIL GIBRAN, FROM *THE PROPHET*, "ON PAIN"

Each time I felt the rage, each time I felt foolish, each time I worried, I would do this exercise. I would feel what I felt and forgive myself. I got to a clearing in my mind. This was a diligent practice I did every time I felt fear. Feeling the rage was a deep entry into the resentment I felt about believing I needed to give so much in life. The anger, conveniently directed at Amelia, was my elixir to be my true, powerful self. Now I knew how it felt to give my energy away. I could feel the moment when I asked Amelia for the signed agreement and she had shamed me. This was a new wormhole in my psyche and soma. I would be able to feel truisms more acutely when with people: I could now be who I am without giving myself away.

My lawyer called on a Friday morning at 10:30. I remember because I was doing my yoga practice on the front deck. I had stopped as I felt overwhelmed with anxiety and was not able to go into poses. I always stay with my practice when I schedule my yoga time, so I stayed on the mat and put the acupuncture ball under my neck to relieve the stress.

I picked up the phone. "Hi, Celeste, it's Robert White. Amelia sold her house. You got your $68,000 back." Silence. I'm ready to do a headstand, handstand, cartwheel, and levitate.

"Oh … my … God." I manage to utter.

"Yeah, there was a long lineup of liens on her property, and somehow you came out on top. It doesn't even make sense. I don't know how it happened."

Then of course I turn into a way too happy yogini and say, "I did meditate on it that I would get …"

"Well I don't believe any of that crap. But, you got all your money. I'll see you in my office Monday morning to give you the cheque?"

Minutes before the call, I had been feeling overwhelmed with fear again. My vacation started the next day. How would I ever relax? That's when the phone rang.

When I was in my twenties, I made a pact with myself to live so authentically that my life would be seamless. I wanted to feel the same way and be the same person in my yoga studio teaching, in front of a large audience facilitating, or having coffee with you in my kitchen. I wanted all areas of my life to arise from what I am and what I am here to do. I didn't want to "go to work" and put on a poised professional cap. I wanted to keep the same head while teaching so that my teaching would never be work, but an expression.

This *is* my life today. By being true to myself and doing what I know I'm here to do—to teach about the body and mind as I am experiencing it—fosters a very strong sensitivity. I can feel when I am not being my true self and following what I don't really believe. When I left the personal-training company (as described in chapter three, "Joy Is a Choice") and continued running my own business, I felt myself fill in again. I became all of life, I was whole and complete. That feeling, that joy buzz that filled me up, is the way a body that is truthful feels. By experiencing how I prostituted my energy to Amelia, I saw how I would lose this harmony in myself and give more than is necessary. I saw where I would be a martyr and overextend myself. Women have been giving more of themselves than is healthy for hundreds of years. I touched down into what it *felt like* to do this. When I saw my face in the mirror as I raged, I saw a hollow, depleted, soulless self. The disbelief and the rage went like this: "Who the fuck does that? You fucking whore! Get out of my house!" When I felt all the vile, caustic emotional energy as I raged in the mirror, the message was clear. Each of the following statements showed me what I thought about myself in the world:

1. "Who the fuck does that?" showed me that at times I feel so alive that I do not see where someone is taking energy from me. (Money is a form of energy.) I actually do not realize that I feel shamed by someone and am cowering into agreement.

2. "You fucking whore!" showed me that I was giving my energy away entirely in the physical sense—I used my entire material worth—I used all the equity I had in my house. *I* was prostituting my energy.

3. "Get out of my house!" (I pictured her in front of me as I yelled this.) I was making a declaration about how I would live in the world and that I would not let anyone in my house (my body *and* actual home) who did not belong. I would feel how to do this. I recalibrated my mind and nervous system to be acutely aware of negative energy.

The true forgiveness I experienced with Amelia was recognizing how I give my energy away. I forgave myself for not honouring the fearful red flag I felt when I asked for legal binding. I sourced where the real pain was. I felt rage because I didn't trust myself to question her or feel that I could. I gave the greatest gift back to myself: trust. Trust in myself.

Today, every time I feel overwhelmed, I milk the feeling. I ask myself, "What's there?" I help myself *into* the feeling. The wormholes of energy open up in my tissues. The emotions coursing through me are given air time. I feel them.

I bring back the joy that is the intelligence in the cells. It's a must. I must feel who I am. When I milk the feeling I am updated by how the lesson has changed me. Joy is deployed and infiltrates the tissues. Every time.

Now, over to *you*. Do joy, only joy. Milk the feeling, come back to who you are. Which is joy. And please, please, watch out for those yoga teachers.

CHAPTER EIGHT

Drama-free Emotional Living

Living in joy is flow. It has the qualities of grace and tenderness. This flowing experience of life allows you to be receptive. When receptive, you can hear compliments, criticism, insults, and loving support. You are with all that happens and none of what happens is personal. You see that what happens is either helpful or it causes you to contract. You start to naturally utilize and receive what is helpful.

No Need to Choose

No discernment is necessary when we are in joy, we choose naturally. We can sense what is right for us. This happens when our emotions guide us. It is only when we attempt to play emotional tour guide for ourselves or someone else that we create problems. Trying to gauge our emotions or control them is nothing less than exhausting, and it traps us. The emotions we experience in joy are different from the emotions experienced in duality or out of joy. We experience the emotions in joy directly. They do not cause suffering. Ever.

Emotions When in Joy

You experience emotions when in joy directly. You feel what you feel with no story attached to it. You experience the emotion and no one gets hurt when you do, including yourself.

EMOTIONS EXPERIENCED IN JOY

- Happiness
- Discomfort (and its offshoot, sadness)
- Anxiety

Happiness and discomfort stem from love, as do all emotions in joy. Yet anxiety slips in there even though it does *not* stem from love. It's surprising to realize you can feel uncomfortable when you feel peaceful. We have been taught that we will *not* feel uncomfortable when we are peaceful.

It's helpful to know we will. When we live in joy, we will meet life and what can happen there. The discomfort shows us the importance of what is happening. The unease is meaningful. If we didn't feel unsettled, we wouldn't know what we need to do or accept. The unease is a prompting.

In the natural world when a baby chick is in the egg, it experiences near death just before it hatches. Inside the shell, a poisonous gas is emitted to cause the chick to peck through and out to go where the life is.

The only emotion that does *not* stem from love in joy is anxiety. Anxiety is a special emotion. It is the metaphorical gas that wants us to peck out of our self-restricting shell. Anxiety deserves its own vehicle. Our bodies are not yet good at housing it. Anxiety's true purpose is to leverage us to change and push us out to growth. For that reason, anxiety is extremely forceful and convincing. It is a fierce emotion.

Anxiety's second purpose is to breathe in the new and shifting environment. As uncomfortable and nerve-racking as anxiety is, just underneath it is deep presence. Deep presence of mind is unsheathed when we experience the anxiety directly.

"In the depth of winter, I finally learned that within me there lay an invincible summer."

~ ALBERT CAMUS (1913–1960), FRENCH PHILOSOPHER

EMOTIONS IN DUALITY (NON-JOY)

All of the above emotions are experienced in duality: happiness, discomfort (and its offshoot, sadness), and anxiety. Duality is the opposite of feeling joy. It is when you separate from what is happening and view it as difficult. In duality, emotional experiences rub you, either mildly or causing great discomfort. There is the potential for the emotion to "ruin your day." Or it can affect your ability to relate to others effectively. Emotions in duality can cause suffering. They include—

- Jealousy
- Guilt
- Shame
- Confusion
- Hatred
- Distrust
- Frustration
- Worry

- Apprehension
- Doubt
- Overwhelm
- Emotional weariness
- And all emotions related to addictive behaviour, such as denial and helplessness

And so many more, such as the emotions that show up when you feel insecure. When I feel my insecurity about shining too brightly, I feel ashamed. *All of these emotions stem from fear.* None of them can arise when you feel love. When in a state of love, which is joy, all emotions serve you. No emotion is wasteful. In duality (non-joy), the emotions are wasteful because they have a cost. All of them cause judgement and expectations.

Judgement and expectations are an equation for one thing: doubt. Doubt arises only from not trusting the emotion, and that means ourselves. When we can trust ourselves to feel what we feel, our emotions always support us.

If you profess your love to someone and they don't feel the same, you feel more love. Not embarrassment. You feel happy that you expressed yourself. You may feel awkward, yet not as though you went too far. You always feel good about expressing emotions when in joy. Every action is honoured. No action is considered risky, or less successful. There is no experience of risk in joy. You truly must do what you are inspired to do, and are willing and interested in seeing what happens if you do. This is only slightly terrifying.

THE DIRECT EXPERIENCE OF EMOTIONS

The expression of emotions allows for honesty. When I feel only what I feel and don't try to filter it, I experience a vulnerability that opens me up to opportunities. Vulnerability allows me to feel like myself. I can experience all emotions and still feel the peaceful me underneath.

How We Think When in Joy

When in joy, I know that what *I* am doing is right. If I am *not* in joy, doing what feels right has all kinds of secondary emotions. Secondary emotions include guilt, self-doubt, and a barrage of "who do I think I am?" thoughts.

"Who do I think I am" thoughts seem to have the most entertainment value. They are at the top of the Self-sabotage Chart in my head when in duality. They cause a lot of insanity in my life. I realize as I write this that if I didn't have these doubt-filled thoughts, I would be finished this book and be on a book tour, I would have said more than "hello" to that guy on the streetcar twenty-eight years ago; my book would be a part of the curriculum on the school board to assist youth in trusting themselves and reducing mood disorders, and I would have picked up that candy that fell right beside my foot at the Santa Claus Parade when I was five. Some other kid picked it up after thirty whole seconds. I wanted that candy. I'm over it, as you can well see.

The image of that candy falling at my feet when thrown by one of those clowns walking on their hands stays with me. (I know they are not walking on their hands—who could do that for an entire parade?—and that they are donning a body suit with a head at their ankles, but back then my child mind *knew* he was walking on his hands!) You could say it haunts me. Actually, it keeps reminding me that there are moments when the candy is offered and I am afraid to take it. Why didn't I pick it up?

The answer to that question has dictated the less-inspired moments of my life. These are the moments when I limit myself. I have an inherent, deep-seated belief that I better wait until everyone else is served before I take a portion. I am so nervous about taking more than I deserve or what I am entitled to that it feels way better to just stay home and be careful. I am downright scared of outshining other women, especially if we know each other, and I can actually feel myself lose my train of thought when an audience is riveted by what I'm saying. When I am conducting a highly successful session in front of hundreds of people or in my boutique studio, I become a deer in the headlights when everyone is with me. Feeling this connected, or how well life is going, scares me.

I can feel this fearful mechanism when I am talking to someone; I feel that they are going to interrupt me and say, "Oh really? How do you know that?" Then my fear fantasy plays out, showing me that I have failed or will somehow fail in their eyes. Meanwhile, out in the real world, this person is simply listening openly.

This notorious fear of shining too brightly is painful and causes a major slowdown in my ability to express myself. This is the greatest form of self-embezzlement, and it's called doubt. Shining too brightly is scary. It feels as though I will crush my mother and everyone knows you don't do that! So when I feel this fear arise, I know I am reaching a growth moment and need to venture forth and say what I need to say. There are also very convincing experiences that go along with the doubt. The three most frequent are—

1. The most popular: deep fatigue.

2. The second most predominant: hunger, especially for a carbohydrate.

3. And the third most popular: a remembrance of all the other things I need to do and an immediate need to do all of them, or at least nine. I get distracted.

A fourth most popular is anxiety. Here again, anxiety deserves a compartment of its own. The Canadian government released a survey showing that in 2013 three million Canadians (11.6%) aged eighteen years or older reported that they had a mood and/or anxiety disorder. "Mood disorders are characterized by a lowering or elevation of a person's mood, whereas anxiety disorders are characterized by excessive and persistent feelings of nervousness, anxiety, and even fear."[1] Other research in Canada has shown that anxiety is now more prevalent than depression. In a survey of my students between fourteen to seventy-eight years of age, over 60% reported feeling intense anxiety regularly, to the point that it affected their lives.

[1]Government of Canada, "Mood and Anxiety Disorders in Canada: Fast Facts from the 2014 Survey on Living with Chronic Diseases in Canada," https://www.canada.ca/en/public-health/services/publications/diseases-conditions/mood-anxiety-disorders-canada.html.

Anxiety has become a fascination in my life as most of my clients are doing it. I too am a specialist at anxiety, although now it only lingers on the perimeter and is less convincing. Anxiety also causes fatigue and hunger, so addressing anxiety has been a big factor when learning to live freely.

Fatigue is a form of distraction. It happens when I focus on an important task that challenges me. When I don't know how to start or continue the task, I feel as though I can't possibly take that time because I haven't put the laundry in yet. Fatigue arises from an expecting mind. This is the opposite of being in joy.

An expecting mind is pulled into future thinking. I am not right here, in this second, as me. My mind thinks about what I *must* do. Even feeling that I must write is a must-do thought. It's different from writing. For me, writing is a decision to offer what I am living. When I feel clear I am engaged, *I am writing*. Who I am and writing are one.

When this doesn't happen and I need to write, all kinds of distracting thoughts line up as if I opened a soup kitchen in my mind. Then I need to be clear and send everyone away. This includes the thought that I am tired and would way rather have a nap—God, that would be so good! And then if I wrestle that one out, another distraction enters. It takes diligence to get everyone out of the lineup and close the door to the distracting soup kitchen. To close the door I need to cancel the thoughts. Then I am present again.

Often hunger arises. And the hunger is real. I feel as though I can't concentrate unless I eat. It takes diligent focus to deploy this one. When I do, I can write.

Then finally, and certainly just as obtrusive, is the feeling of anxiety. Anxiety is fear of the future. Specifically, frozen fear that feels as though I can't take any action at this time that will alleviate the fear. I become a victim. This macho anxiety causes me to doubt what I knew and wanted to write. Yikes, this one is a royal pain.

When I feel the doubt or fear, I am entering duality. Duality is a word I have brought into use because it is the most accurate. I know it's clinical. Duality is when I feel separate in the world. Feeling separate is the *opposite* of feeling –

- safe
- peaceful
- part of the team
- accepted
- loved
- included
- alive
- connected
- seen
- beautiful
- appreciated
- recognized
- liked
- honoured
- and like I want to exercise

Joy is to live freely. Joy is being in life directly with absolutely no fearful thinking driving my actions. All my actions happen from an inner inspiration that invites support. As an extra bonus, they feel good to do (even if not always pleasurable), and they can be done efficiently. Extra bonuses include feeling that I'm in flow, focused, engaged, vibrant, and radiant, and I make more eye contact. I wear my favourite clothes.

When living freely, I am fully who I am. No matter what happens in the world outside of me, I still feel alive and present. Doubt cannot assemble in my mind. I am completely safe no matter what is happening. There is no way I can be affected by any hunger pang, nervous stomach, or gorgeous man. I actually stay on track, no matter how sidetracked I get, or scared I feel—meaning nervous.

Although I still get nervous, I don't *believe* the nervousness. It doesn't convince me. This is one of the most powerful aspects of living in joy: Emotions inform me rather than define me. Emotions are super useful.

1. Emotions are superficial like a wash that glides over my being. Emotions are like the wind that roils the top surface of the ocean. They guide and *do* me. If I feel something like fear, I am not actually scared; I am just informed that there is a need to take

a particular action. The emotion is a nudge towards what to do. I can't *feel* scared, but I know what it is telling me to do. I feel a certainty. This allows for clarity.

2. I am also more sensitive—in a healthy way, that is. I am not a pushover. I do not need outside cues for permission to do what I want to do. I don't need to wait for the right time, or believe fearful thoughts such as I don't have enough experience, time, or money to do what I am thinking of creating or starting. I am not able to embezzle from my own firm.

I discovered that when in joy, all emotions are supportive; nothing can register as "bad." Even if it's nasty. When apparently uncomfortable emotions such as anxiety occur, I cannot experience them as negative. Instead, the squeeze of the emotion directs me towards the next best action.

In joy I never feel bad when experiencing an emotion. Yet joy doesn't seem like a liberated state. I feel an uninterrupted state of being with what is. I am only being, I am not "accepting" the discomfort in the emotion. Instead, I am purely being. ("Being" is directly experiencing what occurs without doing any battle with it. Stay tuned for more on the state of being in chapter eleven.)

No matter what I experience, all emotions occur alongside what I experience, and then are finished. The (emotional) experience is completing as it occurs.

This means that anger creates clarity and inspires the best action. I feel clear to state a boundary or to change a way I am doing something because it doesn't work. No secondary emotions arise out of it, such as resentment or self-doubt. I experience anger and then it is over. I would feel slowed down if any other kind of emotion rode on the coattails of the initial anger, which would be a secondary emotion, such as guilt or blame.

I discovered it is actually not possible to blame in non-duality. There is no environment for it to arise in. This goes for all the secondary emotions, which occur after an initial emotion. Common emotions and their secondary accomplices include –

1. Anger: guilt, blame, shame, regret, jealousy
2. Expressions of love or appreciation: embarrassment, guilt, shame
3. Sadness: depression, apathy, shame, guilt
4. Grief: apathy, depression, guilt
5. Anxiety: overwhelm, frustration, tension, confusion, moodiness, anger

When I experience my fullest vitality, I –

- barely need any food;
- sleep well;
- have a heightened perception of beauty, or amped up appreciation;
- trust life;
- feel as though I have just finished a cleanse (my system feels clean and clear);
- feel like a high-functioning human being;
- am accountable;
- really show up;
- have no agenda or preconceived ideas about what I am supposed to accomplish;
- do not feel affected by a past that is informing that moment (no baggage); and
- have no intention (it is unnecessary to intend).

When I say I have no intention, I mean that I know myself moment by moment and what this self wants to do. Intending would slow down the streaming energy in my mind. This kind of focus is completely unnecessary when you are yourself. This is how fast living in joy is. Because I am true to myself, my actions are clear and rapidly take form in the world.

When Facing the Impossible

When I feel overwhelmed with great loss, I experience empathy for what I feel, which is to honour it. The greatest loss in my life is my daughter's disappearance. When Sarah was twelve years old, she disclosed to her piano teacher that a relative had sexually violated her. Upon further investigation, I discovered that Sarah had been raped from the ages of four to eight. Sarah lived with the relative at her father's, where she visited every other weekend.

When I first found out, I was stunned. It wasn't just unimaginable, it's that what happened inside Sarah's mind caused her to separate from herself. Her psyche split as the suppressed recall of the violations surfaced at thirteen. I saw her literally disassemble. She had no sense of value for herself. She often didn't care what happened to her or what men would or could do to her. She eventually hated herself and was filled with rage and resentment.

I did everything I could to help her in any way she needed. It was devastating to watch her when she began to despise herself and close me out.

She didn't know how to be here. By the age of eighteen, it was clear that Sarah couldn't cope. She was diagnosed with borderline personality disorder (BPD). Years ago, BPD was more commonly referred to as multiple personality disorder. This mental exceptionality (illness) is most painful for those affected by its on-again off-again perception of reality. Sarah would feel certain that something in life was going to get her. The boogie man was everywhere. Especially if someone got close. I was the closest and became the biggest suspect. If Sarah and I came together and she was able to let me in, any close intimate contact could trigger the memories of the violations. If we made healing breakthroughs, the venomous aspect of her split mind would push me away, and all that had just been resolved would break apart again. She could turn on me in an instant. It was heartbreaking.

Sarah became more and more separated from herself, and then completely from me. She moved to her father's. She would rarely see me for the next seven years. All attempts on my part to reach her were unsuccessful.

At eighteen, she moved from her father's to the streets. By this time she had left my life completely and I had no way of reaching her. At twenty-four, and still living on the streets, Sarah called me. I met her at a coffee shop. She was almost unrecognizable. She led us to an alleyway that had a small patch of garden for her and her Labrador, Luna, to sit. We sat, I brought Sarah two ice cold smoothies in thermoses. She started to eat one. I was relieved she had accepted it. She was eight months pregnant. I hadn't seen her in three years. The last time she was with me she had attempted suicide and I had called the ambulance. Again. She disappeared from my life that night and I hadn't heard from her since.

I was completely unable to love and help Sarah and give her anything she needed without enabling her unhealthy behaviour. I wanted to hold her. I wanted her to know I would take care of her and her baby boy, who would arrive in the next month. At the same time, her escalating behaviour showed me how angry she was when with me. My love was not received. I knew I could not help her where she was. I knew this in my body. I felt an alertness that was showing me what was possible. I couldn't feel the *ability* to keep boundaries. It was simply too painful to deny her. What I did was feel the discord that created such a rise in my nervous system that I knew what I *had* to do.

I was being held hostage emotionally. Yet it was impossible to *know* this. As her mother, nothing in me could deny her what she needed. I wanted to take care of her. Yet I knew it wasn't possible. If I did, I would be agreeing to take her back when I could see she was still angry, abusive, and blaming me for her life. I had to separate the sadness and desperation I felt in my heart. And *not* act from these. It was the only way I could take the action I did, which was to say I could not take her back into our home.

Love is warm and allows for total acceptance. In Buddhism there is the idea of using the Buddhist sword to cut through illusion, and state the truth, which is loving. Some may call this tough love. It is pure love. It is only love that can do what is best for me and for her. I had to dig deep under my emotions to hold the integrity of this decision to say it to her. It felt awful.

This decision was *not* inside of me. I had to mechanically state it. A hollow disembodied me spoke. I felt busted and broken as I drove away. I couldn't stop feeling the desperate disbelief that I had to let her go, yet again. It was unimaginable. I was feeling a sense of responsibility for the choices she was making in her life. I felt guilty and just wrong. I could feel these emotions corrupting the truth of what I knew. It was hard not to feel wrong about myself.

It was devastatingly sad to not love her. The unexpressed love was crushing my body. The meeting had gone very badly. I could barely feel how to speak I felt so much pressure. She clearly needed me to separate from her. I didn't know how to do it. I drove away devastated. I was broken.

Half an hour later, on the other side of town, I pulled over on the street to offer a woman a ride. She was walking along with her cane. It was 33 degrees Celsius in the record-high heat wave in Toronto that afternoon. She was carrying her McDonald's bag of dinner, bent over her cane, a tiny soul out to get a cooked meal on a day that you don't fire up the stove. She received the ride immediately. As I drove her home, she talked about how she just wanted a prepared meal. There were not many souls on the street her age as most people were huddled at home in the comfort of air conditioning.

As she spoke I felt myself start to feel somewhat alive again. I felt a part of me reassemble and ground back into life. I was traumatized. I felt so much pain that I didn't know how to *be* in life. Some may think this sadness is a rejection of the circumstances. It was deep hurting. I would not have been able to feel even remotely alive if I hadn't felt the hurt. The sorrow of the hurt connected me to myself.

As crazy as that may sound, I felt just as present as I had before I met Sarah, when I was filled with the love and enthusiasm of seeing her and the wish that I could help her after all this time. Now I felt crushed. The squeeze in my chest was all these desires collapsing into me. I felt as though I couldn't move. Her painful words kept playing on my mind. Hearing this older woman tell me about her day brought me back for a moment. I felt the desire to be with my daughter. It helped me see in real life that we need to receive help. And this need connects us.

When we are open, we are able to connect to the moment. This is the vulnerability I felt, the quickened awareness of pain and the necessity of my impossible choice. My love for Sarah landed in another place that day. That old woman connected me back to the love I feel, which is the life inside me, and showed me it's still there, ready to be lived.

HOW I SAID THIS IMPOSSIBLE "NO"

If we can*not* think when we are emotionally corrupted, there will be a palpable intelligence in our bodies—especially the belly brain —that guides us. This intelligence will lead us to be with the person, right there, and say what is true for us. We will feel the pressure in the painful words and feel more capable of softening into our needs. This could connect us to them, but it's hard to say. I was unable to help Sarah that day.

NON-DUALITY IN EMOTIONAL CORRUPTION

As I was telling Sarah that I couldn't take her back, I felt an anchoredness that was bearing down against the pull of desperation to hold her. The clarity of it was actually grating. I knew what I had to do, yet it was not "logical," clear thinking. The clarity of it was hurting me. My emotions were too powerfully convincing for me to *feel* any sense of clarity. The impossible "no" came out from a completely shaky truth. My non-dual state—the place in my being that was present—created a stalling that would not allow me to move out towards desperate agreements that were not helpful. I spoke from my broken heart, not from my "mother."

To feel present in our lives in impossible situations, we compassionately recognize what we are feeling. Usually when life gets out of control, we try to help the situation. Sometimes we create entanglement.

A mind in joy will feel an ability to be in the situation and hold space for the truest outcome. We can receive anything that can enter. If we can stay present in the upheaval, our presence is powerful enough to promote what is the truest outcome for each soul. It may not be at all what we want. It may be impossible to trust that we are "doing the right thing."

I certainly didn't feel I was doing the right thing. Our only task in impossible situations is to be there as fully as we can. This is more powerful than we can know. Doing nothing may be the truest way to be there with them.

ALIVE IN THE HURT

After I found out that Sarah had been raped, it took more than a decade to feel into the immense layers of loss and grief. It is beyond the expanse of this book to express accurately how I turned to face the agony of the effect on Sarah, and later, myself. I did come to grips with the loss of our loving bond in a way that I could continue to live fully when my life with her felt broken. I came to rout the emotional paralysis and inability to feel joy. Allow me to share a stark recounting of how I re-entered feeling the ability and right to feel joy again. With no way to heal the relationship with Sarah and no closure, I did it in her absence.

Once I released the disbelief, the grief, the anger, and the pain, I hurt. Hurting felt like an upgrade. (It took about four years after our last meeting when she was pregnant.) I felt tenderer in the hurt. Grief is a total takeover. Grief stops everything. As C.S. Lewis describes in *A Grief Observed*, "There is a sort of invisible blanket between the world and me. I find it hard to take in what anyone says. Or perhaps, hard to want to take it in. It is so uninteresting. Yet I want the other to be about me. ... If only they would talk to one another and not to me. ... On the rebound one passes into tears and pathos. Maudlin tears. I almost prefer the moments of agony. These are at least clean and honest."[2]

His final line was my reprieve. There is movement in agony. I felt alive when I felt the full tear in the loss. There was a tonic in the hurt. I felt released back into life with the hurt folded into me. Hurt is softer than grief. You want to land in what you are and not do any heavy lifting. Hurting allows the emotional convalescing to occur. I wanted Life to move all around me and not look to me.

The four-o'clock-in-the-morning shadows were working through the emotional turbulence. I was rolling through my days in an emotional wheelchair. I needed to be slower in life. Hurt slows you down if you let it. If you don't, you're in pain.

Pain is hard. Pain congests you, crushes you, and defines your moments in the day. Pain keeps you pulling up your socks and getting "back out there." "The show must go on!" becomes your motto. You say silly hollow things, such as "it is what it is." Your game face gets more familiar. Pain keeps you from parties and you need to stay close to home. There are fewer options.

Hurt is softer. I did less. What I did felt more whole. I felt a reverence and respect for this honest pace. I could feel what life had to offer. I could feel again that even in this ouching place, life had so much to be with. Hurt can elect a ministry in your being that

[2]C.S. Lewis, *A Grief Observed* (New York: The Seabury Press, 1976), 1, 2.

connects you back to life. You can administer emotional pauses and cry when you need to. (Bathrooms become sanctuaries.) The crying feels like an emotional wash on the Etch A Sketch of your heart. You feel others' hurts magnanimously and really "get" them right away without running for the Kleenex box.

Tribes and villages open around you. Hurt allows for sloppy. You can feel awful, incompetent, as if there's curlers up there on your head and that you're a shoe-in for Charles Schultz's Pig-Pen, complete with dirty cloud about your feet. Yet if you trip in the dirt, help is there to take you up.

The more I owned how I felt, the more the cavalry arrived. I reached out and felt support by an expanding constellation of folks everywhere. I respected my introvert as I went through my most tender days. Permission was the key. Hurting is a gateway into how you feel life now. Joy is also in the now. When they can meet, they do. They will.

When Joy Gets Interrupted, Do Nothing, Only Feel What You Feel

We now know that joy is *not* an emotion. It's an inner anchored-ness that tethers us to the moment while the world swirls around us. Joy remains no matter what happens outside.

So what happens to joy? Why are we grumpy one minute and grateful the next? Best question yet. The Reason: Feelings corrupt joy. The joy buzz gets mugged by a feeling. A feeling such as anxiety is a top choice to mention here as it takes up more airtime in most people's heads (especially women people) than any other emotion.

Often you are feeling neutral and start your day off reasonably happy. You go to work and something happens, and this "bad" thing sets you off. It's not your fault, it's bad. So you start to feel anxious. Let's say you found out that you won't receive an extended leave when you really need it for your family obligations. Or bigger, you find out about a health bad, such as a tumour, or that your blood work is positive for some incurable condition. All in all, it's bad. And anyone would think so, even self-realized people know it's serious. So there you are in the "bad" category.

What to do? Do you try to accept it, as all the self-empowerment teachings prescribe? Do you prac-tise a contemplative Gestalt or meditative approach, meaning to "sit with it" and "process it"? Here's what you do: *Nothing. You do nothing.*

Rather odd, isn't it? When all this (life)time we have been conditioned to be in control. We have been taught to self-manage, regulate our emotions, and work things out. We have been told to be "on top" of things from the beginning. Now, after all that conditioning, you can forget all about all of it. And do *Nothing.* Let me exemplify since you could possibly be experienc-ing some disbelief—and other forms of resistance. Just a hunch.

Before I exemplify what it looks like to do nothing, I will define "nothing." Nothing means we *may not* take any action. Nothing means we experience what's happening. We don't have a "take" on the experience. We choose to only, and simply, experience. Directly. Directly experiencing is the only way joy knows how to live. Directly experiencing is my telling the man I love that I love him and finding out he doesn't ... well, love me. I hate that.

Yet I still feel good. Really good actually, because now I know. The man in question—and not in question—because I said what I felt, is a superb man named Rob.

Directly experiencing is us doing what we need to do and doing it no matter how many people tell us to settle down. It took me three years to tell Rob that I had strong feelings for him. It took me this long because he was working for me in my home office. Our day-to-day exchanges showed me how much I respected and adored him. I never entertained addressing what I felt because of our working relationship. Then a few years later, as life does love to help us along, I got in touch with my feelings as our relationship shifted into colleagues with no shared office. He became the star in my dreamy romantic brain. So, of course, I called him.

I told him I had strong feelings for him and wanted to see him. He said he felt the same. I love that! He said he had never expressed it because I was his boss. Voilà, same page. We met. It was super lovely and fun. And I was really nervous. I never managed to fully relax and be myself. Even after our second time getting together, I just couldn't seem to let go completely. I loved him and who he was. I just didn't know how to let my full self unleash when with him. Soon I could feel that we weren't getting into each other.

I called him. After we did our initial "How are yous?" I got down to business. I told him I wasn't sure whether we were both on board and that I felt unsure about us. I shared that I truly loved him, and that I sensed we weren't growing together. He listened openly and I could really feel him on the phone.

Then a clarity rose in me and I found my mouth saying, "Rob, do I keep on feeling this love for you? Or do I need to move on?" There was a short silence, and then he said, "You need to move on." My throat tightened and my forehead felt light. I felt such relief. I also felt my heart caving in. The ball at the fair dropped through my very earth. A tear rolled down my left cheek. (I only cry out of one of my eyes when it's a tiny cry. Check that out next time you cry, I'd like to do a survey.) At precisely the same time, I felt so alive and free. I knew I would not be dragging along in my slippers in a nursing home mumbling, "If only I told that hot Rob man how I felt …" No. I was done with the need to find out and was clear with what could happen between us. It was now complete. I felt awesome. The sadness was a complete downloading overhaul in my heart and throat. Then it was gone. Far, far away.

I love that. It is so clearing to say what you feel. Joy gets to pervade your body (and thereby your mind) again when you're done. Rob was the best man at my wedding years later.

Joy has no "takers." It cannot be taken. Joy experiences. Directly. It doesn't think you are a moron for expressing your love to someone, or overly romantic and that you should be more calculating and less a risk-taker, or are desperately aging. Joy loves that you shared what is true for you. For joy still has wants. It's just that simple.

Fear: What Is It?

We fear being vulnerable. This results from our seeing power as external. We feel we must control ourselves and our environment. We see vulnerability as a loss of control. But doesn't being vulnerable imply a capacity for carefreeness, innocence, willingness, and openness, and an ability to take so-called risks?

Is there really a risk in being open to someone or to opportunities (same thing)? What specifically are we risking? If we give everything—all that we are—doesn't that leave everything? If I don't hold back and am completely open and honest, am I not allowing myself to express more of my true self? Does this not provide an opportunity for me to become more of *who* I am and articulate what I need and want to say to others?

You could feel a current of sadness after telling the Robs in your life how you feel. *And* you wouldn't feel different. There would be absolutely no drop in how *you* feel. This means that this inner steadiness of a joy hum never diminishes.

Take relationships for example. When we are in a relationship with someone we love, we invest. We give our complete attention, care, support, and probably lots of money. If it ends, we still feel joy.

Again, joy is not invested *in* a relationship. Joy is. It is not pending.

Back to the failed relationship (just kidding). If the relationship ends, then you are still you, joyful, with an experience. In this case, specifically with a relationship experience. You will most likely feel sad. Or you may feel, as I did, utter disbelief. The ending of the relationship may feel so painful that you have absolutely no idea how you will go on. (What exactly does that mean, to *go on*? And who started that ideal anyway?)

Your concept of "future" is now blasted open, and you have no idea what to do next, whom to speak to, whether to go home (which may be completely redefining), or if you can go to your next appointment. Perfect. The pain you feel is the shaking of your foundation. This sense of floundering is the invitation for change and adaption to occur.

So you start (I'm back to the failed—just kidding—relationship). You may start by pausing and going for a drink. You may call a friend for support. You may go sailing; you may go and work out; or you may clean the drawer, and all the other drawers, and your neighbour's drawers if they're home and sympathetic. It's hard to say.

You may go and get into someone else's drawers to ease the pain. Anything could happen. You have all the choices in the world. Even if there is joint custody; even if you own a condo, a home, dog, a boat, and tandem bike together (personal note: tandem bikes are tricky), and it's time to get organized, separated, and settled. You are still you, the same joyful person who started this relationship, signed for the condo, and brought them the extra car key when they lost theirs. It's still you. Except you've been upgraded. You have had an experience.

You may ask, "But what do I do with the love? What do I do with the love I feel for this person, when I thought they were *the one*? I feel so alone, broken, lost, confused, unloved, and unlovable?" (Or perhaps ashamed, if you feel you are to blame.)

First of all, I have posed too many questions. Let me back up. You may have all or many of these questions. And I will pose just one: "How do I continue to *be* love?" Not find love somewhere else, or be able to trust again, or feel the comfort you felt there. Those are all fearful freaking-out thoughts. They are you trying to *not* shift. It's not that you're not willing to shift, it's that it's painful and you don't want to feel the pain. Your life is changing and it feels painful because you don't know where it's going. So you scramble to be here in your life, yet it feels impossible. You will have freaking-out thoughts because you feel so crazy right now that any highly charged thought feels right.

Notice the word "thought." You are having freaking-out thoughts because you don't *know* what to do. The basic fundamental reason you are freaking out is always one thing: You feel separate.

Feeling separate is the opposite of joy. You feel separate because you need to know what to do next in your life. Then you disconnect from yourself, your inner intelligence, and/or from the person(s) involved. This is created by your freaking mind. You are not actually separate. You *feel* separate. You can never be separate. You are life; you cannot separate from life. Only the feeling of fear causes you to separate from life.

What are you separating from? Feeling one with life as it is. This creates the next belief that you need to *control* your life. This is fear. In fact, it is more fear piled on top of the initial fear, which was your reaction to the changing circumstances. This gets us kind of busy. The freaking-mind order of fear looks like this:

1. Fear of change.
2. Fear of not knowing what to do.

It's *not* your fault that you are *not* talented at experiencing fear. We were taught to be in control since we were shown how to put on our shoes. Control is the belief that you need to know what to do.

We are quite attached to certainty. When we cannot help our

situation by freely taking action, or need to wait on others' actions, we often feel overwhelmed, anxious, and trapped. When an emotion takes us over, joy gets cancelled. When joy is cancelled, we feel separate. We feel separate because the circumstances are cracking us open. Separation occurs only when what is happening causes us to separate from what is happening. If we can experience its awfulness—if it's awful—then that is a different moment. We feel awful. And in our terrible feeling is the upgraded, changed, altered us. This new us is a vaster human with a feeling folded into it. Knowing what we feel allows us to feel alive again even if it hurts.

Thanks for hanging in there. I needed to point out all the parts of suffering. We're so good at it that it comes naturally, yet it requires a lot of energy to follow through with it. Feeling fragmented causes us to feel broken because we believe that our life circumstances cause us to feel the way we do.

It never occurred to us that we could *be* a feeling (joy is a great choice; I highly recommend it) and actually *be* that feeling, and only that one. I'm offering that we can actually have that joy feeling inhabit and consistently run through our veins, just like oxygen does. Oxygen always runs through us. It is not a temporary visitor gracing us on good-hair days, or when our veins are more open. Oxygen is in us when we have the flu, when we hold our breath, when we sing a long note till the absolute end of our breath. There is still always oxygen inside us. It simply never vacates.

Joy is the same. Joy never leaves. It gets overtaken by the other feelings, which are emotions. But joy is not an emotion. Joy is the oxygen. You can get a nasty cold and not breathe well, yet oxygen will continue to inhabit your lungs, cell tissues, and brain. Joy can be sideswiped by grief, anger, and anxiety (top three emotional tunes in our society) and still remain. The emotion of sadness will wash over you and temper and buffer you because of your new experience, yet you will be you, filled with joy, while you are sobbing, snot everywhere, and perhaps even heaving (I noticed on one occasion).

And that's the wash of sadness, of unimaginable or just frustrating circumstances that are ultimately an usher's kind hand and nimble body in the Life Theatre pointing the flashlight so you don't trip.

At the times in our lives when we experience devastating loss, we are being exposed to greater circumstances than our minds can comprehend. When we recognize that it is scary, hard, or worrisome, or that we feel we can't do anything, we are being shaped into change. We are being led to the next occurrence that will support us.

I have been learning how to be in my life with the hurt I feel of not knowing where Sarah is. A part of me is here, writing this passage, for example, and the part of my human that is her mother sometimes hurts. The "hurt" me is the soft me who knows that this was all necessary for the mystical expansion of my consciousness that I could never "comprehend." My "knowing" surpasses faith as it is not a belief. I don't have faith that Sarah is all right and that we will connect when she's ready. I know it. I also recognize that anything can and will happen.

If pain is life, then the hurt is showing me life in this version. The captured hurting-heart version that thinks of her daughter. That is beautiful, compelling, and tenderizing, and I connect to her. (Now, feeling the hurt is a homecoming.) I have actually willed the part in me that feels overwhelmed with loss to feel love for her. That took about four years. I had to grieve first.

CHAPTER NINE

Belief System or Religion

"Religion is the opiate of the masses."

~ KARL MARX (1818–1883), GERMAN
REVOLUTIONARY, SOCIOLOGIST,
HISTORIAN, AND ECONOMIST

Beliefs are held constructs that give structure to how we think. Beliefs arrange how we think. They can guide us. They can help us stay on course in our lives and feel our integrity. Beliefs are not wrong; we don't need to avoid beliefs or have beliefs about beliefs! What is *unhelpful* about them is that they may not represent our fullest selves.

Beliefs that are healthy, such as "trust yourself," can be helpful. The problem is that at times you may have no idea how to trust yourself. You may feel overwhelmed and need someone to take over. If you have prescribed to the belief of "trust yourself," you may isolate yourself to feel the answer inside, when in fact, you are quite confused. You may feel that you need to be "mature" and figure this out on your own. You may feel too "needy" when you think of asking someone to help you.

"What we call religion is merely organized belief, with its dogmas, rituals, mysteries and superstitions. Each religion has its own sacred book, its mediator, its priests and its ways of threatening and holding people."

~ JIDDU KRISHNAMURTI (1895–1986), INDIAN
PHILOSOPHER, SPEAKER, AND WRITER

Beliefs limit us by defining "a way." In joy, no belief system, tenet, religion, affirmation, or even eating plan can represent you. Nothing can represent you. You are so awake and interested in your life that you know what you need to know. As it's needed. Needless to say, this requires trust. That's the catch. To trust that what we need will be known is a giant leap in our way of *thinking.* It is a way of changing into a new way of directly experiencing life without relying on any way of thinking.

"True knowledge is not attained by thinking. It is what you are; it is what you become."

~ SRI AUROBINDO (1872–1950), INDIAN
PHILOSOPHER, YOGI, AND POET

Awareness

To be aware is to have the ability to be alive in this moment, free of any beliefs that steer our thinking. To experience joy we feel aware in each moment. Awareness is the energy of the mind before it gets shrink-wrapped into a thought. Without thoughts to direct us, we are belief-free. When we are belief-free we can be thought-free.

The ability to be thought-free occurs only in a mind that is in non-duality. A non-dual mind operates from a pure conscious experience of each moment in our lives. A free mind is capable of uncensored experiences. We see with open, awake eyes. Only a view that is a belief, ideal, opinion, or fear of what is happening takes away from our experiencing this clarity. Actually, any view is a form of either egotism or fear; in fact, egotism is fear. It is a stock-pile of all the beliefs and constructs we (possibly unknowingly) subscribe to. It's good to know that we have this vanity because we need to feel as though we are on top of things or in control. Yet the ego that keeps viewing life keeps us slightly less connected to experiencing life directly. This is a massive loss. We truly experience less of life when we carefully screen it. We don't trust that we can experience life directly without any filters. We develop fears and talk about what is hard and what we noticed rather than what we experienced. Fear develops and hardens into ways that lead to our avoiding life and opportunities. Fear puts the brakes on in our lives. We miss out on the ways we would have been upgraded to a larger version of who we are. We may even develop phobias. For example, let's say you are terrified of snakes (fear of snakes is the most popular phobia in North America). I used to be a crazy snake phobic. I lost all rationality and would even slap my hands to my face if a snake appeared on the screen in a movie.

When I had my daughter, I decided that I would stop the face welts. One weekend two years after Sarah's birth, the Herpetological Society was holding a "zoo" at the library. Snakes galore of every size were on display. What could be better? I threw munchkin into the car and we headed off to what I expected would soon turn the library into an asylum. I was a snake phobic driving to the library to enjoy snakes. I will never forget that day. There was a huge turnout. Wall to wall parents, forty kids sitting cross-legged on the floor and looking up at the wiggling burlap bags. My stomach was trying to turn me around to head for the door. I pulled up my calmest terrified voice and told Sarah that we would soon see a whole bunch of snakes, and wasn't that exciting? She was *so* excited. I sat cross-legged on the floor with the other tykes and Sarah on my lap. If I hadn't been holding her, I would have been wringing my hands. My heart was racing and I asked myself to just try looking at the bags to see if I could do this. Could I just view the long table of burlap bags as if it was just another experience? Could I simply look at them and not feel an inner freak out? It was hard; it was really, really agonizing with my heart rate going berserk, sweat sticking my T-shirt to me.

I convinced myself that I simply *had* to do this. I had to get over this phobia and be a normal, snake-loving or at least not snake-freak in front of Sarah so she could at least have a neutral experience of these horrid (whoops) wiggly, demonic (sorry) creatures. I was ready. I felt as if we were at the starting gates of ... I didn't honestly know what. The burlap bags had my full attention.

The herpetological dude came out, all happy-like and excited about starting the tour of the bags. I was wondering if he might hand out anything, like alcohol, but instead he just launched right into it. (Couldn't he see me?) He started out small. He picked up a rather cute little burlap bag, about the size of a paper popcorn bag you get at the fair. He pulled out the first snake. A garter snake, describing how numerous they are in our province. I made a mental note to stick to the pavement and forget future trips to the ravine with Sarah. Then he went to the next bag. It was larger, about the size of a potato sack. He pulled out a rather thick snake and it wound up like a ball around his hand, hiding into itself. The snake was scared! This was amazing to me since I thought all snakes were so scary that they could never actually be afraid. Something in me suddenly felt compassion for this little creature. I had feelings for a snake! I had feelings for a snake that wasn't terror. The herpe-tological dude said he would come around now, and he walked towards the kids (and me) sitting cross-legged on the floor so we could touch it if we wanted to. Sitting like that with Sarah on my lap gave me absolutely no time to bolt. The dude was coming towards us; my whole body didn't even have any time to get scared because what happened next cancelled the fear. Sarah jumped up to reach out and pet (oh my God!) the snake. She touched it and turned her lit-up face to me and said, "Tuc it, Mommy," in her baby voice. I was so enamoured by the moment, by her momentum, that I reached out and *touched the snake* (cue the dramatic music and the singing choir). It felt incredible. It felt amazing. I petted it again and couldn't stop. I gave the guy a dirty look when he said my turn was over. I was in snake awe. I had only known snake terror, so snake awe was the most incredible switch of internal wiring I can ever remember.

The very next day, I swear to God, Sarah and I were out as usual on my bike, she in the kids' seat on the back. We were riding along the Spadina Avenue bridge, a two-lane bridge, during rush hour. On the very narrow curb, barely room for a bike, there was a snake. Without any hesitation, I said with glee, "Hey, Sar, look at the snake!" She looked down from her child's seat as I slowed the bike down so we could take a longer look. Our new snake moment, me free of facial welts, she bonding with nature, and everyone safe from harm as Mom did not freakishly drive into two lanes of rush-hour traffic and cause a spectacle, not to mention impending doom. This was the day after the Herpetological Society had shared their burlap bags with the Leaside Library.

Feelings of fear or even terror can be cancelled on the spot, allowing for a cellular transmutation to occur. This transmutation is like a rewiring in the nervous system. Once the old habit has been broken, the nervous system can make new neurotransmissions, and new choices and actions follow.

The immediate shift in feeling occurs when the break in the old wiring leaves a space for a new experience to enter. The break occurred when I was presented with the snake and without thinking, touched it.

Because I didn't think and only acted by reaching out with my hand, I experienced a brand new moment in my life. I had never reached out towards a snake. This fresh new action was the instant when all my old beliefs were cancelled and replaced by a new experience. This is how we experience non-duality, or pure consciousness. We enter a unified field. A new ability enters us and takes us over. If we are open to life in all moments, a new ability or experience can enter us. We experience; we don't censor.

It takes the "thinking" mind 1/10,000th of a second to label what we experience.[1] For example, I have a tandem bike. Riding a tandem bike is such a kick as people are caught off guard as you go by and they stare without meaning to. An adult will look and smile— or they sing the song "Bicycle Built for Two." Young children, though, will stop in their tracks and their parents can't budge them. They can't stop staring. Their pure uncensored consciousness has never seen a bike with two people peddling. They are in awe. Adults recognize it is a tandem bike. Their thinking minds name what they are seeing as a "tandem bike." No biggie. A mind that is in joy— pure consciousness—lives in a unified field where all occurrences are experienced without naming them. This is unimaginable to us. Because our thinking mind (the ego) authors our thoughts, it decides for us what we are seeing and what to do.

The only way to arrest this quick censoring is to catch that you are thinking a thought. I mean you have only 1/10,000th of a second to sense that you are thinking about what is happening. You are viewing what is happening and rating, naming, or deflecting it.

---

[1] David R. Hawkins, *The Eye of the I: From Which Nothing Is Hidden* (City: Veritas Publishing, 2001), 124.

(Remember that naming what is happening could reduce your direct experience of it.) What are the chances that you won't label what you are experiencing? Not so good. It would take years of training your mind to notice that you are thinking thoughts about what is happening, and then focus mentally to catch the 1/10,000th of a second when you do this. Then you need to stop your mind from naming what you are seeing. This is far too complicated. (And not fun—I've met these people.) The other way to do this without taking sixteen years of meditation training (I actually worked this out with an avid teacher of consciousness—it could take sixteen years if you meditated four hours a day. Four hours!) and then return to pure experience without a view. This practice is an exercise of mindfulness training of your consciousness that takes concentration, contemplation, and a humility that is grounded in compassion. It also takes time, as mentioned above. I have another idea: How about feeling who you are? How about feeling what it's like to be you, which is what feeling who you are is. This does *not* take time. It's instant and a complete takeover of your physiology. Your entire physical body and consciousness fill in with a sense of completeness. Nothing can beat how this feels. This is you. How do you feel this *you*? I'm so happy you asked. *By touching down into the place that chooses your favourite ice cream and doesn't know about calories. It's the place of pure permission and delight in life.*

This experience of who you are is also thought-free. You are not defined by who you think you are. For example, man, woman, tall, funny, serious, or having fallen arches. You are you free of labels and, yes, uncensored. When you are this thought-free you, there is a space. In this space is light—pure consciousness with the interface of joy. You experience this pure consciousness if you were to wake up on the first morning of a vacation—say in Cuba—you wake up and hear the sound of waves. Your ears perk up. You then register that it is the first day of your two-week vacation with no responsibilities. You feel alive and delighted! This is how a thought-free mind feels. This is how constant joy, or non-duality, feels. The experience of joy feels the same way each time. And differently. That is, joy always feels the same: alive and energizing and as if you are being invited and welcomed into the next moment. It is different every time as each moment becomes unique.

A mind in joy is pure consciousness. "Pure" means it is not contaminated or designated to parking spots of thoughts. To think, we choose a thought. Once the mind starts thinking at around three years old, we begin to have many thoughts. There is not a single thought conveniently directing us. Now we have moved from directly experiencing, which is pure awareness (no thoughts to juggle), to selecting thoughts. So how do we operate?

We are living in an age that Nietzsche called a period of comparisons.

How We Think Thoughts

- Thoughts develop the need to think and choose one thought.
- We choose thoughts.
- We categorize thoughts as good or bad, enjoyable or difficult, and this sorting becomes a habit.
- Our thoughts create a perception of life.

We create this more difficult existence because thinking means we consider how to take action. When we *think*, sensitivity is lost. Thoughts often direct our actions, yet they may not be *our* thoughts. When we do what we are *supposed to do*, for example, we are less involved in what we are doing. When we are *not* thinking about how to take actions, we sense what to do. Being sensitized, we don't think so much.

Although we can switch into non-thought or awareness and be open to whatever can occur, it's not exactly like that. It's vaster than that; it's better than a switching, as that would be mental. Awareness is an interest in listening fully. Awareness is the ability to watch everything that occurs in our lives but not *choose* one thing. It's a parent's love that watches over all the little guys without favouring one. Yet awareness chooses an action, *without* your mind doing it. *You know* to tell the little one to stay behind the curb, but you don't need to *think* about that.

The actions of awareness—which is non-thought— arise from love. Life is pretty alive and interesting. You don't end up telling catastrophic stories about kids who won't stay behind the curb. They just don't catch your attention anymore. In fact, your mind's attention is open for more experiences. You see more.

So-called "bad" experiences don't get snagged in your mind. Being aware allows *you* to move freely in your life. You can move from a barely workable situation to an extremely efficient flow because you sense what to do. You can feel what is right for you (not right as in right or wrong, but true for you), and you move with this naturally occurring discrimination.

There is only one way to live in an aware mind that is free of family traditions, religion, habit, beliefs, judgements, expectations, control from others, and puddles. Only one way: *Catch when you feel any thought that is not joyful.*

When you notice the thought—maybe you are worried about your mother—then notice how you feel. Notice how the worry thought brings you into more worry thoughts, and now they're having a giant party in the basement. Of your mind. Like the unruly teenagers they are. Remember being a teenager (a warm welcome to any teen readers; you are in an excellent position to drop expectations early and help our planet, no pressure) and how much you wanted to break out and have the room to do what you want? That's what these worry thoughts are doing. They are making a mess. We get concerned and create tension in our lives when we feel scared— or angry—about what is happening.

Awareness shows us how much we need what is happening to be different. Being concerned will mess us up. It will perpetuate misery, and we won't help our mom. We'll mess *her* up with our concern. Way better to notice you don't feel joyful. Then have compassion for yourself and realize you're scared, angry, or want to make her life better. You will see what you're thinking and what you need.

Discovering what you need is enlivening. Discovering that you wish Mom was okay is a beautiful need. Maybe it can't happen, yet touching down into the love you feel for her *is* enlivening. This is awareness. You connect with her. You only want what is happening to be different to help her. Simply feel the space in you that loves her. That is where the beauty lives.

Beauty is awareness. An aware mind is beautiful. A feeling of beauty is a homecoming and connects you back to life with all its magnificence and painful heartbreak. You open.

"If you're really listening, if you're awake
to the poignant beauty of the world, your
heart breaks regularly. In fact, your heart
is made to break again and again so
that it can hold evermore wonders."

~ ANDREW HARVEY, AUTHOR OF
THE RETURN OF THE MOTHER

Building the Yoga House

Ten years ago, I was about to build an addition on my first house to add to my yoga studio. I was walking with my friend the day before we were to break ground. In the ravine close to our homes, she pointed to a house at the top of the hill looking down over the trees and said, "Why don't you buy *that* house? It's going on the market soon and you could get it cheaper off the market." I wondered which house she meant and she specified the house number. I told her I had already looked at it and it was too small. "Then build your addition on it." She said waving her hand as if I was the millionaire among us. My immediate thought was, "Nice idea, but that would take all the financing I could muster just to buy that house, with nothing left to build an addition." It seemed monumental. Also, I had almost paid off my current house, so why would I take on so much debt?

Over the next week, I met with the owner to see the property. It really would need an addition as it was so tiny and dark. Yet as soon as I walked in, I pictured the yoga studio taking over the whole main floor looking over the gorgeous ravine. *I* could see it. My brain couldn't. My brain saw extensive, outrageous costs of an architect, plans, permits, demolition, and red tape at City Hall. (And I hate that.) Just the thought of the project was daunting.

When I was able to stop *thinking* about it, there was no question. I wanted to build a gorgeous yoga studio in nature. I bought it.

It took two years to build the studio. Part of that time was simply waiting for permits. During the construction I had big trouble with the contractor and had to sue him. I "lost" more money than God has. The wiring and plumbing had to be redone as they didn't meet the code. Brand new walls were torn open and drywall redone and repainted. (I could go on, but I'll stop.) It turned into one of those *Holmes on Homes* episodes. I was an emotional wreck. I developed a muffin top. I borrowed until I was at the peak of needing to abandon the whole project, and then borrowed the rest from the Bank of Mom and Dad.

During that time, I "saw" only the studio. There was never a question about its completion. I can say now that my love of nature and wish to bring students to a yoga studio with a gorgeous view was an absolute known. I felt that the ravine view was the backdrop to the stage where I would teach. I saw myself leading the classes with my cast behind me. This was not me manifesting a clear vision in my mind. It was a "knowing" in the very cells of my being. I could not see exercising, yogaing, or meditating in a room that did not have such a vista.

Without "thinking," we have clarity that brings alive what is in us to do. What we want to do is known. By doing so, any belief or idea about *how* we need to live is lifted and we source the true inspiration in us.

Beliefs are based on what we know to work or aspire to work. This cannot be known or mystically evoked. If I had known the costs I would incur, the issues I would have with the zoning department, and the emotional insecurity I felt when being attacked by neighbours (but, as you can see, I'm over it), I would have bailed and gone fishing, with cheese popcorn.

To return to awareness in our lives we notice how our thoughts *feel*. Keep coming back to the thoughts that are lifting you instead of those that remind you to "settle down" and be realistic.

*"The constant assertion of belief
is an indication of fear."*

~ JIDDU KRISHNAMURTI (1895–1986),
INDIAN PHILOSOPHER, SPEAKER,
AND WRITER

When we experience joy-based thoughts, the thoughts direct us completely in a silent way. We don't feel them moving us, *we* feel moved. They create crystal-clear clarity. We do not need to figure out what to do. We know. In joy, we still think thoughts. We still think joy-based thoughts. For example, when I feel overwhelmed with my responsibilities, I know I am not experiencing the reason I started the projects. That means I have developed expectations about *how* they need to be experienced. This will never bring joy. "How" or "the way" we want to live will not create joy-based thoughts. In joy, any degree of overwhelm or frustration doesn't actually bother us. Instead, the frustration pushes us like a butterfly coming out of the chrysalis to a new, never before experienced action of flying. The hard feeling delivers clarity about how to proceed. Either immediately or as you need to know. Joy-based thoughts can be angry and fuel our clarity and need for boundaries. Joy-based thoughts are *not* positive thoughts. They are joy-based, which means they are your real experience of what's happening. You experience your life directly. You sense what to do as you go.

Six months after buying The Yoga House property, I remembered saying to Sarah *nine years earlier*(!) when we were walking through the ravine that I wanted to buy a house there. I pointed to the very property that I bought! I had completely forgotten about saying this until I was driving on the 401 highway six months later. What we say or think that is pure inspiration is so valuable.

Let your dreams rip and say them to yourself, or to a stranger in line while waiting at Canadian Tire. They have no way to exit or time to judge you.

CHAPTER TEN

Mask Self and Ego

You begin life feeling perfect and whole in your humanness. Your mind was curious, open, and constantly learning. This is your brain before it knew how to think. You had no illusions about your greatness. You knew you were great! You didn't think about demanding a bottle, you demanded it! The idea of receiving love based on your behaviour couldn't register. Your Baby Job Profile was to make sure your needs were met. You wanted everything when you felt the need and the deadline was now.

Then, at about eighteen months, the mind develops the ability to discern. You learn how best to make demands. You recognize that certain ways of demanding elicit a negative response that doesn't result in your having your needs met, and that other ways elicit a positive response to your needs. You learn to repeat the best way of demanding. Now your brain has changed how you ask for what you want. *You use the energy of the mind to think of a required response.* A gap, a hesitation is created between the need (which is natural) and the contrived way you request it (which is unnatural). You learn that sometimes you have to wait to get what you want and that you may have to ask in a certain way—or ask for what you know you *can* get, even if it's not what you really want. (This is a real crazy-maker.)

There are two types of responses: negative responses and positive responses. "Negative responses" can cause us to feel bad or as if we are wrong. This stress elicits the flight-or-fight response, causing an elevation in cortisol levels and a rise in the sympathetic nervous system. "Positive responses" affect the parasympathetic nervous system, releasing serotonin and other nurturing hormones. We feel reassured, comforted, safe, and worthy.

We record these effects in our nervous systems. We like to keep these records so we don't repeat the unsuccessful requests. We learn to ask when we see Mom in a good mood. As the mind learns to discern more details, we remember to ask Mom only for a second cookie if we asked for a third cookie last time and she got angry. The discerning mind adds this event to its memory bank and refers to these responses in the future.

This is a paramount moment in the development of the mind. Simply put, we begin thinking. The mind begins calculating how to ask for what we need. The mind stops spontaneously asking for what we want. (This is why we don't walk up to someone and tell them we think they look lovely. It's awful, really. No wonder no one is dating in real life. I digress, with joy.)

In this hesitation, the mind takes the original need and compares it with similar memories in the mind bank and decides on an appropriate way to request. Of course the current situation may not require us to be careful. We may be able to ask for exactly what we want.

In one of my intimate relationships, when we lived consciously and were interested in helping each other grow, my partner would often say, "You've got your scared voice on." He could tell that I was afraid to ask for what I needed.

Marshall Rosenberg's Nonviolent Communication (NVC) approach to living addresses how we can ask for what we want without feeling feeble and shrinking. He suggests you use your Santa Claus voice and say ho, ho, ho followed by your request in a booming voice. So this is me asking someone to pick something up for me (although I admit I do the ho, ho, ho in my head): "Ho, Ho, Ho, you lucky soul, you get to pick up toilet paper for me on the way home!"

So now when I ask someone for help or to pick something up for me, I use my Santa voice. I even have a friend, Robert, who regularly picks up toilet paper for me from Costco with his membership. I actually think this is helping me stay regular.

By regulating how we ask for what we want, we create secondary feelings. Secondary feelings arise when our needs are *not* being met. These feelings are often unexpressed and lie repressed in our tissues. (For example, you may feel greedy or unreasonable for asking for what you want. So you don't ask. Then you blame yourself for not feeling content and accepting your lot.) These secondary feelings take on a life of their own. They become encoded in the cells of the body since they are *not* being expressed.

The body becomes a map of these suppressed impulses. Normally, we would express these feelings, but having been denied airtime they lie dormant. This creates crusty tension and, over time, body armour. The suppressed feelings can lead to resentment and judgement of others who *are* asking for what they want. My family could judge the choices I made as a single mom. I knew I was going beyond the family concept of What Was Allowed. It was tricky and scary for me, and I often thought I was a selfish bitch. (I didn't really think I was, but when I was around my family, the silence I experienced caused me to feel that I must be.)

By monitoring how we ask for what we want, we develop a false self. *The false self thinks and monitors our behaviour, dividing us from our needs.* We become a contrived self that calibrates everything we can ask for. Because, of course, we still want to have our needs met. And toilet paper.

When we refer to these memorized childhood images or to past responses, we create false conditioned responses. These conditioned responses make up the *mask self.*

> The *mask self* is the careful façade we present
> to the world when we don't know how to give
> them the real us. Or ask for toilet paper.

The mask self keeps us busy calculating our responses by moving out into our world and back into our minds, calibrating what's acceptable. The mask self's request may not represent our true feelings, but it helps present our request in a way that our caregiver can hear it and perhaps be willing to fulfill it.

The idea of controlling our needs is introduced at a very early age. We learn we *must have* some control over our needs. (Yikes! Scary music just started playing.)

How We Become Numb

During the early stages of our development, if our needs were not fulfilled we got tired of asking, gave up, and fell asleep. Falling asleep is symbolic of what we do today. When we don't address our needs, we "fall asleep." Instead of trying to satisfy the needs in ways that we *can*, we numb ourselves and pretend it's not possible, or that it doesn't matter. We get really gifted at convincing ourselves that "it doesn't matter." We give up. We try to distract ourselves with other sensations or substances such as food that give us instant gratification. Or we may suppress the need altogether. Eventually we get busy. We identify with our responsibilities, which can give us a sense of control, completion, or temporary satisfaction. At least we're being useful.

It's awful. I have to stop writing about how we develop this false, contrived mask self. It's depleting. So everybody, yes all of you, please stand up and let's stretch and breathe. You too! I'm not writing one more word until everyone stands up. We need to decompress from all this dehumanizing conditioning that has corrupted our ability to ask for what we want. Stand up. Now raise your arms high above your head, look up. Still looking up, say, "Yay!" Louder if no one's home. "YAAAY!" With arms still up, side bend to the right—then left. Jiggle everything: arms, legs, wrists, and especially wiggle your ass. Okay, sit down, and I'll continue. If you didn't do this exercise, please don't continue reading. Take a break from the ridiculous and dehumanizing genocide-of-the-imagination mask self you just read about and take this stretch break. See you in a minute.

The mask self develops early in life and is so learned by age five that we usually have the act down to a science. Since we have been living from our mask selves for so long, we can actually lose sight of what we *really* want. We get used to tiptoeing and being careful. We lose our spontaneity. We become less intrigued. Now we consider what is *possible* or *realistic*.

Soon it gets comfortable ("comfortably numb" as Pink Floyd would say) to wear our mask selves. We don't feel as alive as we did without them, but at least we feel in control. We watch others do flash-mob performances. And by the way, aren't those guys good? We can hide how we really feel. We conveniently desensitize ourselves from our feelings. The mask self births ideas, beliefs, and concepts that become our religion. This mask self reduces who we are and suppresses our genius.

> The mask self births ideas, beliefs, and concepts that become our religion.

In my own life, I can feel my mask self when I need to ask a teacher to vacuum after their class in my yoga studio. I feel worried that they may not comply. What is really happening is that I don't feel I have the right to ask for what I want. Often this reflects my other learned limiting behaviour—

that they will never listen anyway. In that moment, my mask self is telling me I need to be nice to be liked. I think about the *other person* and if what I am asking is reasonable. This makes it difficult to focus on the reason I came to them in the first place: I need them to clean the studio. Now I start to feel confused and wonder if my request is reasonable.

When I don't ask for what I need, I know my mask self is trying to convince me that it doesn't really matter. Who do I think I am? I feel as though I am making way too big a deal out of what is happening and *should* simply accept what they do. This, of course, means I am not being honest with myself.

The mask self keeps us dishonest. We are dishonest with ourselves, and this means with others. When we stop being honest with ourselves, we get cerebral. In our masks the energy of the mind is trying to operate "objectively." We are thinking. Thinking causes us to value an ability to override the senses and get things done in our lives.

Our society commends those who are able to complete their tasks with ironclad composure. (There's that body armour again.) I was recently at a family funeral where the twenty-something-year-old niece of the deceased sang a number of songs. When she began singing, she was overwhelmed with grief and her voice wobbled as she began to cry. Afterwards she was apologetic and felt she didn't "perform" as well as she could have. It was one of the tenderest moments in the service. It was at this fragile, shaky moment that her breaking voice helped me feel connected to her, her message, and why we were all there.

When you unmask yourself, you discover what you need, and you ask. Doing so, you step into your integrity. It could take about a year for this to feel normal (or eight). You can do it.

Going Past What Is Allowed:
Busting Conditioned Thinking

When I was building The Yoga House, I was aware of the zoning requirements for a residential business. I designed the floor plan to reflect these requirements. Then life happened.

I changed the plans completely during the demolition phase. After the workers tore off the back of the house and I saw the valley, I knew I could not follow the plan to build the kitchen on the main floor, like a normal person. When I saw the ravine on that sunny June day, and those giant hundred-year-old oaks, I knew that the entire main floor had to be the studio. Unfortunately, the zoning inspector didn't feel the same. Yet during the next three-year period, with the help of my dear friend Manny, I worked together with the inspector to provide plans that would meet the zoning regulations.

This was a tumultuous time as it was costly to produce a number of new plans to meet their changing requirements. The main difficulty was related to a neighbour who was trying to shut me down before I could open. I discovered that his allegations were keeping me from closing my building permit and passing code. That was the costly part for me. I felt judged and unwelcome. I felt attacked and bullied after I discovered many of his actions. I went to this neighbour's home and invited him to mine, clarifying my plans and addressing his concerns. Even after inviting him, even when he had prints of the house designs, I discovered that he had continued to present false allegations to the zoning department and our neighbours.

Eventually I decided to face this directly. I was nervous about how to proceed. I had already had a grand opening for my yoga studio and programs had begun. But the glare from this neighbour and his cohorts was hard for me.

He behaved inappropriately towards my family, friends, and clients when they came to my home studio. His silent petulant bullying and snarls at my clients provided little documentary evidence. I would not find out about his actions until long after they had occurred, and for this reason I couldn't address them at the time. I knew I had a case against him from the actions I had documented. But I felt this wasn't the way to proceed.

Instead, I went down to City Hall with Manny. I met with the inspector. I have learned that, as a woman, when meeting with a man to bring a man. I wish I didn't need to write that, but this is how it is at this time in our human evolution. After sitting with the inspector and introductions were completed, I turned into an excited child.

I remember a time when I picked Sarah and her friend up from school. When we went to get in the car, we discovered a wounded monarch butterfly on the windshield. Its wing was tattered and it was fluttering about on the glass. Sarah and her friend Nathaniel oohed and aahed and picked up that dear creature and brought it into the back seat. We drove straight to the library to find out what we could do for that little guy (not much Googling back then). When we entered the library with our little battered buddy in a container, Sarah and Nathaniel could barely contain themselves. They burst towards the librarian at the checkout desk, butting in at the front of the line. They exclaimed excitedly that they had a butterfly to save!

This is what I must have looked like when sitting with the inspector, Paul. I was so excited to tell him why I didn't want to put a kitchen on the main floor and keep it as an open spacious studio. This was the issue. There was no other house that had passed code with only a studio on the main floor. I simply had to have a big open space looking over the ravine in the city to bring people close to nature. I was like the seven-year-old Sarah saving the monarch butterfly to release it back to nature. I wanted to bring people into a nature sanctuary with an unobstructed view! I wanted to save myself from being boxed in.

I saw the inspector's eyes light up when I burst out with the description of the studio and how people walked straight to the back French doors to see the ravine. "It is so bright and open and beautiful, to put up a wall that separated the room would break up the whole view!" After I spoke, I watched as his demeanor fossilized into an objective professional returning to the forms in front of him.

Then he actually picked up the forms and changed the deed of my house to a residentially zoned yoga studio! I thought I would pee my pants. I tried to appear calm. No, that's a lie. I know my face was bursting and my knees were clapping under the table.

Paul explained that the zoning would be amended and copies would be sent to me to sign. I managed not to kiss him. I actually can't remember much after that; instead, it felt as if in that entire moment the archaic zoning by-laws that were no longer representing the people were moving forward. It felt as if the refresh button had been activated.

We Have a Strong "Knowing" That Guides Us

Eighteen years before this meeting, I sat with a dear friend, Miguel, to film a visioning session. He wanted to help me sense how to move forward with my teaching. I was teaching exercise and yoga in corporate settings, working with people after accidents and surgery, doing prescribed exercises and rehabilitation with clients post-physio, teaching life skills to youth in the school board, and many other diverse projects. He sensed that I was scattered. (Ya think?)

We started our session with a meditation. Together we touched down into how I felt at that time in my life and how I would deliver what I had to teach.

I knew I wanted to bring people into nature to practise yoga, raise consciousness, and experience an empowering environment that would entice each soul to feel alive. I wanted to bring them to a nature sanctuary. I also wanted to have a studio in Toronto, so people wouldn't need to leave the city.

I imagined the space that would evoke the truest teaching. I felt as if the environment, as I envisioned it, would be the platform that would bring about the fullest representation of what I wanted to share. I have always loved Toronto, and I must be in nature.

I didn't recall this visioning session until years after buying the property on the ravine and building The Yoga House. This is the innocence of a child. It is the innocence and genius in joy. When my nephew, Matthew, was three, I asked him the ridiculous question, "What do you want to be when you grow up?" He looked at me with a twisted quizzical face, as if I was nuts, which was fair, and said, "I'm going to be Matthew."

A child doesn't want to be anything other than what he *is*. Children learn and grow through abandoned play and frolicking expression. Through curiosity and expression we learn how to progress and create what is inside us to do.

I need to play in nature. I need to do yoga outside. Building The Yoga House meant I got to do both each day without ants in my pants. Seriously, those red ones hurt.

Ambition is different. Pure, focused ambition is a linear desire for results. Expression allows us to develop through conveying our personal truths. That is play. Our personal truths are the creative expressions inside us. My personal truth to build a yoga studio in nature actually altered the zoning code in the City of Toronto!

How I Came to Know the Body's Wisdom

At first I worked with elite athletes. Some were nationally ranked, some were Olympians who had been on the wrestling and basketball teams at college and later at the university I attended. They just happened to be in the athletic centre where I trained, and I happened to know they needed me to train them.

I seemed to do that a lot. I would get a clear sense of what I wanted to do, and it would drive me. When I realized I wanted to begin teaching exercise, I knew I needed to have formal training, yet I felt an illogical enthusiasm to go ahead anyway. After I mailed physical-education directors proposals, I would call them, saying I was going to train their athletes. I didn't ask when I called, I just told them. I was following a thread that pulled me to a destination. This way of informing them would usually attract their attention. I think they probably met with me out of intrigue more than anything else.

I clearly remember one day, at the age of eighteen, when I walked into the phys-ed department of Humber College. I asked to see the director of the evening programs, Bill Pangos. After a few moments, he came from around the partition and said hello. I looked at him and without even reaching out my hand in greeting said, "My name is Celeste Shirley, and I am going to teach the women's weight-training course you offer in the evenings." (In retrospect, this was a particularly *interesting* statement because there was already a qualified Russian instructor teaching the program.) He grinned and said, "Then I guess you better step into my office." As I went around the partition, he pointed to a chair and said, "Please have a seat." I said, "I can't sit down, I'm too excited."

These encounters were free of cockiness. I just couldn't help myself. I had been weight training since the age of fourteen and felt I knew everything I needed to know. I took coaching certification courses at night. I was so inspired by the results that training had on the body and mind that I had to share it. I felt a physical prowess that instigated my need to teach.

Back then, living my aspirations was all about strength and physical endurance. I was building a physical armour to make my way through this world, where I felt hard work and determination were necessary to reach goals.

That went on for eleven years. By the time I was thirty-three, I was struggling to keep up my personal status quo. Things didn't seem to be making as much sense anymore. I started feeling what I can best describe as vulnerable.

I knew something in me was wrong. I felt it. I kept trying to muster up more energy to "go on." I kept altering my diet, revving up my nutritional supplementation, "doing" more meditation, getting more rest. I kept trying to bargain my way out of this sense that I was sinking fast.

It started as a lack of physical energy to teach another exercise session. Yet I loved teaching. I lacked the energy to take my daughter to the park, yet I relished this magical opportunity. I persevered for years. Then (what felt like) the ultimate happened. One day I couldn't get up. Not a lack of desire, a physical reality. I was unable to raise my arm. Sipping a glass of water felt like I was holding a dumbbell. I had to save my pee. Getting up to go to the bathroom was torture.

I had all the tests done. My blood tested as "very healthy," yet my skin was turning more and more yellow, and I was losing weight and looked like a deflated sack of freckled bones.

It was ridiculous. Here I was running a fitness business, teaching about physical vitality, and I couldn't stand up. This went on for three years. I took about a year off and then most of the next two. During this time I slept. I couldn't read or watch videos to make me laugh, even though I knew the power of laughter, and taught laughter yoga (check it out, please see the resources section). Even viewing something took energy. The thought of answering the phone and attending to day-to-day activities filled me with an immobilizing anxiety.

The doctors diagnosed my condition as chronic fatigue syndrome and fibromyalgia, many prescribed antidepressants. I declined. I *knew* what was wrong, although I couldn't describe why it had affected my body to the point that it was agony to stand. I knew I had to listen to my body and do exactly what it requested. I knew in my heart that my body was revealing deep Akashic records of instilled wisdom. (The Akashic records can be thought of as the collective consciousness of all knowledge and emotion that our souls are here to experience. It can be accessed when our minds are still.)

The only thing that I was able to "do" during this time was meditate. I used no formal practice of focusing on the breath or styles of posture. I simply lay in bed and went within. The deeper layers of my mind started to surface, I had been meditating for years, but this was different. It was a deep tunnelling into the mind that would blast forth insight and revelation. A burst of consciousness blast was like a shimmering, icebreaking feeling of light that would expel any thought or constructs my mind would engage in. A day in my life would play out like a TV show. I would watch, recognizing the scenes and feel their relevance and the pressure I had put on myself that day. I could feel a pressing, idealizing mentality that pervaded every scenario. My life was flashing before me so I could see what a crazy person I was being. I would often break out laughing each day after a "TV show" had ended. I couldn't believe the intensity I was living and the speed at which I was getting all my tasks done. It's a wonder I didn't have some kind of psychic rug burn. I continued to meditate. (I had no other options; the fatigue was a complete takeover.) Any thought was a distraction. I knew I couldn't distract whatever this process was with thoughts. I couldn't panic or worry about my current situation in life. Any thought, be it a worrisome thought or planning, was a discourse, preventing further tunnelling into this mind that now had so much to say it was rendering my physical body inactive.

One message that kept coming up was, "You're not going anywhere, girlfriend. You're staying right here!"

I experienced constant muscle pain that could keep me from falling asleep, even though I was exhausted. I knew this pain. It felt exactly like the time I had run a triathlon and crossed the finish line. I clearly remember saying to myself that I couldn't take another step, even if someone put a gun to my head. I felt exactly like that now.

I also had a dream that I never forgot. I was driving along in a tiny, bizarre, boxy car. I was in gridlock in downtown Toronto. I needed to get somewhere and was in a real hurry. I knew I wouldn't make it. As I sat in traffic, the panels of the car started to jiggle and fall off. All parts of the car started to malfunction and crumble to the street underneath me, including the bottom of the car. The steering wheel came off. I had no control. I was like Fred Flintstone and tried to use my feet, paddling under the car. (I wish we could do that in real life, save on gas and get great gams!) I manoeuvered with my waist, jockeying the weight of the car over towards the side of the road where there wasn't even a proper shoulder. I leaned sideways and tried to sleigh ride the car across the lanes. No one was letting me in. I woke from the dream.

(Eleven years later, in real life, I saw the exact replica of the car, the Mercedes smart car, driving along the street. It was the same car as in my dream, only a different colour. I couldn't believe my eyes. The driver must have thought I was on acid.)

The symbolism and meaning of the dream was instant when I opened my eyes. The car was my body. The interior my soul, my Ātman. My physical vehicle was done driving in crazy traffic. My soul wanted to dance in the streets, express itself, and stop forging forward.

This depleting fatigue made me feel like a foreigner in my own country. I couldn't understand the street signs anymore—the signals from my body. I didn't know how to act on them, they were so powerful and unfamiliar. I didn't know how to be ambitious anymore. Every attempt on my part to progress in any way felt pushy and wrong. I didn't know how to do things anymore! I didn't know how to *do*.

I didn't know how to initiate projects or stay with something until it was completed. My only choice at this time was to let everything go, ask for the help I needed, and have faith that it would all work out. Faith was the biggy! I realized I was not used to operating on faith.

This came as a surprise to me. I was considered to be a positive person, but I now understood that being positive and having faith are two entirely different existences. Having faith means you are not trying to think in a certain way (positively) or move towards something that is tangible. Having faith has no "seeing" sight. It is blindly present with "what is." It has no particular allegiance with any belief.

I later started to understand that faith is not a belief, but a way of living that doesn't need to understand what to do. This can provide us Type A individuals with a sense of great relief since we can loosen up the reins a bit. Suddenly I felt as though I had more room in life. Room for anything to enter. A sense of expansion could enter, or that everything would be okay.

Because of the muscle pain the only way I could fall asleep was by meditating. The pain had a clear message: "You have been dancing as fast as you can and you cannot dance this staccato anymore. Your dancing is choppy and ungraceful; find the grace." The grace I would learn would be this new faith, the ability to listen to the body's signals and let them gently guide me rather than ignore them until they manifested as symptoms.

To live a peaceful, harmonious existence requires our attention. This can be done in gentle, smart ways that do not turn our lives upside down. Drama is so eighties. Learning to listen to our bodies and the subtleties of our minds is sensitizing. We learn to listen and really feel what we feel, and then we know what we need.

Body Wisdom in Pain

On a long weekend in May, I dislocated my shoulder. That got my full attention! My arm was out of the socket for an hour. I had nerve damage down to my elbow. The pain was intense, to put it happily. I did physio on myself for the next three months. My physiotherapist told me, just to prepare me, that I might need surgery in the future.

As I convalesced I felt an intelligence in the joint. Although my range of motion was minimal, below the radar of pain, I had an *ability* that was eager to move. I kept listening and building on it. It was tricky as I needed to be careful not to dislocate it again, which is likely with this particular injury.

Whenever I felt the fear, I would go back to the sensations in the joint. There I could feel a hum of low-grade pain. It was a sensation like Santa's workshop in the tissues. I realized that the torn ligaments, tendons, and nerves were repairing and that that was part of the tight catching feeling that was causing the discomfort. I also noticed that when I got stressed the hum would amp up.

I decided to feel the sensations with an interest, as if they were cueing me. By deciding *how* I would experience the sensation, I was able to really tune into any catch or pull when I moved. When I felt nervous about the damage and what this could mean to my career, I would realize I was buying into all the stories around me about how surgery was most likely necessary and that I would have arthritis and a lifelong weak shoulder. I would then switch back to being curious about the sensations.

The choice to feel the sensations stopped any alarm bells that would go off in my nervous system, creating the reduced immune system of the fight-or-flight response. The stress response reduces the capacity for tissues to heal by tightening the fascia. Fascia is the connective tissue that Saran wraps over our bodies. When the stress response is excited, the fascia tightens like shrink wrap. I sense that is why less scar tissue developed. If we can trust the pain to guide us into reasonable movement, mobilizing the reassembling collagen fibres and muscle tissue, it can rebuild with less injurious effect.

By feeling the scary pulls when I moved, I sensed how to increase my range of motion with attentive interest. I didn't identify this as a "shoulder-dislocation story." We can meet an experience when we don't make it into a story. Today the affected shoulder is actually more mobile than the other. I am aware that cancelling the fear factor and being thankful to the body for sensations is our way to be guided by its innate wisdom. As in all injuries, repair to tissue is best done with solid relaxation and listening to the amount of sleep the body is asking for. In a sleep-macho society, we rarely notice how tired we are until we're exhausted and our adrenals have gone on vacation. I found that during my recovery I was extremely tired, and I could feel it was from the nerve damage.

Nerve damage trumps other tissue injury and is to be respected. As I recovered and I could do more, I felt that I *should* do more. Although I could use my arm again for gentle actions, I could feel that there was no real life in it. I resisted believing I needed to get caught up with my responsibilities and continued to rest.

Daily I am amazed at how intelligent our bodies are. When I felt the enthusiasm, which I felt ever so slightly through the pain in my shoulder, it was a whisper of guidance. I would not have felt this subtle sensation if I had kept trying to keep going at the same speed as I had before I had torn it. Pain, in all its forms, assists our consciousness to listen deeply. The mind's experience of pain is where we need to slow down and *feel*. Pain, when felt—when we can drop into all its guises—assists us in how we need to move, act, and receive.

PART THREE

Constant Joy

"A self-respecting artist must not fold
his hands on the pretext that he is not
in the mood. If we wait for the mood,
without endeavouring to meet it halfway,
we easily become indolent and apathetic.
We must be patient, and believe that
inspiration will come to those who
can master their disinclination."

~ PYOTR ILYICH TCHAIKOVSKY
(1840–1893), RUSSIAN COMPOSER

CHAPTER ELEVEN

The How of Constant Joy

Direct Experience

According to Google CEO Eric Schmidt, "Every two days now we create as much information as we did from the dawn of civilization up until 2003."[1] When you experience your life directly, you are in joy. *No thought* directs you. A thought occurs when you need to prioritize and direct your actions.

An alive mind, in joy, does not need to prioritize what is important. It senses what is important. It doesn't need to choose the "better" thoughts. (Hallelujah!) A mind in joy has thoughts that are congruent with feelings. We are in sync with what we feel. Our feelings help us understand what we need to do as we go along. We trust them. (There is no actual drama; it may take all your energy, but it won't be the crazy-making drama.)

---

[1] M.G. Siegler, "Eric Schmidt: Every 2 Days We Create As Much Information As We Did Up To 2003" (August 4, 2010), TechCrunch, https://techcrunch.com/2010/08/04/schmidt-data.

As our lives progress—or what silly people call "aging"—we develop more desires, apprehensions, preferences, and affections. Our lives get complicated. It is difficult to realize what *we* really want.

A mind in joy is *not* pulled by *outside* desires that are not what we want. Outside desires are the ideals we may have bought into. We may take on these external influences and forget what is really meaningful to us. My mom's generation is focused on successful marriage and financial security. (Just for the record, I would love to have a husband who contributes to the bills; is caring, loving, and brave—in the true sense of the word; gives foot, back, neck, and shoulder massages; recites Walt Whitman; runs after me when I'm hurt; draws a colourful hopscotch on the front sidewalk for me to jump in; takes me to the Cayman Islands; shows me all parts of himself so I can be with his fears and lift him up; takes me to the skateboard park to delight in the guys with rubber ankles; takes out the garbage; addresses my unruly neighbour; and says "let me do it" at opportune moments. Just in case he's reading this.) I choose to feel alive and discover how that looks as I live.

A mind in joy is fuelled by inner inspiration. We know what *we* want. (As outlined above.) The goals will not be external carrots. We will be propelled by an inner knowing that *does us*. We will feel the goal inside us. And it will feel delightful to bring it to fruition. We do not need to *think* (thoughts) about this inner goal. It is alive in our minds and itching to come out as our expressions. Affirmations are so boring when you feel alive.

We still need to work our buns off, and it can take everything we have, financially and emotionally, and cause us to question our sanity as we watch the family leave. This is a good thing.

The Mind's Energy When We Think
(Rather Than Be)

When we think, the mind's energy collects into a thought. Thoughts initiate mental focus. The mind's pure consciousness narrows to a pinpoint. We begin to think rather than *be* in our lives. For example, if you need to make a decision on the spot, and you really need more time, then the mind's energy must speed up and tighten to concentrate. We become logical and make a list of pros and cons in our mind. We enlist an expert to guide our decision. We forget to trust that we know what to do. We don't even know that we know anymore. We force ourselves to focus when we complete a task that we were *not* inspired to do. We postpone what feels relevant. This distorts the mind's ability to create what we know is true for us.

Now our obedient mind reads outside cues for direction on how to live life correctly. If we listen to others and do what is "right," we disassemble this clear inner knowing. We still know what we want, yet we don't act on it. Our inner knowing is still inside us, yet it becomes dull and may fade away. Yikes, this is such a loss of what makes up who we are. These "knowings" can fade until we lose sight of what we know. We may do some of the things that are important to us and bargain with ourselves that we can't do the biggies. We live with an on-again, off-again switch of our imagination and bravery.

> The doing mind, which chooses a task and focuses on completing it, and which is less alive, curious, and spontaneous, separates us from ourselves. To feel who we are again, we trust that we know what to do.

Being a Knower

Knowing occurs when we feel who we are.

Being a knower is *not* living with a sense of certainty. Knowing has a much deeper quality than this. Knowing occurs when we feel who we are. This sense of self knows what to do. This is felt. And it is solid.

"In the ordinary life, we try to know what is good or right, and once we think we have found it, we somehow try to implement our thought. The supramental consciousness, on the contrary, does not try to know or to decipher what it must do or not do; it is perfectly silent and still, living each second of time spontaneously, unconcerned by the future; then at each second, the exact required knowledge falls like a droplet of light in the silence of the consciousness: 'This has to be done, that has to be said, or seen, or understood.' Supramental Thought is an arrow from the Light, not a bridge to reach it."[2]

~ SRI AUROBINDO (1872–1950), INDIAN PHILOSOPHER, YOGI, AND POET

[2] Sri Aurobindo, "Chapter 15: The Supramental Consciousness," https://sites.google.com/site/mandrivnyjvolhv/indu/piznishi/sri-aurobindo/satprem-sri-arobindo/17.

In this passage, Sri Aurobindo speaks of how the supramental consciousness is free of thought. This pure consciousness makes up the knowing inside us.

We Know What We Need

Before I learned how and what it is to live joy constantly, I thought I had good days and days that were harder. Mary changed all that.

In 1995 I was contacted by a rehab consultant representing an insurance company. The consultant, Carol, asked me to start exercise rehab sessions with a woman named Mary, who had been in a catastrophic car accident. Carol did not have any physio or medical reports to outline Mary's injuries. She explained that her injuries were extensive but her ability was epic. The spirit of Mary's nature that Carol enthusiastically outlined brought us together rapidly and we became fast friends on the phone.

Carol told me that Mary was the most courageous person she had ever met. Nothing that Carol expressed could have prepared me for the exceptional, life-changing effect that meeting Mary had on me. Meeting Mary showed me *Brave*.

Mary had been hit by a driver passing a transport truck. He had been driving at 130 km/hour, and he and his daughter had been killed on impact. Mary had been driving home from her cottage on Highway 55 on a Sunday afternoon. Her family convoy was made up of three vehicles. Her mother and father were a few cars ahead of her. Her husband, Bruno, was driving their 4×4 behind her with their youngest daughter. Mary had their four-year-old son, Anthony, beside her in the double-seated passenger front seat, with her brother, John, beside him, and her five-year-old daughter was in the back seat.

The speeding driver hit Mary's car head on, and she was crushed behind the wheel. Anthony experienced fatal injuries, and her husband, Bruno, in the car directly behind her witnessed the entire accident. (Her mother and father were a significant distance ahead of them. When Mary's mother saw all the emergency vehicles whizzing past them, she told her husband to turn around.) The intensity of the crash completely destroyed the front of Mary's car. The car's hood was smoking and flames were licking the front end when Bruno ran to pull everyone out. Everyone, that is, except Mary. She was pinned inside the car and appeared to be dead as her head was severely damaged and her lower extremities were crushed. He tried desperately to open the driver's door, but it was pinned shut. He ran to the passenger's side, and pulled out his brother-in-law and his son, whom he thought was dead, from the front seat. He then pulled his daughter, who was conscious and injured, out of the back seat. He then tried again to open the door on Mary's side. No matter how he tried, he couldn't pull it open. At that moment, two men arrived on the scene, and with their combined brute force, they managed to pry the jammed door open. The flames had already burned much of Mary's body and face, but she was alive. Her son, Anthony, died in the hospital three days later.

Mary's husband and the medical staff didn't tell her that Anthony had passed. The doctors felt she would not survive the news. She had lost a vast amount of blood. They waited a month to tell her. Each day, Mary would ask Bruno how Anthony was. It is unimaginable to consider the stamina, resilience, and courage it took Bruno to visit with her and sound encouraging as he carried the knowledge of their son's death.

Mary spent the next six months convalescing in the hospital. Her lower body was literally rebuilt. Her leg and knee were reconstructed with numerous surgeries and pins, plates, and screws. She also had multiple skin grafts performed over her entire body. The fact that she survived was considered a miracle. After these procedures were done and she had been allotted time to recover from them, she had many more reconstructive surgeries. Among them were jaw surgery, hair transplants, and many more. Her injuries, including the burned areas of her body, affected her face, arms, torso, pelvis, legs, and feet.

I started working with Mary one-and-a-half years after the accident. It had taken that long to rebuild her. (I came to call her the Bionic Woman.) She was the most faith-filled person I had ever met. I worked with her three days a week. Every day that I showed up to do exercise therapy, she would smile.

To this day, I still remember how she taught me the intelligence of pain. When I would lift Mary's left leg and work on increasing her range of motion, I would watch her face to see if it was too much. "Too much" was so unidentifiable to her. She would work with whatever range her leg would give her and my guiding arms would sense. She did not resist. Her face was always relaxed. She even lived faith on a cellular level. I had to beg her to tell me if it hurt! "Does it hurt, Mar? *Does* it hurt?" Mary surpassed pain. She experienced any painful sensations as she relaxed her body to allow for the greatest range of motion. Her willingness enhanced her physical ability. This capacity to feel pain while opening to whatever range of motion is possible is pure cellular intelligence.

I adored her style of faith. It was not Pollyannaish. One day when we were walking outside to increase her stamina, she shared with me about a woman who told her she was going to sue the city because she had slipped while on the public sidewalk and incurred injuries. You should have heard Mar! She had zero tolerance for this woman's minor injuries and major complaints. I loved her so much in that moment. Her disdain for this woman's quibbling showed me that she wasn't positive. She was real.

Mary showed me *real* every session. She worked with her body. At each session I would ask her how her body felt. I knew the pain from her extensive injuries and burns must have been constant. She would rate her body sensations with a straightforward report so we could measure her ability on any one day. That was it. She didn't see a painful day as anything that rated reporting.

As I got to know her, I became more curious. I wanted to know if anything had bothered her *before* the accident. Was there anything that she thought about that wasn't right in her life or that kept niggling at her? We hadn't yet developed a relationship that was conducive to such a question. I didn't ask until one day when we had started to talk about the accident. She said, "*Yes!*" She had noticed something that had been a real wakeup call.

One evening around nine o'clock, a while before the accident, she was running upstairs carrying Anthony's bedtime bottle and *noticed* that she was running. She tried to remember the last time she had actually walked up the stairs and not sprinted. She couldn't. In fact, she couldn't remember the last time she had moved at anything but top speed during her day. She also noticed that her fanny pack was still clipped around her waist. She hadn't unbuckled it when she came in the door at dinnertime.

Each work day she would drive the kids to daycare early in the morning, drive downtown to her work a half hour away, and then rush across the highway at lunchtime to bring her kids home, and drive them back to daycare, and then drive the half hour back downtown to work, and then do it all again after work. She would travel four times a day on Highway 401 to and from the suburbs to downtown Toronto to design windows in the Eaton Centre. It was incredible that she did this in the time that she did. She was always in a big hurry.

So it was here, on the stairs, pausing with baby bottle in hand, that she realized that she had been speeding through her days. Rushing to get to work, rushing to be a mom, always running. But it wasn't until she was standing on the stairs that she realized this. It wasn't until she was *running* up the stairs, carrying Anthony's bottle, that she realized this.

After the accident, Mary could *not* run up the stairs. It wasn't physically possible. Her left knee-joint had a plate in it and she could barely bend her knee. To get upstairs, she would patiently step up with her right leg, and then hoist her left leg up with an outward swing. It took synchronized diligent maneuvering for her to move up the stairs, one swing at a time.

We looked at each other when she shared this realization with me. No more running upstairs, no more rushing. Life had halted the speeding. Speed had ended the speeding. Now Mary stays at home and cares for her children since the accident and the many following years of surgeries and rehabilitation changed the pace of her life.

Mary had shared these details while I was stretching her left leg. Afterwards, we were silent. The power of her recognition of this knowing hung in the air. A tear that was travelling down my face dripped onto her. I have never forgotten that moment.

The little inner hunches, these little pulls on your mind's attention that say "*do this*" are not that little devil or angel character sitting on your shoulder. They are you sensing life and what you need to do right now. We can listen to these "knowings"; they will *not* ruin our ability to keep up or get everything done.

Mary felt the knowing on the stairs. She felt it when she told me. Our bodies are so intelligent. They know what we need. We can listen. Mary gave birth to a baby boy two years later.

Doing and Being:
A New Model for Discipline

"To be what we are, and to become what we are capable of becoming, is the only end of life."

~ ROBERT LOUIS STEVENSON
(1850–1894), SCOTTISH AUTHOR

There are two ways we live our lives. We are either doing or being:

1. Doing is moving from a place of not having to a place of having.
2. Being is inspired action.

When we are doing, we set out to start and finish a task. Think of taking out the garbage.

Sexy, right? It can be. When we are being, we feel ourselves complete the task of taking out the garbage. One day I spontaneously took out the trash early in the day so I wouldn't need to do it in the evening. I had never taken it out to the curb this early, but on this day, I saw a neighbour I had been thinking of and a beautiful butterfly flutter across the rays of the late afternoon sun. I was occupied with taking the garbage out. A *prompting* had moved me.

Being is alive and has more charge to it than *doing*. When we are *doing*, we focus to acquire, gain, or complete. When we are *being*, we *experience* what we are engaged in doing. When we are *doing*, we finish one thing and think of the next. When we are *being*, we feel no beginning or end of each experience. All of our moments are experiences. There is nothing we need to gain from the experiences.

Being is the same experience as love, as St. Bernard of Clairvaux illustrates: "Love seeks no cause beyond itself and no fruit; it is its own fruit, its own enjoyment. I love in order that I may love."

When we are being, our action is true creation. This creative impulse feels like a "knowing." It is a kind of certainty that doesn't rely on outside feedback or affirmation to be certain. This knowing occurs with such clarity, such precision, that we need not question it. We simply know it is true.

Being is a spontaneous movement of the mind. When we are being, we do not think about what to do. (There's that "no thought" occurring again.) It's worth repeating: There is only "knowing." When we can be with "what is," we can "observe and act." When we "act" in this way, our action is free and right; it is right for us. When we are being, we –

- are gentle and inquisitive—we are interested in what we are doing;
- lose our need to judge whether what we do is right or wrong— when we stop judging what we need to do, we simply do it;
- free up all the mental energy we previously used to try to talk ourselves into doing it because we simply do it; and by doing it
- realize we can rely on ourselves.

Let's explore the difference between doing and being further so you will know when you are doing and when you are being.

How Do You Know When You Are Doing or Being?

The late Ursula Le Guin writes about the vital difference between doing and being. When doing we are "busy"; when being we are "occupied with living." Being is to enter and occupy what we are accomplishing. Doing is a response to our world. Doing is a reaction to something outside ourselves. This could be a family responsibility, or any obligation.

In this doing, there is thought. The thought directs us to configure our next move. The brain works in movements when it operates this way, movements from starting points to desired finishing points. This is very different from being. When we are being the creative impulse, or what is in us to do, creates the action.

Conversely, when we are doing, the desired finishing points are rarely, if ever, complete. Once we reach one finishing point, we begin thinking about the next one.

We are never truly satisfied. A chain of desired finishing-point thoughts keep racking up. The mind is a stockpile of our desires. We feel only temporarily satisfied when we fulfill one desire and then return to the backup in our heads.

This movement in and out of the mind causes a fragmentation of the conscious energy. The mind must choose if it will attend to the inner (stockpile) dialogue or the person we are talking to. We are rarely aware of this mental division. It is difficult to feel present in our lives.

When we are being, the energy of the mind is whole. We are one directed arrow. Isn't it splendid to look up and see the *V* formation of geese flying in the sky? Their unified, directed formation is cooperatively beautiful and inspiring. The geese are *being*. They are flying south with the world's geography mapped within their very cells. This is how it is with us. We are directed when we feel the inspiration of expressions animate us.

Living by the Inner Promptings

When we directly experience life, we will feel an impetus that moves us. I call this the "inner prompter."

HOW DOES THE INNER PROMPTER FEEL?

The feeling of inner prompting is enlivening. When you feel an inner prompting, it is a concrete feeling. There's no confusion. An inner prompting occurs when you spot your child in the play on stage and your heart lights up. Inner promptings can occur when you start talking fast about the ideas you have. Inner promptings are love in action. A prompting can also be unsettling, confusing, or outright terrifying because you don't understand why it is prompting you to do something that makes no sense. No sense at all.

Inner promptings can also be frustrating. One client I work with is getting clear messages to stop eating at McDonald's and to cut back on alcohol. Inner promptings may not be fun, but you know they're true. They can be real bummers. (Especially when your husband is looking at you quizzically with a bottle of red wine tipped in air to pour your Friday-night reward.) However, stay with the insight that the prompting is revealing. Be a deep listener and suspend disbelief.

Inner prompting will move you physically. The prompting takes you over like water filling a firehose. I have felt the prompting lift my arm as if *I* wasn't doing it. The power in the prompting feels like when you pull hard to open a drawer because it is normally stuck, and it whips open easily and you practically fly across the room.

Emotionally, the inner prompter is raw expression. Or it will feel as though an emotion is directing the words that come out of you. Like when I told my husband I wanted a divorce and it was a feeling-truth speaking. (You can read about my joyful divorce in chapter twelve.)

> Spiritually, mentally, and relationally the inner prompter
> is a fresh knowing that uplifts and ennobles you.

I feel the inner prompter as a wash of energy like a stream rushing through me when a twig has been removed. It is richer than an aha moment as it isn't just a flirt of inspiration in the mind. Most aha moments are cerebral and the recognition that something needs to change. That is more a product from the thinking mind; the inner prompter affects the entire body, mind, and spirit. It interrupts and enlivens your nervous system.

The inner prompter is a whole package deal that hums in you and launches you into the next "next" in your life. This could be your next moment, intimate connection, idea, insight, realization, feeling of love, or assignment. When you do feel the inner prompting, milk this feeling. Hang out there.

- Is the feeling positive? (It will be.) Exciting? (It will be; it is never discouraging or negative. It can be scary yet absolutely not discouraging.)
- How is the feeling helping and directing you?

For example, if you are considering whether or not you can stay in a relationship, feel your mind chattering "should I stay or should I go?" How is it making you feel? When you consider staying, do you feel alive? Do you feel overwhelmed? Is the prospect of staying sinking you into a pile of needs you now must sort out and communicate to your partner?

I felt this way when I was trying to decide whether to stay with Sarah's father when I was pregnant. I didn't really need to decide! I knew the answer; the inner prompting was moving me to leave. I just didn't want to know it was true.

If we give ourselves the time to explore our thoughts and their accompanying feelings, the inner promptings are there. We always know what to do. No one knows like we do.

HOW TO FEEL THE PROMPTINGS

First, to feel the promptings you may be aware of what you *don't* want in your life.

This could be an outworn relationship, job, or way of eating. It could even come out as a judgement. Feel the message in the judgement. For example, when I judge my mother, I realize how I wish to parent Sarah.

Following this you may get real about your situation and feel a deep insight. The actual experience of the inner prompter is that it has meaning for you. It lifts you up and supports what is important to you. It creates breakthroughs. The essence of the inner prompter is power. As the late David R. Hawkins wrote in his book *Power vs. Force*, "Power is always associated with that which supports the significance of life itself. It appeals to that part of human nature that we call noble, in contrast to force, which appeals to that part of human nature that we call crass. Power appeals to what uplifts, dignifies, and ennobles. Force must always be justified, whereas power requires no justification. Force is associated with the partial, power with the whole."[3]

When we feel whole, we feel powerful. Power is a field that does not move. Everything moves around it. This means that when we feel our inner prompter, we feel the impetus inside us to do what it points to. The inner prompting is complete unto itself. It is not partial nor does it compartmentalize like it does when we are weighing the pros and cons about what to do. The inner prompting is complete knowing. The only reason it may feel as though it is wavering is that we don't trust ourselves enough to do what it is showing us and delay. The inner prompting is solid; it's that we are afraid to act on what it is showing us to do.

> The inner prompter is a trusting-knowing. It is the ability to trust that each moment we can directly engage with what is happening. This trust allows us to know what we need to do.

IS THE INNER PROMPTER A GUT FEELING?

In my experience, the inner prompter is *not* a gut feeling, although for many it is. I tend to feel it as a whole package deal. The gut, or solar plexus, houses its own brain. The gut is more than an organ

---

[3]David R. Hawkins, *Power vs. Force: The Hidden Determinants of Human Behavior* (Carlsbad, CA: Hay House, Inc., 2012), 95.

of digestion. It is a sensory apparatus with a nervous system of its own, intimately connected to the brain's emotional centres. It is referred to as the "enteric brain." When we feel in sync with ourselves, the intestines are influenced by the parasympathetic nervous system, which is the relaxing side of the nervous system, as opposed to the fight-or-flight response.

We will *feel* what is true for us. Often when the gut, or solar plexus area, is stressed, our belly-brain feels tight and distended. We can feel confused. This can cause inflammation leading to bloating, irritable bowel syndrome, moodiness, brain fog, poor digestion, and the related fatigue and other "stomach in knots" feelings.

I have felt the inner prompter as a movement in my psyche that caused me to turn around and go back into a weight room. I felt weird going back as I was done my workout. Upon entering the weight room, I went around a corner to the bench-press area. Within seconds a young guy started to lose control of the barbell that was above his head. I swished across the room and pulled the barbell back up onto the rack. If I hadn't been called back, the barbell would have fallen on his neck.

He started to freak out, and exclaimed I had "saved his life!" to the other guys in the weight room. I hurried out to keep the calm feeling that had taken me there. I felt that I didn't want to hear any talk of it or to be recognized. This kind of collecting oneself and being inward with the power of these promptings allows us to stay solid and powerful without frittering our energy away.

HOW COME I DON'T FEEL
THE INNER PROMPTER?

We resist going deep within ourselves to access the knowing that is our inner prompter. We have *not* been taught to simply trust ourselves. When we do, we can access the tender assistance in the body and mind that knows what to do. (This is how we experience an intelligent body.) Because this prompting is often buried in us and we have become numb to the prodding, it needs to be excavated. To access the promptings, we let our feelings direct us towards true action.

When we reach into its knowing, we feel free of bossy "mind-chatter." The opposite of this knowing is having others' ideas invade our minds, which is the essence of neurosis. That is, we do it to ourselves. The invasion of other people's ideas creates the conditioned thinking of the "mask self." The mask self is a collection of ideals we believe we need to follow, as outlined in chapter ten, and it will sabotage your inner promptings.

WHY WE DON'T LIVE BY
THIS INNER PROMPTER

The resistance we have to this inner knowing is clever. It is conniving, like a controlling lover who is afraid we will leave. It is our unhealthy ego. Our unhealthy ego tries to convince us that we cannot take risks. Inner promptings could scare us. We are being led beyond our limits and comfort zones.

Our defences rise to convince us to take an already familiar route that will GPS us back to the safety of familiar habits (that are tainted by our personal politics). Yet if we really tune in at that moment, we will be swept up by (carried really) a clarity that creates action. (We trust ourselves and don't delay any longer.)

Direct action is the result of being tuned into the inner prompter. It organizes and directs our lives, *our* lives. Its power is so complete that *we* are moved.

When we stay tuned to this power—which is how joy feels—a shift occurs that enables us to follow through. When we stay in the feeling tone of joy, we can stay tuned to it and live it at all times. This may sound grand. And it is. Yet it is not a grand task that requires diligence. Although this is necessary, it occurs naturally.

You don't fall in love with someone, drive over to their mailbox, and get distracted by Dairy Queen. You drive like a madwoman, and you put a love letter in their mailbox. You reach out and give them *you*. You give them a piece of the affection that is rocking your very soul.

This is you. This is you at your finest and this is what you give yourself when you are rocking in your own life. Your sensuous, celebrated life will reflect who you really are in an unsentimental way.

Let me elaborate. Our actions directly reflect how we feel. Feelings look like action. Actions look like feeling. I know what you're thinking: What about when I feel really nasty? No worries, this can be felt too without your being discouraged. Nasty feelings are where we lose steam and, most importantly, our self-esteem. Shame or doubt enters our building. That's when I loan all my equity to my yoga teacher. (Note: Every time you lose steam, something happens to support you in this returning cycle called Life.)

When I feel disgruntled and "off," I know that I am wasting energy and pouring it out where it isn't needed. For example, when I feel insecure around a gorgeous woman, I know I'm looking for affirmation, and I don't feel it here because I think she looks better than me. Which means I am (still!) believing I'm not good enough. Which is exhausting. This kind of existence creates a barrage of fleeting feelings that ultimately will never convince me that I am okay. It also means I will have to find ugly friends.

Nasty feelings point out where we have energy leaks. They point to the sticking points where how we feel about ourselves relies on some outside affirmation. When the support isn't there, we feel let down. This is why our relationships are so fleeting. We feel "love," and then when the person doesn't "notice" us, we feel neglected. When in fact they're just thinking about Dairy Queen.

We can follow New Age, mindfulness, and other such guidelines and "not take it personally," "take deep breaths," and "reframe the situation," which may work—on some days—when we remember to use it. On others days you may be too immersed to notice you have spiralled down the *nasty* hole. This is why you have to get stellar. You need, I don't like to sound all bossy, but you really, really need to notice these nasty holes in the golf course of life. Find out where they are in your day and notice why you feel that way. (Hey, that rhymes.) Then be interested in what the script is that's feeding them. Then meticulously dissect the script.

Okay, let's say you feel beautiful, and useful, and then, wham, you fall down the nasty hole and feel anxious, bloated, and disorganized. This nasty feeling is real; it feels as if you can't shake it no matter how many deep breaths you take or walks you force upon yourself. *This is when you are really onto something*; this is where the juice is. It is super important to recognize that at times like this, you *expect* (and want) to feel differently.

So if you feel anxious, you believe that you would be better if you felt calm. Yet feeling calm may not appease or fix you. The anxiety is useful. It shows you there is something that needs to change in the way you're experiencing life.

Can you stay with the anxious feeling? (Not a confidence builder, I know!) I have been working on writing this book for thirty years … Jesus! When I attempt to write what I know, I can feel anxious. I feel a massive amount of enthusiasm for what feeling joy constantly actually feels like. Yet when I sit down to write how I live this way, I feel as though I'm trying to write instructions. I don't want to write about *how* to live joy. The how is lived by *being* in joy. Yet that doesn't help *you*!

The anxiety I feel reveals an insecurity that says I cannot be so empowered and know *this* much. (Yet again, the ol' Imposter Syndrome.) The anxious feeling shows me that I don't know how to be this big and liberated. The feeling is ever so convincing. It takes diligence to feel this anxiety and then go write anyway. Because I am right. I know what I'm saying! When I feel this way, I feel the "right" to write what I know. Under our anxiety or any other discomfort and agitation is a fierce boldness. A clarity of how we want to live, act, love, write, create, relate, govern, contribute, and any form of expression.

Please, please join me. For your own sake, or God's sake if that does it for you. (Same thing; you're God.) Let the corked, stuck, frustrated impulse in anxiety and discomfort out. Write. Say what you need to say. State what you need. Say it again if they didn't respond. It doesn't have to make sense. Express that you don't know why you feel anxious. You don't need to know. This is not a test. Actually, it is a *kind* of test. You are being tested to see if you will suppress the anxiety, or if you will draw on a courage to feel it. If you can feel that you don't know what's wrong (seriously, honestly, it doesn't matter), you can feel all nasty and know that there is a deployed, congested inner prompting that wants out.

This stymied expression is one thing: You want to feel connected. You feel separate. You're not sure if you're doing this life right. I understand. Feeling separate is hard. It creates anxiety and uncertainty—as if you're not doing enough, as if you didn't do that thing yesterday and it's already Wednesday. Feeling separate is the impossible place we go when we feel anxious or uncomfortable.

Stay right there! In that stuck feeling. You don't need to do a thing. It's so weird, which is a kind word for unfair, that living joyfully, when you really do it, is shaky. Living joyfully is like meeting your darkest shadow self and knowing *you* are still there. (That's massive faith!) It's a toughie. It's not for sissies.

I could give you many examples of how I have done this in my life. I could tell you many more stories about how to feel joy no matter what. I won't. Life is super quick. And this book is long enough already. So *you* tell me how to feel inner promptings to keep yourself living true to yourself! You tell me how you do something that was really hard and you did it anyway.

You don't need to be absent of uncomfortable feelings to be moved by inner promptings. You're still here—the you who is experiencing the nasty feelings. So stay here. The nasty feelings, when felt, will reveal a need. Please, stay here. It takes monumental discernment to stay with the discomfort. People will stop thinking Dairy Queen and remember to care. In the meantime, *you* care. *You* care for you and feel everything with curiosity, interest, and empathy for yourself. Punch a pillow, smash the shopping cart with running speed into the dominoes of carts in the parking lot, or scream in the car. Please, please make sure the sunroof is closed.

Joy Doesn't Deal

When I first experienced joy at the age of twenty-one, many considered my experience to be miraculous, as if I had been blessed by divine intervention. (Which does sound cool!) It was definitely the most alive I had ever felt, but I was very much grounded in my mundane moment-to-moment existence. It's that *I* was divine. The divine inhabited me because I was being who I am. I felt very much a part of life. I was not in any way removed from my environment or lifted to a higher level of awareness or realm.

If I had experienced some extreme difficulty, which I cannot remember experiencing, I was not exempt from hard feelings. It's that the difficult stuff didn't rub me out of joy. I sense that that's why I have no recall of difficult ordeals. All the gritty details were not markers for how I felt or for what I dealt with. I didn't deal.

When I'm congruent with life as it is, I have no sense of separation from it. This actually makes it *impossible* to view anything as difficult.

Why I Had to Make People Sit on the Floor

When I first started studying yoga, I went to a yoga studio, like everybody does. I hid at the back. I was very inflexible and knew nothing about what the teacher was going to do (to me). With my tight bum, I didn't want to "get in the way" of her teaching. It never occurred to me that I would be learning about *my* body and how to work with and *breathe* it.

I believed I was supposed to follow the poses the teacher demonstrated. Not unlike the classrooms we all grew up in. Yet after about eight years, I noticed I was becoming more like the people in front of me. I could *do* more of what the teacher was doing. I could stay in the poses without my hamstrings dialling 911. One day a woman whom I had always admired who was training to become a yoga teacher was in the class. She came up to me afterwards and told me how incredibly flexible my forward bend was. She had never seen anything like it.

It was official: I was *flexible*. I was now one of them, of the higher echelons of the Stars of the Yoga Ladder of Gumby Success. Yet I felt very much the same. Except I felt way more sensitive. A precision in my thinking was missing. I felt an absurd willingness to be changed by anything I was seeing. I lost opinions. I felt an appreciation for whatever was before me. I wanted to listen. I was feeling an expanded experience in each moment. My senses were dilating.

What really seemed unfair was that I felt fragile. I felt exposed to the outside world. My body armour made up of ideals and ambitious expectations had cracked and peeled off and must have been in a puddle somewhere. I felt an enthusiasm that was not being met. This open, empathic enthusiasm lived right alongside a magnificent feeling of gratitude. I felt a constant appreciation for beauty and truth in life. I didn't know how to feel so alive and untethered without a landing pad for this enthusiasm. I constantly felt all inspired for no reason at all. I was like Anthony Robbins without the pump.

I felt as though my yoga practice was opening me up, and yet I wasn't sure if it was dangerous to live in its closed society. Where do I go with this openness? I felt rather flimsy in this dog-eat-dog culture. I felt I had better tone it down a bit. I looked too eager. I needed to constrain this joyful, vibrant sense of freedom that was buzzing through me, willing me to burst out to any interested soul who had questions.

Would I start accosting strangers in the park, on the jogging trails, and in line at Shoppers Drug Mart to tell them about how liberated they were? I felt as though I might erupt to them then and there and reveal how amazing life really is before they could get away from the crazy lady.

Yes, I had to do something that was not evangelical. So I made the main floor of my home into a yoga studio. I got rid of all the furniture. Yes, I was concerned where my parents and other normal people would sit when they visited, but I could not stop this ... prompting. I had to share what I was learning. Crazy is good. It's normal people who are frightening. Let's get crazy (ode to Prince). It's time.

Becoming more of who you are can change your life drastically, and you might end up getting rid of furniture. Becoming more of who you are may feel unnerving and not provide the sense of confidence you may have thought it would. I know! Who knew that doing what is true for you may feel really, really uncomfortable and cause massive self-doubt. It truly seems bizarre (happy word for "unfair") to connect to life so completely; give up on a secure, reliable living (i.e., a paycheque); and risk everything only to feel more unsure.

As you continue to do what you know you must do, certainty will lose its anchoring appeal. You will feel a pull into vaster potentiating possibilities. As an ambassador of living your truth, I implore you, again, to feel the shakiness and trust yourself to feel what is important. Then start.

Doing Creates Unnecessary Effort

When we are *doing*, we are forcing ourselves to take action. The only way to do what it takes to change is to accept the fact that it will be uncomfortable, and you will feel uncertain. It's super helpful to be awkward and hold space for change to enter when you don't know how. To actually act in your life with this feeling of uncertainty, you need to respect yourself so strongly that you are not willing to be anything less than impeccably true to what you need to do. This holding space means you allow for a chaotic learning curve that welcomes mess. Clean people need not apply.

The only way to do what it takes to change is to accept the fact that it will be uncomfortable, and you will feel uncertain.

The part of our psyches that is not willing to experience discomfort is the wounded aspect of ourselves. It is the childlike self that wants pleasure and comfort. It cannot see the bigger picture. It cannot give up pleasure and comfort to provide a fuller experience of ourselves later. Brave living is rare. Brave is trusting what we know.

When I was writing this book, I went through months of nausea as I collected the decades of writing to bring to an editor. (Which took eight years! I thought I couldn't take it to an editor until I'd edited it!) When I set time aside to tighten the writing and organize the structure, I felt awful. I felt overwhelmed and anxious and thought I had better clean the house. And your house if you were home. I felt a desperate need to sleep. The feelings cut into my writing time.

When I tried to nap, I couldn't. I didn't know how to settle the hungry-but-can't-eat-anything anxiety I felt. My sleep was affected almost every night. Then I remembered a conversation I had with my friend Barbara Marx Hubbard. She said that when we are pregnant and giving birth, if we didn't know we were pregnant we would be terrified and treat the birth pains. We would never tolerate such intense pain without trying to do something to stop it. (Just to be ever so clear, even when you know you're giving birth, you would still do anything to stop it.)

In the past when I looked at what I had written, I saw that I was so caught up in delivering the message *well* that I lost the potency in the message. I kept attempting to "get it right." And each time I needed to come back to trusting myself to write what I knew in the way I felt it.

When I reflected on this writing-down-the-bones process, I recognized that I felt an impending "I'm wrong!" lurking in the stratosphere around me. This "other shoe" that felt as though it would drop through my very earth had been my nemesis and annoying buddy all my life. It always viewed what I was doing and questioning it like a petulant god. Pretty sure it was Mom. Yet I did all my John Bradshaw work in my twenties (releasing my wounded child and cling-ons of shame). What is *she* still doing here? I thought I had workshopped her out? Really?

I did strong direct clearing with my mom in my twenties and early thirties. I cleared old, unhealthy, unspoken agreements that had affected my self-esteem. We did a real sell-off. Wall to wall we released the hurtful statements, the shaming events, and the ways I felt ridiculed. I called my mom, who was in Barrie, from Toronto after I watched the movie *The Joy Luck Club*, a rendition of Amy Tan's book. In this mother-daughter movie each of the characters strives to say their hurts and break cultural and unspoken, restricting codes of conduct. When I called my mom I was a splotchy-faced, snotty mess. I had just finished bawling my eyes out, double-pump style—that's when you do that gasping drawing in of breath real quick so you can let out the next wail. I was so sober with the release of my realizations that I must have sounded like the voice of God when I called her and said I wanted to see her. The last time I had called her was to tell her I was pregnant (I was single).

The next day I drove up to Barrie and spilled the beans. I sat with my mom in the sunken living room looking over the bay. This room was usually used only for guests and parties. I had been with her in this room maybe three times. We sat on the hot-pink love-seats facing each other. (My God, this sounds like a western.) I told her that I didn't blame her. At all. I told her that I was coming to her because I knew that if I went to what felt like the source of my lack of self-esteem, I could really, truly move on.

My mom was amazing. I released every particle of my painful story. Then she took me to Hooters for dinner. I thought that was weird. My mom was so understanding and loving. She really owned how she had parented. I have always dearly loved my mom. She is an incredible mother of six(!) children and raised us with attentive care. When I told her all the things I felt in my life that were shameful and how I doubted myself, she heard the ways I had felt she had shut me down.

I remember what she said and how it affected me. For years, when I made "mistakes," I would echo self-recriminating statements in my mind. If I wasn't successful I'd say to myself, "How could you be so stupid?" These were the criticisms she had said to me. I told her I had worked since my twenties to rewire my brain to deactivate the way I felt about myself. She not only listened openly, she also owned another painful event she felt bad about that I had completely forgotten. She was truly the most supportive mother I could have experienced that day. She didn't cross an arm or a leg, or cross back over the line of her own ego and defend herself. She listened so deeply. That talk was the most powerful time I have ever had with her.

(Mom, if you read this book, when you read the entries where I share my pain and how what you said affected me, know that your critical eye and fast words made me live an accelerated life where I can detect in an instant when someone is shaming themselves. I am grateful to you for having the mind that could catch all the ways I could be better. I know I am better because of you.)

It took ten minutes to tell her how that pain I felt in my life was related to the way she had spoken to me. And with the telling, I felt as if I had lost thirty pounds from my shoulders, rib cage, and gut. Maybe that's why she took me to Hooters.

I still won't speak to her about certain subjects. I'm sure that's standard procedure with moms and their grown children. I realize as I write this that my mom would often quip after I shared deeply about my life that I was "analyzing everything to death" or she would quickly move onto another subject as if I had just put a rat in the punch bowl at the party. Around my mom and family, I can often feel as if I'm silly, ridiculous, too granola, need to "lighten up," and *should* just have a glass of "whine" and be done with it.

Trusting what I know to be a true way of living has been like foraging through the terrain of my life with my own compass and making sure I didn't meet my family. This is the universal conundrum. (That is one of my favourite words. Conundrum.) Living in duality and back into non-duality (or joy) means I live in a conundrum daily. Conundrum living is separating. Not to be confused with "condo living." (Which is also separating, but I digress.) It means I feel clear and confident and true to myself. Then the next minute, those healthy feelings are gone. They disappear when the pride police come and all the feelings of greatness hide behind the self-conscious bushes.

Demarcation of conundrum living: I am afraid of feeling great. If I feel *too* great I'll be in big trouble, and that lurking petulant god will send me back to the trenches for shining too brightly. I feel I must *settle down*.

After "analyzing this to death" all my life—thanks, Mom, seriously, it helped me to question myself and then trust myself again—I know that when I am afraid that I am shining too brightly, I need to continue doing what I'm doing. I now know I am becoming more of what I am. Becoming more of what I am is code for living with beauty and grace and honouring the very life force in me.

Please join me.

CHAPTER TWELVE

Using Emotions as Ushers

To really *be* with an emotion and feel it doesn't mean you mechanically accept it. Absolutely accepting what happens is a strategy. When the mind creates strategies to handle emotions, you have to rely on that strategy.

Being with the emotion is different. You are stretched open and feel what is happening. *When you do, what happens next will be different.* Feeling the emotion allows more depth in your experiences and for you to be altered by it rather than resist what it is giving you. You actually experience more joy when you don't use strategies to discriminate against what is happening. You are able to experience more joy because you are able to experience pain and loss.

The most prevalent disruption of joy is "negative emotions"; however, I use that term to make it relatable; in truth, no emotion is negative—it just doesn't feel good.

The following emotions (and their offspring of secondary emotions) cancel joy. To make this arduous task of looking at our difficult (negative) emotions more interesting, I include their "purpose" here:

Primary Negative Emotions	Purpose
Sadness	To help you realize you feel pain, loss, or a sense of separation.
Worry	To show you that stale concerns rewind in your mind and hold you hostage; you don't know how to address them. You need support to start and to stay with taking care of them. You need to feel safe. Reach out and ask for help, or schedule time to be with someone who can listen without feedback so you can air your concerns, and/or express them in ways that release the negative energy—exercise, write a letter you don't send, paint it, or make any other physical or artistic display.
Anger	To show that you are taking things personally; you need to address someone, something, or yourself to learn what is disrupting your ability to be real and honest; you need to set boundaries.
Frustration	To show that you believe you are being tripped up by someone or something else, you need to take responsibility for your own sense of joy. Identify what the frustration is. Name it. Then you can see you are having expectations for the situation to be different than it is. (If you are, you are creating your own suffering.) Once you have identified your expectations, you can name your needs; for example, if you need someone to listen to you, then you know you need to feel understood and connected.
Impatience	As with "Frustration."
Anxiety	This emotion is very popular! It shows you that you believe you need to be somewhere that you are not now and pressures you to get there (this feeling manifests particularly in your solar plexus). See also "Worry" and "Frustration."

Desperation	As with "Anxiety," with the addition of a tight timeline.
Disenchantment	You realize you are having expectations. You are freeing yourself from false beliefs or illusions. It may feel lousy, and it's good that you now understand yourself better.
Lonely	To show you that you believe you are separate when you want to feel connected. Feel the need to feel connected and this will allow for the courage to express to another what you need.
Secondary Negative Emotions	**Purpose**
Grief	This emotion goes with sadness; it shows you that you are experiencing change and a shift in your life due to a loss. Allow the grief to usher you into a tenderer, dignified way of living that lets you move at the speed and in the ways that you need.
Nervousness	This emotions goes with anxiety; it shows that you are feeling flooded with emotions and caged in. You identify with time, and a sense of urgency is taking over your nervous system. See also "Worry" and "Frustration."
Confusion	This emotion goes with anger or sadness; you feel overwhelmed and as though you can't take responsibility; it shows you that you don't feel you are good enough or that you can address any actions or decisions at this time.
Jealousy	This emotion shows you that you are comparing yourself to others and believe that you come up short.
Hate	This emotion causes you to separate yourself from others and shows you that you are being judgemental.

If you read the above chart with interest, you will be able to recognize the emotion's purpose as it arises in you. You can experience its contribution to your growth and identify your needs. This is extremely helpful and healthy—and even better than taking your Flinstones vitamins.

When you experience the emotion directly, you can actually "be" in your life. You experience all that the emotion gives you. I have noticed that even when I experience deep sadness and start to cry, the release of tears is a tenderizing wash. I feel clear and *in* my life as I feel my body opening through the release. The sad feeling is there, but barely. It's more that *I* am there. It is only when I enter the story about the sadness and go back into what happened that I suffer.

Part of joy is feeling awful. You feel terrible when you lose someone; you are heartbroken or sad when relationships redefine; you are clobbered by self-doubt when you need to finish a project. You may even feel guilty about feeling so good (especially if you're female). It's still all there, and you wouldn't actually want to miss it, because although the clobbering hurts, it reveals how you and all of us have ideas about how this life is *supposed* to play out. It causes you to suffer because you define (and identify with) it as pain. You don't see it as being informing, and so you put it in the heartbreak category. When you choose to live in joy, your heart expands, and it is impossible to avoid collisions and sometimes explosions (I have noticed). Hearts will get smashed open. Then the experience permeates your nervous system, and you grow. You are shaped by your experience, which creates awareness and (what we perceive as) wisdom.

> **Newsflash**
>
> This just in: I have asked my awake friends about living a life with such dilated senses, and they have all said that their hearts break daily. You can use this newsflash to inspire you in knowing that daily heartbreak allows for a massive amount of love, support, empathy, compassion, insight, wisdom, resolutions, communing, creativity, integration, healing, flow, and grace to enter. I have noticed.

This is more powerful than when you had a smaller heart or were more careful. When you know who you are, caution cannot even assemble in your mind. When you feel what you feel, everything is exactly as it needs to be. It is perfect.

How can it be perfect when you are going through something like a divorce? I'm so glad you asked. My divorce was completely unexpected. I could not have seen it coming. I was in our bedroom with my husband, André, trying to communicate how I felt about his treatment of my daughter, Sarah, the night before. I wanted to talk to him while my feelings and experience of the night were fresh. It was our first chance to be alone.

In my view, he had been a dictator, demanding that she stop her antics with no real reason for his request. She was playing around at a community drumming circle we had initiated in a local church basement. She was having a blast up on stage being a wacky clown and making us all laugh. She would appear from behind the curtain and then put on a dramatic face, pretending she had been grabbed, pulling her head with her enclosed hand from behind the curtain. The typical "hook" joke. I was laughing so much that she kept going. André told her to stop and that she shouldn't be on the stage. He was angry and visibly frustrated. She got down from the stage and went on to other parts of the auditorium to continue clowning around.

I knew the truth: His inner child was playing out. He was angry because Sarah was free to be her funny, actor-self. He wasn't. I could tell that he felt compelled to control her actions and shut her down because someone had shut him down.

That afternoon, up in our bedroom the morning after this event, I asked him why he had done that. He made some feeble attempt to say that she shouldn't have been carrying on like that. I couldn't feel any conviction in his words. He made no eye contact; he kept looking up and around and down. His words were defensive, and he kept referring to what she "should be doing." This made no sense. It went against all the inner values that had brought us together in the first place. He wasn't angry with Sarah. He was angry with himself.

A strength grew in me. A boldness surged through me like an arrow hitting its target. It felt as if I was being cracked open. A stunning clarity arose in me. "I want a divorce." I felt alive and certain. At exactly and precisely the same time I felt crazy and could not believe the painful, shocking words coming out of me. Out of *my* mouth. Had I spoken them? Did I say that? I could never imagine leaving André or him leaving me. It was simply not possible. I could feel my chest and stomach start to collapse. I was crumbling inward. I think I fell to my knees. Yes, I did. I fell to the floor, head in hands, sobbing.

"Please, Celeste!" André pleaded. "Please be patient with me!" came his desperate plea, in his thick, French accent. He was sincere. He was listening. He wanted me to give him a chance. I remember what I said next so clearly it was as if God rose out of my mouth, the words were so crystalline and concise: "Patience is permission and I can no longer permit this."

André looked wide-eyed at me; my words had stopped any plea he was about to make. He looked as if he had been slapped.

Everything went dark. I couldn't see. All around me was pitch black. André might have said more, but I don't remember anything after that. I became a limp puddle on the floor. The arrow that entered my body felt like truth serum flooding my respiratory system. I was being taken over by pure consciousness that created a pinnacle of clarity. There was no room for confusion or cruelty, only honest action. I felt exhilarated and then broken. These feelings occurred almost simultaneously. I felt utter disbelief and crushed. Yet I felt no doubt. Only the powerful awareness that it was true; he had to go. I could not live truthfully alongside the choices he was making.

His treatment of my daughter was tainted by his painful past. He was taking it out on her. Nothing in me could allow his projections. Not even the undying love I felt for him. The alertness I felt in that moment had allowed me to take the clear action of asking for a divorce. I felt disbelief that I had asked, but not confusion.

The weight of my words were breaking my heart. Yet I felt no "hurting." I was in pain; hurt would have been miniscule compared with what I was feeling. This pain took over my entire body, saturating my cells and making me unable to see. I was like an emotional ink pad—a dark blackness was spreading through me, saturating my tissues. I felt a total physical dark-night-of-the-soul kind of energy take over my entire body.

I do not experience channelling, but what I felt was similar to what I hear people who do. The truth was coursing through me and out of my mouth. I simply had not known those words were there. They were absolute and felt powerful. I felt no sense of self-preservation or defence. I only felt the potent, heartbreaking truth: I could not share my life with him.

In the state of joy, there is only life. During this entire experience I felt so awake. The heartbreak did not take me down. I felt vividly, vulnerably, and fully alive. For the next two weeks I went through the due diligence of our initial separation. During this time, I wept constantly. I would weep while driving, while on the subway, while teaching yoga. I became a professional, silent crier. When with people, I would shrug and say, "Allergies."

I remember teaching became a joy. Each moment in my life felt adventurous again. When I would teach a corporate yoga class, I would feel a fresh, flourishing enthusiasm as if I were beginning my career again. It's exhilarating to feel broken and alive. It felt as if I had nothing to lose. By following what I knew I had to do, I became the true me, alive again. I was no longer *trying* to communicate with my husband. Now the ways that I had felt myself constrict when I saw how he was treating my daughter were lifted. The renewal back into life showed me the effect I was experiencing by not being in coherence with someone and living with them.

We could both be real now. Within a day after André's departure, he called and told me he had met a wonderful woman who was so happy with his work that she was going to connect him to her entire network of accounts. He was soaring with a sense of amazement and gratitude. The humbleness and awe in his voice helped quell my heavy heart and the sense that *I was to blame*. This was only one day after our separation! The period following that was uplifting and inspiring.

He told me that when he met this very passionate French woman, she said, looking deeply into his eyes, "You've been touched by an angel!" When he told me this, I was utterly surprised. Someone outside of our relationship saw the effects of our recent actions. The love that predominated during that time allowed us both to step into the stunning hurt we felt and move into action. André was angry, and I was clear. He knew what I had done was necessary. He respected my choice. It was hard.

I felt fragile *and* clear. I did not feel solid in my decision in the way we might think certainty feels. Instead, I felt like a foreigner. I experienced jabbing pangs of disbelief that were the street signs of the unknown in this new land of singlehood. I would never have believed I would be single again. This new status was like suddenly arriving in a new country and wondering where you had been dropped off. I was in psychic shock.

Shock allowed for confusion. I was able to reorder and feel what to do next. Nothing felt familiar because I had never been married and now separated. I felt exhilarated in the heartbreak, and open to life.

The moment of anxiety, of discomfort, or where a seed of anger is felt, is the moment where a vastness reveals a breakthrough. If we can catch that instant where a strong uncomfortable emotion is trying to permeate, we can stay with its prompting and let it *do* us. It *does* us by revealing what it is for. It has a purpose. It is here to reveal a prompting that is true for us. We would not feel or know this way if we didn't have the emotional upheaval. The upheaval catches our attention, slows us down, and interrupts our lives.

To live freely, keep an open-ended curiosity. It is in that mystical, willing-to-be-ness where nuggets are revealed in the difficult moments. When we are interested in the emotions, they stop being interruptions. We will sense and know what to do. Or not do.

Feeling the Joy of Sadness

Sadness never seems to get any good press. In our productive culture, feeling sadness is seen as a disruption in our day. Paying homage to painful emotions is a healthy ritual. (Usually we want to sweep them out the door like an unwanted guest.) If we pretend we don't feel sad and pull up our bootstraps, do the dishes with a forged perkiness, or God forbid, make dinner, then the food tastes different. Stuffed-down emotions stockpile in there. We end up with a sore neck, a parasite in our gut, and we wonder why our knees hurt (inflammation in our gut affects our soft tissue, such as our joints).

The inner circus that is my fantasy mind entertains ways we could live an emotion when it happens. It's really quite fun. You could join me. I play out what I would do to *that* person or what policies I would administer if there was a choice. Imagination is not illegal. You can have a little breakout session when the world gets crusty. You can imagine what you would do, even if it is simply to dance an anger dance when you get home.

When I was building The Yoga House and had problems with the first contractor and I needed to hire a new contractor complete with new costs, as I described in chapter nine, I was a messy, hurt, angry, disbelieving, deflated, exhausted puddle of my former self. At the heat of my stress, after addressing the issues, I danced out the chaos. I had set some hours aside. I put the contractor in a chair in front of me (in my mind). By then most of the tools and equipment were no longer in the yoga studio. I opened up the French doors to the ravine. I put Peter Gabriel on full blast. I danced for hours. A rage dance: screaming every form of disbelief and vile, caustic, venomous emotion in there. I would spin and turn to the imaginary "him" tied to the chair and point right onto his imaginary face while screaming my disbelief. I don't know how long this went on. I only know I lost myself in the release of anguish. Madonna would have been proud.

I danced until there was nothing left to dance. The (imaginary) contractor (tied) to the chair was stunned into a tiny, cowering, disenfranchised man. When my body stopped moving, I felt a new energy. I felt as though I had come out of surgery. The hate was removed from my gut. I was a puddle on the floor. You could have poked me with a yoga block and I wouldn't have flinched. I got up and took care of emails. *I* was back. No lawyers, no extensive fees (as if I had money left), simply a released Celeste then able to dance any dance after that.

Emotional sanctuary is absolutely critical to live a joy-ability in your tissues. When Sarah was young, our home was an emotional sanctuary. All emotions were felt and given airtime. The free reign to feel everything that happened allowed for swift emotional riffs that were gone by dinner. One time Sarah came home so angry she couldn't speak. Back then when I lost my shit, I used to buy a large bag, or two large ones, of "healthful" (I'm feeling defensive) cheese popcorn. That could be dinner.

I told Sarah this and said that if she ever needed to feel like poop and didn't want to talk, she could eat a bag of popcorn (her drug was Cheezies) and that would be just swell. She wouldn't need to be interested in eating salad.

One day about a year later as she came in the front door after school, she looked at me as if to say, "Can you believe those guys?" (meaning those people out in the world) and threw down two large plastic bags from Shoppers Drug Mart. Inside was a large bag of Cheezies and, oh yah, two bags of cheese popcorn! She went up to her room. I didn't see her until after her "dinner."

A house policy was that Sarah was always allowed to stay home from school if she felt poopy; for instance, if she woke up and was still concerned about something going on in her life, I would suggest that she could stay home and we could discuss it or she could take it to the park and play it out.

There are seven days in a week. Five of them are school days. There are forty-six weeks of school days in a year. Of the eleven years of school that Sarah was with me, she stayed home only one day. Actually, only half the day. One half day! And I'm certain she came home early because Rob, who was working for me at the time, was the greatest guy on the planet, and she just wanted him to pick her up from school. She knew I was teaching. I couldn't have agreed more; the guy's a peach.

When I came home from teaching, she was sitting on Rob's lap at the computer in my home office, and she smirked at me coyly from under his chin. If she was any happier, there would have been two of her. She wasn't sick. She wanted to be with Rob.

We need to feel what's going on inside us and, if needed, come home from work, or school. We need to leave school and go to the beach. We need to say what we feel and interrupt dinner. We need to have rituals that honour sadness, hurt, disbelief, anger, embarrassment, and unimaginable, disturbing occurrences in our day.

In my fantasy mind, we have rituals for sadness, anger, and any other emotional riptides. When Sarah was in grade one she came home from school one day super angry. She told me what her teacher had done, and we just fumed together. The anger-evoking situation involved another student, Daniel, who was being a real bonehead. I asked Sarah if she was really mad at the bonehead. She nodded. I said, "Come here," waving my hand towards the living room. We had just moved in with another single mom, Shona, and all the furnishings belonged to her. I picked up a couch pillow and said, "This is Daniel." Then I punched that pillow with glee. Feathers flew everywhere! The room was now white fluff! Sarah and I laughed our heads off. I found the vacuum cleaner and we restuffed the pillow. I went to get a needle and thread. She recounted the whole frustrating episode while I sewed.

When I was growing up, having nasty feelings was treated as depression. Depression was forbidden. Something to get through before lunch. Or, God forbid, dinner when the family is together and everything needs to be fine.

Years before joy had become the default in my bloodstream, I was angry. When I was young, messy emotions weren't allowed in the house. By the time I left home I was such a tough guy that I didn't have any room in my psyche for disruptive emotions. I would feel angry because hard emotions would all get thrown into the only one I knew. Anger was the most accessible and it felt so necessary. Where's the room to feel this crippling disbelief and incommunicable disease called loss? In my family there was rarely, and sometimes never, the room for us to take it easy and feel the hurts. Depression was treated as a demon to be swept out of the house with the aid of medication. Even the four weeks it takes for the pills to take effect were considered a nuisance. Life could return to normal once we had self-medicated and joined the gang of *Everything Is All Right.* ("Self-medication" often took the form of pretending everything was all right.)

I value hard feelings. They are uncomfortable, *and* they usher us forward in life. In joy we let the discomfort in hard emotions show us what we need. We can feel hurt, deep loss, and angry and know that this is a relevant wrench in our day. We can know that the emotional squeeze and turning of this wrench is steering us towards actions, realizations, or changes that we need to make. We experience the emotion directly. The shrapnel of our former selves, the parts that knew the previous reality where everything was good need to land and reassemble.

Am I Too Needy?

In my family, "she never complains" was considered to be the hallmark of success. If you got through the day, and it was a wicked one, if you didn't talk about it, you were Rocky Balboa and it was the best indication that you had stamina.

It is so valuable to know that communicating your needs allows you to be brave. Communicating your needs is a beautiful moment. It is not a needy moment. Feeling a need is a homecoming. You can be more of who you are.

In our anxiety-driven society, we may forget how to *feel* a need. Needs are often perceived as "giving in," or being needy. This never feels good. However, stating a need with power and clarity allows you to be free. It feels good.

How to Learn to Receive

Learning to receive is code for learning how to have needs. Judgement of ourselves and others stops when we feel what we need. We stop thinking about the other person and what they did or said.

We are in touch with ourselves. We feel what we need. Once we are aware of what we need, we can ask. This may take some practice. Possibly eight years. I wish I was kidding. If you are female, perhaps nine. But let's stop that, shall we?

To feel what you need and to ask may take some real practice. When I started asking the people in my life for what I needed, I was hooked. When I had foot surgery, I contacted all my friends six weeks ahead of time and asked them to bring one meal a day to my room on the top floor, and then do the dishes afterward. I had eighteen friends help me during the five weeks of convalescing. Each person would come and we would sit up in the Tree House of The Yoga House. We sat in the glass room looking over the ravine. Friends would end up staying for hours. I tasted every kind of vegan, gluten-free, chocolatie, Ayurvedic dish they had ever made. We shared what they created in their kitchens. I hadn't seen some of these friends in ages. The sacred, undisturbed time was a welcome solace for us. It was a slow, steady party. I highly recommend doing this.

Go ahead and begin to do this with the people in your life now. You could ask for someone to bring in the garbage cans when they come up the drive. Then move on to asking them to pick up batteries on their way home. Then to asking for some validation and appreciation for the lunch you made them. Why not? Live a little.

But, really, truly, deeply practise. Communicate and ask for what you need *very* specifically. Men *and* women love that. Woman need to be clearer to end their resentment. What is most beautiful about asking for what you need is that you feel more like yourself. When you feel your needs, you cancel the feeling that you are being weak or ridiculous. Instead you recognize you feel depleted and overwhelmed. You invite others to recognize what they're feeling too. Now they can have needs.

Life after Judgement Day

When you stop a judging thought, you see what your act of judging is telling you about yourself. All the energy you used to judge is now free. Now you have way more mind-energy for free will. I have practised this inner awareness of feeling my energy, and I notice that as soon as I judge I feel tired and, of course, separate. So when you or I stop this, all that mind-energy is available for solutions and insights that we couldn't fathom when we were all ruffled or pooped. Please join me.

When you stop judging, you can't even pull up frustration. Post-judgment living means you feel your needs and you truly fill in again. You fill in with *you*. A need becomes a beautiful moment to connect with someone, or life.

CHAPTER THIRTEEN

Milking Emotions

Shame Is the Poopiest of All Emotions

Sarah and I lived in a basement apartment in a gorgeous triplex across from Casa Loma in Toronto. When she was one-and-a half years old she used to be up most of the night crying, and I would rush to her because a guy visiting on the floor above us would thump on the floor if he heard her. This would scare her, and she would cry even more.

One morning after I had been up most of the night soothing her, and I was exhausted, as I was changing her diaper I said, "You were up last night crying and screaming." She took this in then replied with glee, knees kicking, "I kwy I scweem! I kwy, I scweem!" in her baby voice. She was so happy. She was quite delighted to know she was so active during the night. I realized that I had said what I said because it really had more to do with what I had experienced. Actually, what I had said was only for myself. What she had shared with me was how *she* felt about it!

Sarah hadn't thought about the night before or how she had

behaved! How could she? She wasn't thinking about anything she had done. I realized with profound clarity, with a poopy diaper in one hand, that I could have shamed her. Which makes sense because shame is the poopiest of all emotions. Shame is the most crippling emotion. Shame is one of the first emotions we develop in our repertoire of painful emotions. Shame has the ability to stop us from living. Because we are shamed so early in our development, shame is one of the first corrupters of joy.

To catch shameful thoughts, notice when you feel as if you're "not allowed," or simply doubting yourself. If you do, you'll know you're in the shame category. Use the energy in the shame. Milk it. What is the milk, or nutritional fuel—since everyone's off dairy—that comes out of the feelings of shame? I'm so glad you asked.

The message in shame is "do it anyway," "do it," and "start now." Now, anytime you feel doubt, know that shame is in your building. Anytime you believe you had better "settle down," "get real," "be responsible," or you believe "that's just the way it is," then know that you are thinking about what you want to do, and your mind—being in duality and all—is shaming you. To silence the shameful thoughts, start now. Right now. See you later.

Shame

Shame is the most crippling emotion. Shame's sabotaging effect reduces our physical, emotional, and spiritual development. By spiritual, I mean our sense of feeling safe, empowered, and that we belong in the world. When we feel spiritually enlivened, we *know* what we want and move forward in our lives with a quickening propulsion.

When we are *not* spiritually enlivened, we separate and check off the "to do" list. Our actions are all about getting 'er done. We do the dishes, go to work, pay our bills, and call our brother. We don't feel a warmth or an engagement with what we are doing. This is coping. Shame causes us to cope. Coping is groping along in life at half-mast. Joy cannot feel shame.

Feeling the Fear and Asking Mom Anyway

Once when I told Sarah why my mom was angry, she asked, "Why? Hasn't she ever asked for anything in her life?" (Bingo!) I was sitting on the swing beside her in my sister's backyard with the low afternoon sun skimming the back fence of the suburban neighbourhood. We were living with my sister in Scarborough as we were in between houses. I had just called my parents to ask for an additional loan on the down payment for my first house. Sarah was nine.

I sure hadn't wanted to make that call. I was terrified. I had twenty-four hours to raise the money. I could actually hear my mom at the other end of the line gritting her teeth. I was taxing her to the hilt, not financially, emotionally.

How I felt when going to my mom was the fear I feel when I am growing. Am I allowed to ask for so much in the world? My fear revealed a membrane of permission I had created in my tissues. If I felt afraid to ask for something, it meant I was sure I would be turned down because I *should not* be asking. I *should* just keep on taking care of myself and Sarah. If I felt afraid to do something or ask for something, it meant I was including others.

On my own when I bought a car or made decisions, I didn't feel this fear. Working with others or asking for what I needed was the scary place. I feel inside me that I am sure they will reject me. Solitary confinement is much safer.

Feeling the fear showed me that I needed to learn how to work with others and to know that they wouldn't think, "She's not good enough" or "She's greedy and brazen." I can write about this here and I feel as though I'm a psychologist in an office naming why I didn't do what I wanted to do: "You didn't speak up because you are afraid of what he thinks." It's safe to name the fear after it's over. That's easy, convenient, and analytical. The testament is feeling the fear and saying, doing, acting, moving, pausing, and being transparent in the face of the fear.

So *how* do you feel that you know what you know—and act on it in the world? It's always about trusting yourself. Start, just start. Then start again.

I bought the house. My mom and dad loaned me the money within twelve hours. Mom was tight as she did it, *and* she totally supported me—just not emotionally. It was so hard for my mom to see me on my own with a child of my own and making these decisions. I know she just didn't know how to support my autonomous living.

I paid my parents back in two years. Three years later, I had a housewarming for my family. I don't like to rush things. My mom was so proud that her eyes shone into me. I have never forgotten that look.

When You Feel Dismissed, Live Your Great Big Self

One day a friend's behaviour in the audience of a workshop I was giving made me feel uncomfortable. Peter was sitting in the front row and had that nasty tight look on his face as though he didn't believe me and he wasn't going to listen to me, whereas other participants were giving me nods of understanding.

As I scanned the audience, every time I passed by his face his expression became more and more resistant, until I thought he was going to speak up. Which he did. He said that it was fine for me to speak about my experience of joy, but he had never had such an experience and didn't know if he ever could. He didn't see the value of my speaking of my experience if he could never enjoy it himself. The rest of the audience fell silent. He appeared to be alone in his view. I listened and felt for the message. What was his view showing me about myself? He quickly provided the answer. He said, "When you are talking about joy, you keep using the word 'you': When *you* go into non-duality *you* will experience." He said he wanted me to speak in the first person so I wouldn't be delivering a promise that might never be fulfilled. This feedback was immensely helpful! I had been suffering from the fear of proselytizing. I felt afraid that someone would think I thought I was a holier-than-thou type or that I was offering a belief system to subscribe to. I was feeling insecure, and because he knew me well, he called me on it.

It's not always the easiest task to feel the nugget in the feedback. If you can feel the heat of the discomfort and know that you are feeling anger, or any other hard emotion, then the catch of its difficulty will reveal that something helpful is being imparted. Wisdom is reaching out to you. All moments are helpful. You milk the uncomfortable feeling.

Best-selling author and Buddhist priest, Pema Chödrön, speaks to these charged moments in her book *Practicing Peace in Times of War*. She asks how we can stay with the "seed of anger" and not "*fan it*." How can we not get "hooked" when anger-evoking circumstances get to us? "Whenever there's a sense of threat, we harden. And so, if we don't harden, what happens? We're left with that uneasiness, that feeling of threat. That's when the real journey of courage begins. This is the real work of the peacemaker, to find the soft spot and the tenderness in that very uneasy place and stay with it. If we can stay with the soft spot and stay with the tender heart, then we are cultivating the seeds of peace."[1]

---

[1] Pema Chödrön, *Practicing Peace in Times of War* (Boulder, CO: Shambhala Publications, 2007), 29.

When we are tender with, adaptive to, and present with what is happening, we experience an ongoing curiosity with life. At the very least, we live with a steadiness to directly experience life with less emotional upheaval. Peter showed me that I had to own my joy-filled mind. He demanded that I speak what I know and say it with strength.

Milking a Feeling

When I had Sarah I continued to run my fitness-consulting business. I started teaching early in the morning and needed to bring munchkin to a private in-home daycare as I started teaching before the daycare opened. I was done teaching by noon and would spend the entire afternoon and evening with her. I left my paperwork and all housework until after she went to bed so we could have maximum playtime together. I kept meals super simple, and my house was a mess.

On some days I had this niggling compulsion to "Get Ahead." I felt I couldn't afford this luxury of spending so much time with Sarah. Why wasn't I teaching more and saving for her college fund and signing her up for piano and dance classes? (Guilt and shame were often my nemesis again.) Our days were filled with trips to free events in the city, the library, and the park.

We lived a truly charmed life. I remember one summer day as we went off to the art gallery, a car pulled over and the sophisticated driver told us how lovely we looked. We were wearing matching sundresses printed with celestial-blue flowers that looked as happy as the sky. I felt I was doing the most important activity. Ideas about future planning were all around me. I really needed to continue to trust my heart and keep my business small. I wanted to be with Sarah. This was inspired; it was not a moral decision. Often I couldn't feel the trust to continue to live this way. To help myself I would pull it up. When I did continue to spend this much incredible time with Sarah, it always felt right and exhilarating.

A child is naturally intelligent. By spending time with Sarah, I learned about the world and its harmonious ways. Really being with her allowed me to visit the world hourly with more frolic, spontaneity, interest, and playfulness. Those early parenting years showed me how important it is to listen. By listening to Sarah, I watched her grow and learn to trust herself. I learned that listening meant I was more in touch with the abandoned way that is the life that children know. This reminded me to do the same, and I felt the ability to trust myself to keep following my heart.

As I write this, I realize that being alongside her I learned to trust the way I was living. Rather than being caught up in financial planning, swimming lessons, and moralistic parenting, we lived gently. We connected to nature and I fostered the true intelligence in her. It was hard to trust that I could parent this way. I sometimes felt guilty for living so simply and felt I *should* get with "The Program."

I had not followed The Program myself. Could I do this with my daughter? My program was to be true to myself by teaching what I knew and was discovering. I had turned down countless job opportunities in teaching and managerial roles in organizations where I would have to follow their policies and protocols. It was tricky to actually feel I was making the right choice. The right choice for *me*.

So why couldn't I feel the right to live freely? Raising Sarah this way showed her that life is safe. I discovered that when I slowed down the world was more benevolent than I ever could have known. I relayed this to Sarah by showing her to trust herself and do what was important to her. By being Sarah's mom I remembered to keep re-trusting this myself. We live in a desensitized culture in our Western society. We are driven by anxiety. We do not foster our imaginations. It takes imagination, trust, truth, and beauty to live in joy and believe what you know. Feeling trust in yourself is one of the precursors to living joy constantly. Feeling trust and supported by life took practice. I had to live by what I knew was true, and this meant I felt isolated and displaced at times. I learned that being true to myself can be a unique path and there may *not* be a lot of other participants.

In the early years of Sarah's life I felt cynical, displaced, and at times angry, overwhelmed, and lonely. Doing what I wanted to do in the way I needed to could cause me to feel as though I may not meet anyone who knew the same politics. I learned to express this frustration like an angry tantrum in ways that felt as though I was kicking it out. Writing, and daily intense exercise, were my chosen arts. I never missed my exercise. It was my daily prayer.

When Sarah was nine I remember after feeling, milking, and releasing the anger and cynicism in my life, I would feel lonely. Rapidly. Often this occurred when Sarah was at her dad's for the weekend. I would actually have time to myself! Yet I could feel a hollow discomfort about being alone.

One weekend I was about to rent a movie. I could feel a sense of urgency rising in me. I asked myself what I was feeling. The urgency was saying that I needed to connect with someone, that I must get "out there." When I touched down further into the feeling and practised being with it, I noticed there was this *idea* that I *should* be with someone because it was Saturday night (and "I ain't got nobody").

I could see that my thinking was compulsive. I was desperate to fill in this time with someone to make sure I had fun. I was actually in business mode, ready to check off the social category. Yet there was no real need to be with someone. *I* felt good. It was the *idea* of being alone on Saturday night that was driving this loneliness feeling.

I decided to call a few friends and share what I was feeling so they could see what I believed, and they could mirror back what they saw. I called three friends. I left three messages. Within the hour they had all called back. My message went something like this: "Hi. It's Celeste, I'm feeling lonely tonight and I need to share what I'm feeling, if you're able, could you call me?" After leaving the message, I remember I felt raw and tender, and my vulnerability immediately started to ease the feeling of urgency.

By the time the first friend called back, I was more interested in the feeling than actually feeling lonely. He shared how he feels lonely sometimes too. He asked me what had triggered it. His attentiveness allowed me to be interested in it too.

I stopped feeling as though there was something wrong. I felt held in the feeling by his attentiveness. Feeling held allowed all the inner churning of the emotion to surface. It was as if a cauldron of stewing emotions was now being allowed to pour out. I didn't feel as though I had to get over the emotion or fix it. I had time to feel it. The urgency completely stopped. Without the forward march of the lonely feeling, I felt only a presence. I felt as though I made sense. I didn't feel silly about having the feeling. I felt human and the joy of connecting with another human. That was extremely helpful.

By the time the second friend called, I was over it! When the third friend called, I was just ready to party. It felt as if when the three firemen had shown up the fire was so out. The support and validation of experiencing a feeling without needing it to change or go away is how we feel alive.

Having a witness and being heard is incredibly releasing as the message within the feeling is experienced. The experience showed me that I believed I was more attractive, or at least wanted, if I was out having a "good time" on a Saturday night. Yet the truth was that it was the only night I had to be with myself and enjoy doing what-ever I wanted to do. It revealed to me that emotions show us what we are thinking about ourselves. This means you feel the emotion directly, and by doing so you are freed from its effect, and only a clear greater sense of yourself remains. I have never been lonely since.

Since then, I practise calling friends. In the last many years, I've noticed I don't call very often. I now know how to feel the emotion myself. Yup, just little ol' me and the big bad emotion. It's not so big and bad now. Often I can feel its energy template without needing validation or a witness as backup to help support me. I feel the emotion gently, with respect and interest, as if listening to little Sarah when she was scared. It has become my way to honour and milk emotions. This is rote now. The emotion is important *and* it doesn't define me. Feeling the emotion tends to make fewer waves. Often I can feel a hard emotion and be so directed by it; that is, it is its purpose and it propels me into the truest action.

CHAPTER FOURTEEN

Allowing Awesome

"You're not going to believe this!" I say to three-year-old Sarah as she toddles downstairs early in the morning. "It's a beautiful day!" I enthuse with outstretched arms, the front door open out to the street. This is how I started each day with my daughter. One year later she would run to the front door, pull it open with all her might, and say in her baby voice, "You're not going to beweeve dis, Mommy! It's a bootifow day!" She was four years old and telling *me* now.

When friends say they can't believe how well their lives are going, I pause dramatically and urge with a waving palm, "Believe it!" It has become "normal" to *not* believe how effortless and beautiful our lives can actually be. We can't believe it because we are hardwired to believe the "other" way, which is that effort, and struggle, are necessary to make things go well.

Our inability to believe reveals that we need to *choose* to change our setpoint to a new junction and eventually off a continuum of what we consider realistic. We could even go crazy and forget to have a setpoint for our experiences. If we did, we could live in a vaster field of potential. We could trust that what doesn't feel right for us—real danger factors—will be felt viscerally.

"Believing" instead of our usual "I can't believe it" could become the new norm. We could soon believe anything. Let me be specific. Believing in anything means being open to everything. This doesn't mean you are a pushover. You see all options. You can listen and be interested in any radio station when in someone else's car, yet when in your own, you choose rock.

Using What You're Not "Good" At

When I was thirteen years old, my swimming instructor took me aside and asked me in confidence if I was coming to the final exam scheduled later that month. I looked at her quizzically. She knew I had been training for months, swimming one mile each day to meet the requirements of the physical tests. The exam was for an advanced level of life saving and required deep-water rescues carrying bodies to the shore while performing mouth-to-mouth resuscitation. It was heavy duty. I looked at her, "Why do you ask?"

"You're not going to pass," she responded, deadpan.

Without missing a beat, I said, "Why?"

"You don't have the strength."

I nodded. I understood. I had no idea that this was true. I got out of the pool that night and snuck into the weight room. The YMCA policy allowed only those over fourteen in the weight room. I squeaked in behind a guy who had wide enough pecs to cover me. I started weight training that night. I was a volunteer at the Y and for years had given tours of the weight room, where I had watched the guys train. When I went in they would give me tips.

I had two weeks until the exam. I trained every day until the day of the exam (and for the next forty years!). I failed. She was right. I made the grade in the stamina department, but I didn't have the strength to haul those adult clothed bodies (they *were* alive!) out of the deep water. I continued weight training every day and took the next exam. I passed. (I have been weight training, dancing, running, yogaing, and doing Jane Fonda–like calisthenics to play my body ever since, about six days a week.)

One day, when I was eighteen years old, while riding an exercise bike in the athletic complex at Humber College, a basketball player asked me what I was training for. There was a pool of sweat around the bike the size of Lake Huron. I paused, searching for an incentive to report, "Life" I said, shoulders shrugging.

By nineteen I knew I wanted to plug my love of training into a measurable aspiration. I planned to enter a provincial bodybuilding competition, even though I thought bodybuilders were an odd, macho, rather egocentric lot who belonged on the beach wearing string Speedos and comparing biceps and protein-powder labels. The idea of sculpting the body and meeting proportioned levels of muscular development presented in a dancing performance seemed poetic to me. I decided to become a sculptor of my body. (I described entering my first competition at twenty-one in the preface.)

Following the competition, I still trained at least ninety minutes a day, even though I didn't know when I would compete again. I loved training, learning about nutrition, and developing the most inspired body. It never occurred to me to train less. My training was prayer. Less than a year later, after the competition, I had nagging shoulder pain that I felt from overuse, and it became unbearable. I couldn't raise my arm, and I started physio. My physiotherapist said I would need to stop training my upper body. This was clear to me. Yet I didn't know where to plug in all the incentive I felt to train. I kept trying to find other types of competition that felt inspiring.

Soon I knew that *life* was my sport. I didn't need a specific finish line, the rivalry of competition, or the intense focus on aesthetic presentation. Even the concept of a competition *date* felt inane. Why would I cram all this knowledge about the body into one day's presentation to the world? Bodies could not be judged! Bodies could not be compared!

This seemed frivolous to me. I wanted to train to live in a healthy body that shared its exuberance each day by living spontaneously. I respected the discipline of training and learning how to best fuel this body through the science of nutrition. In fact, the extremely low body-fat percentage required for the competition went right against my sense of personal health. I didn't feel honest being on stage with seven per cent(!) body fat. (I had no menses during the month of my competition, and I'm sure it was because my hormonal system couldn't register that I was female due to my extremely low body fat.) My respect for the body didn't include intense, unsustainable measures like this. I knew that continuing to train with focus was my love and my passion, and it was this time when I had to train myself that fuelled my entire life. My daily investment developed the myriad exercise disciplines that became my fitness-consulting business. It never occurred to me that I would begin to "teach" what I knew, or that someone would *pay* me for this! Wherever I went I shared what I was discovering and soon it became what I lived and do.

By the time I graduated from university, three years after the bodybuilding competition, I was running my fitness business full time. Although I had wanted to be a competitive bodybuilder and go on to compete nationally, I was training to train others. When I recall how exercising this way evolved, it reveals how I naturally operate. It is my nature to inspire, to evoke self-understanding, and to facilitate people's ability to do what they really want to do. That excites me. When we live a non-allegiance kind of existence, we live our passion and rarely have a design of what our future looks like. Often there isn't enough time to make such a plan! For this reason, the professions we take on often happen more effortlessly than we could ever have imagined. Our profession is an expressive extension of who we are. Or as my friend the visionary futurist Barbara Marx Hubbard so often expresses, "We are vocationally aroused!"

This sense of ease of expression is a powerful antidote to the wrangling of the (unhealthy) ego. The ego-mind, or who we *think* we are, may convince us that we are not capable of fulfilling the ideas that this passion un-nestles in us. Please ignore these doubting thoughts.

The Ego Is the Doubter

The ego will try to convince you that you are not in the luxurious position to believe you can do what really turns you on and makes you talk fast. Again, please ignore the unhealthy ego. It's jealous. When you cannot believe you have the right to do what is important, then your mind is messing with you. The thought that you have to "get real" is not only annoying and causing doubt, it is also false. Any thought you have that tells you what is possible is a wee test. The thought is always a test to see if you will believe in yourself.

The shoulder injury I experienced from weight training showed me how I wished to train: I didn't want to align with the competitive standards and the intense one-dimensional ideal that developing lean muscle puts on the body and psyche.

Realizing that this caused me to feel pressure to train my body with stringent focus allowed me to see that any concept of how we need to live our lives is not intelligent. The concept to rehabilitate from an injury so I could continue to compete was an insensitive view. I wanted to strengthen my body and play it every day. I wanted to move this body in inspired ways and teach others how to experience this respectful discipline. By recognizing where the false thoughts disrupt you, you return to your swift inner current of believing that will inform you of the way. The flow keeps you on track and fuelled by an inner inspiration.

The ease is not about *how* you experience; you may feel very unsettled. It's that you are willing and open to having *that* experience too. Ease allows and incorporates all experiences. The ease may not feel comfortable. Good. This means you are being recalibrated to operate in this new time zone. Let the ruffling begin. The ruffling is you being changed. You are being buffered, tempered, and shaped to a new level of ability where you can adapt and meet new requirements.

These new requirements, to trust yourself or to have more stamina, occur as you believe in the current that is moving in you. The current of your inherent inspiration is compelling. You never ever actually feel as if you should settle down or get realistic. You know that the important desires inside you are the necessary next steps you need to take, and you do what you need to create them. So there.

Fear Cancels Awesome

Let me walk you through a fearful moment. A fear I experience is that I am shining too brightly and bothering someone, or making way too big a deal of a need I feel. Basically, I feel as though I *shouldn't* be so needy or take up too much room. This fear causes me to feel an inner contraction.

I feel only discomfort. I even feel it when I am supported by someone who truly believes in me. No amount of reassurance can quell this belief that I am not worthy. The feeling will trump what is actually happening around me. Joy cannot assemble or be felt when there is fear.

My fear of shining too brightly was exemplified in a dream I had fifteen years ago. In the dream I died in a head-on car crash. For some bizarre reason I was the actor Ethan Hawke. Beside me in the passenger's seat was a skilled yoga teacher named Kevin, whom I know and respect in real life. (Just for the record, Ethan Hawke and I are not tight. We've never even met.) Kevin's body was completely uninjured, but his head had hit the windshield killing him on impact. My Ethan Hawke (still no idea) body was completely mangled and crushed behind the steering wheel.

In the dream, as I was about to change states and leave my physical body to pass to the other side, I was asked by the angelic realm (man, were those people pretty!) if I wanted to have a second chance at life. I knew I was having a dream. For some reason I thought that the lucid dream state gave me licence to stall. I knew the angels were giving me the chance to live. Yet I hummed and hawed as if deciding on wallpaper patterns and said, "Do you mean that you will give me Kevin's body and that I could move my perfectly intact (Ethan Hawke) soul into Kevin's body and live?" The angels knew I understood exactly what their offer implied and got irritated. Turns out angels get peeved too. I stalled again, "If you do move me into Kevin's body, will I be able to take on all his yogic abilities and do the poses he can do?" The angels knew I was really trying to buy time and got exasperated. They looked at each other, arms raised out to their sides with palms up, wings actually, as if they were saying, "Can you believe this guy?" Remember, I'm still, oddly, Ethan Hawke. The answer was stuck inside me as if I needed some throat Liquid-Plumbr. Finally, just as I said "Yes! I'll take his body!" I woke from the dream.

It's a terrible feeling. In life—and the dream, I don't know how to accept gifts—or trust myself. I mess myself up. I self-sabotage and life halts or the angels get angry and tired of offering so much. I stop the flow of life's gifts, and therefore joy. I believe I need to keep stalling to ... to what? To get it right? What right? Life? How can that ever be determined?

So, why do I stall? Why do I keep putting off life's gifts by believing I haven't qualified? Why do I believe I can't have it all and that I need to earn it? There is only one true answer. The brain is wired to *manage* life not live it. The nervous system is engineered to notice stress. When there is any kind of stress, any stressor at all, the nervous system steers the brain into caution mode. Careful makes us slow, dull, and calculating.

To stop stalling and say Yes! to life, I need to recognize that it is *not* easier to be calculating, careful, and small. When I feel the fear, I *now* know that I do not know how to do, say, begin, or act on what I set out to do. That's all. I don't know. The fear moment is the stuck place of growth. When I identify that I am stuck and in fear, then I can take action.

The Empowering Effect of Empathy

Empathy brings you into another's life. You sit on a park bench with them and feel their day rise and go down. I'd like to introduce you to Roots of Empathy (ROE), an organization that teaches young children emotional literacy and the power of honouring their feelings. The organization helps children recognize the power of empathy, which is the ability to feel what another person is feeling. ROE is administered in eleven countries around the world. By this year, 2018, we will have reached one million children.

As a teacher for this organization, I saw two eight-year-old boys really hear each other. That day I was teaching how our emotions need to be felt because they are important and not big and bad.

They may just be uncomfortable. As we sat cross-legged in a circle, I had the children share about a time they had felt hurt and someone had helped them.

One boy, Elias, who gets extremely excited and animated when talking about his experiences, shared a time when he hurt himself on the stairs at home and how his mom helped him. He told the story with such expression and gory details that you could practically feel his injury.

After he finished telling his story (which I had to ask him to do!), Anthony, sitting across from him in the circle, said, "Are you all right?" Anthony had become so engrossed in Elias's enthusiastic description that he went right with him down the stairs! Empathy brings you so fully into what the other person is feeling that you imagine what they must be experiencing.

This is different from *understanding* what another person is feeling. Empathy is not cerebral; it is felt. If you hurt yourself and I reach out and say, "Can I help you?" then I am probably experiencing empathy. If you hurt yourself and I say, "You okay?" then I am probably assessing the situation to see if I need to do anything.

Empathy Leads to Intimacy

*"Attention is the rarest and
purest form of generosity."*

~ SIMONE WEIL (1909–1943), FRENCH PHILOSOPHER,
MYSTIC, AND POLITICAL ACTIVIST

Doing something for someone, such as making them soup when they are sick, is the more common practice in our Western culture. We are doers. Sitting with someone in silence after a great loss is an art. Sitting with someone and listening deeply is intimacy.

When we are intimate with someone, we really know *them*. And want to know them. Intimacy occurs after empathy. Empathy brings us close to each other, where we can listen. Empathy is the bridge to intimacy. It is the antidote to the separation that the thinking mind creates.

In an empathy-deficient society, we rarely get to the intimate moments. We are so used to making things better and hurrying back to work that we pay little attention to people's fears or hurts. Sometimes the only time we really see each other is when we say, "Are you okay?" or "Is something wrong?" The speed of living today has desensitized our bodies and senses. Our accelerated living has Bento-Boxed intimacy into "quality" time, when we actually deeply listen and see each other. More often, the most empathy a person can muster is, "What's wrong?"

I'm more familiar with the sound of a truck backing up than the sound of a loon. Our brains and senses have become so inundated with identifiable cellphone rings that we simply feel stacked to the brim in our minds. There is so little room in there to sense and feel and empathize. We're fully loaded, and most of the time spring loaded. Doctors now have an umbrella term for our overloaded minds: "messy-desk syndrome." When we describe to our doctors that we feel overwhelmed, tired, depressed, or forgetful, they may identify this syndrome. A "syndrome" is an acceptable term for epidemic. Our minds are so fully loaded that they are heavy. There is little room for the tender, open, connected living that an intimate mind creates.

The first time I gave a retreat in Costa Rica, I got off our small four-person plane and went straight to the rain forest. I was there for three minutes when I heard my cellphone ring. My cellphone was in Toronto. I am not that astute, and my reception is not *that* good. I was hearing my cellphone in the stridulation of a cricket's body parts rubbing together!

We may become sensitized when we gaze at a beautifully spun spiderweb shimmering against the backdrop of the setting sun. A fly gets snared, and for no apparent reason, we watch it struggle as tears come to our eyes. The tears could be related to someone we love who is experiencing deep emotional pain. The spider's web, the fly, the snag, the snare, connect us to our hurt. This is an enlivening moment. Feeling the hurt is a chance for your body to release the pain. It's an emotional spillage. We will feel more heart-centred and therefore alive. When we let the emotional life inside us out for a spin, we wash clean of accumulated debris. This lighter body can feel more. We become intelligent.

In his book, *Pronoia Is the Antidote for Paranoia*, Rob Brezny describes how the whole world is conspiring to shower you with blessings. In a section entitled "Evil is Boring," Brezny describes a cleansed mind as having less room in its archives for evil stories about bad mayors, terrible traffic jams, and horrible losses. It is paramount that we notice what is on our minds, constantly. What we are *with*, what we are thinking about, determines our moment.

> We are able to live a love vigil. When I stay up with someone all night, rub their feet, read to them, or do therapeutic touch, then the love may enter them again and the grip of sadness may loosen. A beauty moment may occur.

Often when we are with others who are in pain, we begin to profess how we have experienced similar pain. We are trying to commiserate and relate. My sister who is experiencing the ravaging effects of scleroderma finds that if she mentions her disease to someone, they start to talk about the person in their world who has lupus. They start to talk about the people in their lives who can't work. My sister says it is so frustrating to share what you are going through with someone only to hear how they compare it with their uncle's illness. It takes a present mind and gentle spirit to simply sit with another when they are hurting.

"Leave a tender moment alone."

~ SONG BY BILLY JOEL, AMERICAN
SINGER-SONGWRITER AND PIANIST

When I am with a soul in pain, it is *their* experience. I don't need to do a thing. I can be there with her and feel her pain. I feel tender. I get up and make her soup only if she asks. I don't come loaded with a casserole unless she asks (or I'm hungry). To be with someone deeply is a gift for them and for us. We can hear someone's painful story, sit with them, and land in their soul …

"… to toss the reins to the winds
that lift us like seeds
and land us in the soil
of each other."

~ RICHARD GEER, POET AND
ASTROLOGER, FROM THE
POEM "THE HAND"

CHAPTER FIFTEEN

Self-Agency

I love Bill Murray. Recently I found more reasons to think of him and smile. He is not only uproariously funny and wacky, he's also his own boss. Literally. He replaced his agents with a 1-800 number.

In an article in the *Washington Post*, Emily Yahr reported that in 2000, Bill Murray fired his agents for calling him on the phone too often, replacing them with an automated 800 number. As a result, filmmakers who wanted to pitch film ideas to Murray had to leave a voice message, which Murray rarely checked. If Murray is interested in a script, he has it faxed to him care of his local office-supply store.[1]

Living with self-agency is the ability to know how you need to live. Self-agency reveals an ability to say no to the onslaught of opportunities and responsibilities when needed. You get clear about what you want to create in your life. You work from an open focus that invites support.

---

[1] Emily Yahr, "Bill Murray Has Missed Out On a Lot of Big Movies—Here's Every Strange Reason Why," *The Washington Post* (September 16, 2015), https://www.washingtonpost.com/news/arts-and-entertainment/wp/2015/09/16/bill-murray-has-missed-out-on-a-lot-of-big-movies-heres-every-strange-reason-why/?utm_term=.f531e10d1bfa.

Being a Single Mom and
Moving Past Cynicism

After Sarah was born in 1989, I found that other single moms were cynical about men and overly exhausted. Big surprise. Many women were living in poverty consciousness. Poverty consciousness is the belief that we are lacking what we need. It is to work from a place of scarcity, which is a fear-based view. In 1989 the statistics showed that over eighty per cent of single mothers were in the notorious poverty bracket.

Many single mothers were so overwhelmed that it was hard for them to focus on their lives outside of their frustrations, specifically men-related frustrations. How they would make ends meet and trouble with their children's fathers were common conversations.

I cut these women out of my life. I didn't return their calls. I didn't hang out with them at Parents Without Partners' meetings. It was my way of taking care of myself. I didn't feel comfortable with their view. I felt awkward trying not to commiserate with their frustrations. I actually felt a tightness in my throat when listening to them. I had taken legal action to protect myself from Sarah's father and did not want to focus on the energy it took to keep him out of my life.

I remember a single mom I was speaking to right after I had Sarah. She was irritated to hear that I went to the Y every day to work out. She was displeased that I would take this much time away from my baby. It was hard not to feel selfish. She was not my people.

We need *our* people. In the section "Housecleaning Sabotaging People" on page 236, I speak about this need to avoid low-vibration (negative), well-meaning folks and remove them from your life. If you need time to make changes within yourself, which is like taking time to activate new upgrades, then you can communicate this to the people in your life.

Communicating new upgrades is how we help others keep up to speed with us. When we go through inner changes, we don't do the same things. We need to let others know. You may notice that you don't want to do things you used to do. You have the choice and opportunity to communicate this. If I feel tired after being with someone, then it is time for an upgrade. Upgrades are clarifying boundaries. Upgrades occur by recognizing what you truly need and if you can experience it in any particular relationship.

This does not mean that the people in our lives are disposable. It's that we love being in life, and those who are doing battle with life will now have a different resonance from us. There may be very little connection. Discrepancies may become apparent between you and those you love. Allow shifts to occur, as it is life itself opening you to new ways you can share and meet your soul's family. In this way, you can make room for fresh conversations.

Children do this naturally. They take very little of their lives, if any, personally as they learn through play. When Sarah was two years old, the son of one of our neighbours would push her down when they were playing. Sarah took care of this after two run-ins. When she saw him coming, she would bend at the waist, sit her hips back and plop down onto her padded diaper bum. No problem. She was going to end up there anyway, why wait?

Let outworn agreements between you and your friend, relative, or live-in be reworked. Practise nonviolent communication to assist in this process (see the listing for the Center for Nonviolent Communication in the resources section). Give yourself the permission to govern yourself. Honour the clarity you feel and will continue to feel. It does take practice. If you've been living with people who are pained and focused on this, it may be messy to open a dialogue of deep listening and sharing (yet oh so worth it). It can be messy to separate from them. This separation is a loving gesture on your part. It allows you to freely choose what you agree with and what is not true for you.

Again, this can be compassionately communicated with your friend, partner, or neighbour (sometimes! Could someone take care of my neighbour?). Whether or not you will be understood or met is unknown. When you learn to express your needs, you see what is important to you. Even when our attempt to communicate our needs appears unsuccessful, it is a contribution to our growth as we have seen what we need. Feeling our needs and naming them allows us to become more of who we are.

Joy's Mental Oil Change

When you are stuck, disheartened, discouraged, depleted, exhausted, and out of all possible thoughts that feel alive, you must, and I do mean must, choose the way you want to feel. To change how you feel, I recommend a mental oil change.

There is no potential for love, connection, or change to occur when you do not choose to pull up how you want to feel. Ten years ago I recognized the absolute necessity to pull up how you need to feel. One sun-filled afternoon in June I was running through a trail deep in a valley in northern Toronto. It was a gorgeous day and the covering of the trees created a cooling, sun-speckled tunnel around me. Thirty minutes into my run, a creepy feeling rose in my body. It was like a dull apprehension. I didn't feel scared for my safety; I felt a dark, heavy energy in my solar plexus. I ran around a bend and was wondering why I was having such a sudden change in my internal frequency. At that moment I saw a colourful altar on the side of the trail with lovely fresh flowers, a photo, and a newspaper clipping attached to a tree. There I read that a fourteen-year-old girl had been murdered and her body had been found in this spot. Her family had erected a plaque commemorating her life.

I jogged on that spot for a while as a feeling of reverence dropped me into a desire to be there around her altar. When I felt inspired, I started to run again. I thought of how devastating the homicide was as I remembered the reports of it in the newspaper. I felt compassion for her family. Eventually the sadness dissolved as I moved through the beautiful trail.

As I ran, I thought about how my body's radar had been able to sense what was around the corner. Then, at that moment, I realized that if my body and mind could feel a dark feeling, I could attune this affinity to sense what was ahead on my path to beauty and enhancing opportunities. I basically asked myself if I could have a mental and physical oil change.

Since that time I have seen that event as a reminder to amp up my ability to sense beauty and supportive opportunities. Our primal brains are wired to sense danger and protect us. To alter our ability to feel safe, alive, connected, and in joy, I saw, yet again, the need to catch the intense feeling and milk it with curiosity. By feeling the creepy feeling, I saw that I sensed creep more than beauty. There was far more beauty on the trail than any other vibration. I am happy to report that now I have a greater ability to connect to supportive and prosperous opportunities.

It is necessary to regulate what your mind's radar focuses on. Choosing how you feel changes the moment instantly. Or it acts as a waterfall, chipping away at the old habits that keep us stuck. And I swear to God that if you keep choosing how you feel, you will see that this is *not* optimism. Choosing how you *feel* is choice on a cellular level. Choosing how you feel is an evolutionary moment.

Choose How You Feel

When you choose how you feel, you think differently. Choose feelings, which generally occur before the thought, and you will orchestrate what kind of thought you have. For example, when I need to start my daily exercise session and I am exhausted, I start. The rise in adrenaline and epinephrine gets my body to follow.

When you choose how you feel when relating with others, you

will change the potential dynamics that can go down between you and the other person. They simply won't know what's happening.

I repeat: Please know that this is not optimism. Optimism keeps us repeating affirmations we force ourselves to pull up. Even when you don't feel them. When I am trying to be optimistic, I am trying. It takes mental focus. Mental focus exercises the left brain. Feelings arise out of the right brain and affect every cell in the body. Every cell. So feelings are simply the grand central station for acting as a contagion for the rest of the body.

When I presented this solution to one of my students, Shane, she asked, "What if you can't change the feeling? What if, no matter how earnestly you try, you can't feel another feeling?" This is what you do:

1. Give yourself empathy. Feel empathy for yourself as a congratulations for being aware of the negative feelings.

2. Pull up the feeling you want to feel. This may take incredible crowbarring action. Again, you must.

3. To help you do this, have a preplanned memory schema that pulls up the feeling. Have it down so well that it is the fire exit where you go in your mind to enter the hall of the positive feeling.

Today, I notice that the thoughts I have feel true only if they arise from a loving consciousness. I don't need to have dramatic falls to steer me. The messages are there each moment, guiding me as I go rather than escalating into difficult digressions. Today, fluidity and flow punctuate my life and the nasty people have gone missing.

Living in joy allows for whimsy. An extremely frolicky phenomenon is how much love I am experiencing. I find that now, if I have a negative thought, be it a worry thought or any other concern, someone or some occurrence captures me and shows me there is nothing to feel overwhelmed about.

When Sarah was five years old, we had moved in with another single mom and it was not good. I felt worried about finding a new place to live that I could afford. Each time I felt worried, Sarah would look up at me and say, "I love you, Mommy!" It would happen each time I started to think about affordable housing and all the gory details. Every time my mind went there, she would say this! It was so random. She had never done this before. She wasn't looking at my face when I felt concerned, she might have been reading a book. It got to the point that *my mind would interrupt me* when I started to worry. I had developed an innate mental correction that would stop the worry thought, just as Sarah's affection had done.

Soon a worry thought would feel unbelievable and like an interruption. It would stick out like a false idea. Today I feel a congruency with what is true, and any discordance is highlighted. I cannot agree or participate. This is only slightly uncomfortable. It can be awkward to feel separate from the kinds of conversations that go on around me. At the same time, when I don't participate in uncomfortable talk, or fear-based beliefs, then I feel more alive. Even if it is only inside for me to enjoy. Not being able to concur with the conversations and beliefs in our social culture is only slightly awkward. I let any grating feeling slough off the uncomfortable belief that I need to participate.

The delightful aspect of staying true to living in joy is the amount of love in my life. In the last decade it has been metaphorical. When I cut a beet with a knife, there is a heart; when I go to clean the garden, the moss has grown into a perfect heart. Hearts show up everywhere—in the coffee grinds in my strainer, the stain on my canvass bag, the watermark on my yoga mat. I actually leaned over to Chloe, one of the grade-three students I was teaching, and asked, "Is that a heart?" when I saw the stain on my bag. "Yeah," she said, as if it was the most natural occurrence in the world.

Housecleaning Sabotaging People

"I want to know if you can
disappoint another
to be true to yourself.
If you can bear
the accusation of betrayal
and not betray your own soul.
If you can be faithless
and therefore trustworthy."

~ ORIAH "MOUNTAIN DREAMER" HOUSE,
© 1999, FROM THE INVITATION[2]

Your friends, partner, family, co-workers, associates, and people in your life are an integral part of your feeling that you belong. When you feel connected to the people in your life, you feel harmony. This is joy.

You keep the people in your life who support you. You need to discard the people who deplete you or question you in a demanding way, or who disagree with your dreams. Putting people out in the trash is easier than it sounds. If you're lucky, they will leave of their own accord. This type of "housecleaning" need not be vicious or mean in any way. Honest.

If you are close to people who do not support your goals and are having a hard time supporting their own—or in believing they can—and are not conscious of this, they will conveniently, and most often unconsciously, puncture holes in your dreams in case you win first. For many people, life is a game of acquiring goals

[2]Oriah House, *The Invitation* (San Francisco: HarperCollins, 2006), 2. Presented with permission of the author www.oriah.org.

and collecting rewards. It can be painful for them when they don't get what they want "through no fault of their own" as they scramble to believe this.

When people like this start to poke in on your life, back up and run. If this is not an option, such as with a live-in person, then you can clearly communicate that you do not need to be a dumpster for their garbage. Garbage dumping is when they deny you your dreams. They are perfectly capable of denying themselves their dreams by being problem-focused, but not your dreams. You deal with other people's garbage by making it very clear that you won't. You will support them and their dreams, but not their garbage.

There is a big difference between being empathetic, listening to garbage (what's wrong in their lives), and supporting them. Supporting their problems will help keep their problems alive and get you thinking about your own. Which is not what your mind's energy is for. People who are problem-focused are draining, and being attentive to what's wrong in their lives might get you thinking about what's wrong in yours. Then you give your power away and you keep living what's wrong instead of creating what's right for you.

When you are with those who are people-dumping, choose whether you wish to *be* there. Decide if you want to listen or be with them and the energy they are emitting. I find the most supportive way to be at these times is to listen. If you choose to listen, because you sense that the other person really needs that sounding board, then be there and truly be with them. Listening is empathetic and supportive; it means you are validating them. You are present *and* not moving out towards their misery meter and keeping it humming. Hear them vent; daily kvetching is usually necessary for us to feel light and more present with each other. You can be there, hear them, but there is no need to join in the tennis game and serve up your own angst.

To be garbage free (Say No to the Dump!), hear their issues and know that your presence is enough to be supportive. Love, or support, allows you to live your own life among the many lives around you. When you live your *own* life, you are loving life itself, and love will permeate all that you do. You will affect all the lives you come in contact with by the strength of your presence, which will have a strong impact. I know you know this, it's just that we need to validate and commend ourselves for the focus it takes to be compassionate, loving, and empathetic. Or maybe it's just me.

When you are present in your life, rather than moving your energy out to try to help someone (when they don't want help, they want to complain), then you are more valuable to them and yourself. Invest in yourself and you will mentor your support rather than dole it out.

Housecleaning depleting people in your life keeps you clear to focus on your commitment to yourself, which is the most loving thing you can do for both of you. Housecleaning can be done along the way when the cranky people appear, or you may need to do an overhaul and get rid of a season (or years!) of accumulation. By being clear about how you use your mind's energy, you will stop worrying about your own or someone else's problems. You put yourself in a position to receive the support to reach your goals, and you will stop playing in the dumpster and play at life.

CHAPTER SIXTEEN

Living with Joy

Let's pretend now, just for kicks, that we are living in joy. Constantly. We honour what we know. We act from a clarity that experiences each moment. A fresh, moment-to-moment experience of life informs our decisions. And that's what's so refreshing about living this way. You just can't say what will happen because you're not interested in preplanning and figuring life out. You just know what you like.

When you operate from joy, you feel connected. If you fall out of joy, you are identified with *how* you think you need to behave, you feel separate.

One day I was driving into Barrie from Toronto to surprise my parents. As I got close to their home on the water, I called to let them know I was a minute away. I was really excited. I love surprising them. When I called, my Dad answered.

"How are you Dad?"

"Good."

"I'm just around the corner."

"What, you mean you're in Barrie?"

"Yeah! Surprise!"

"Oh, okay." My dad has always been an expressive one.

"Is Mom home?"

"No, she's at Telecare. It's her shift."

"Hey, what's the number? I'll call and pretend I'm hurting." Dad gives me the number. I call.

I did my best I'm-dying voice—all I said was, "Hello?"

My mom says, "Oh, hi Celeste!" How is that possible? *One utterance* and she knew it was me! We know our children's voices. We know we like French vanilla at the ice cream counter. We know we don't eat dried apricots because they are preserved with sulphur dioxide. These are no-brainers. The pure "knowings" that reveal who we really are that make up our unique imprints are us in joy. They are identifiable and perhaps adorable. At times, *and* they are ours.

The many ways we like and need to live comprise how it feels to live joy. They are what people recognize us by. My voice, your way of walking fast, my way of bursting into surprise at a neon beetle, your lingering eyes that follow the line of the horizon as you fetch your camera. We have ways that show *who* we are. This is you in joy.

I am happy to report that if you steer or stumble into who you are, which is constant joy, you will still be you. Even if you drop limiting beliefs, you will still be reliable. Even if you stop judging others, you will still be discriminating if you are that way.

I want to emphasize that if you live in joy constantly, you will not come out of a phone booth as Joy Super Hero. Although that does sound cool. Living in joy does *not* mean that the "isness" that is you will be stylized into a more patient you if you are impatient. Yet your speed in expecting life to keep up with you will become humorous. Nothing is *not* humorous when you live in joy. You can take seriously only the areas that you know you really need to. Like making sure you have toilet paper.

The most notable important detail about living in joy, which means you are not thinking (remember how you know what to do?), is that you will use your left brain as needed. Your thinking mind, your right brain, will still be intact and no one will wonder if you are selling your law practice, buying hemp drawstring pants, sprouting alfalfa in the kitchen, chanting over your toothpaste, or building a waterfall in your living room wall. You can be joyful and mainstream. No one even needs to know.

The fears that I hear most commonly expressed by my students, family, friends, and the many fresh faces I meet with whom I have shared the possibility of living in joy all the time are these: "If I live in joy constantly, won't I be less sharp and progressive?" "Will I still be as motivated?" "Will I still want to work?" Oh, yes, and "Will I be a navel-gazer?" All of these concerns pose *one* question: If I live in joy constantly, will I still be responsible?

The truth is that you will be *more* responsible. You will be capable of living with greater focus, clarity, potency, inspiration, motivation, energy, love, interest, curiosity, passion, intimacy, empathy, commitment, attentiveness, alertness, warmth, kindness, compassion, and a sense of connection to life and others. And I think you'll be funny. Yes, this too can be yours. I feel like an evangelist now, and God, those people scare me.

You will feel this way when you live in a state of joy because you will be focusing on what is meaningful to you and doing it in the way you need to. You will still live with a healthy ego when you live constantly in joy. You will still be you, the same you, only you will live from a point of steadiness.

Comparison between Coping and Living with Joy

Coping	Living Joy Constantly
• You respond carefully to life; tip toeing	• You live life according to what feels inspired; you ask for what you want, you ask for what you need
• You think about what to do next based on past experiences	
• You feel overwhelmed and anxious more than any other emotion	• You feel without self-judgment
	• You have a sense of strong physical energy, endurance, and stamina; you're adaptable
• You don't like yourself at times or much of the time	
• You look for cues from the environment that will give you permission to ask for what you need	• You have a healthy and happy view of yourself and others; if someone is acting like a dick, and you know that, that is just one of their characteristics, it doesn't cloud your view of them, and as a result, you don't feel tense and upset
• If you don't feel as though you can ask, you don't; you shrink and pretend it doesn't matter	
• You spend a lot of your life pretending it doesn't matter	
• You spend a lot of your life pretending to be someone you're not	• You can be around dicks
• You don't ask for what you want	• You respond easily to stress
• You don't ask for what you need	• You are a neutral observer in life and can view it with an open heart
• You don't feel good enough	
• You compare yourself to others	• You feel connected and have a sense of belonging in life, where the human need for interaction is met
• If you're with someone you consider to be better than you, you have a hard time being you	
• You think everyone and their mother looks better than you (seriously!)	• You feel supported by life, as if you have a lot to offer; you feel inspired by who you are
• You feel separate and isolated (feeling separate means you need to take care of yourself rather than feel a part of a family or community that cares)	• When you feel negative emotions, you are curious about what it is showing you about yourself (this was learned)
• When you feel that you need to take care of yourself, it often means you feel tough or severe and have an outer shell	• All your actions come from love
	• You experience strong, intimate connections
• Ultimately, you are your own worst critic	

Last night as I was sleeping,
I dreamt—marvelous error!—
that I had a beehive
here inside my heart.
And the golden bees
were making white combs
and sweet honey
from my old failures.

ANTONIO MACHADO (1875–1939),
SPANISH POET

An experience I once had with a parking-enforcement officer is an example of how the mind can work when we have a healthy, non-thinking, innocent, joy-filled mind. Yes, I did say parking attendant, although that's not what I normally call them. I was parking my car on busy King Street in downtown Toronto. I put enough money in the meter for exactly thirty minutes and went into a café to have lunch. I came out twenty-five minutes later, and as I was walking towards my car, I saw the officer writing a ticket on his pad. My first thought was, "Oh, some poor sod got a ticket." Then I saw him walk behind *my* car to write down the licence plate number! I was really miffed. I couldn't understand why he was by my car. I came up beside him and said, "Are you writing a ticket for *this* car?"

He didn't look up. He kept writing. He was standing facing me with his back to the meter. Behind him, the patio of the café I had just left was full of patrons. Every seat was occupied on this sunny June day at noon. The patrons were waiting with forks in air for the outcome. "Yes," the officer said with a firm jaw. I was stunned and felt an innocent surprise.

"That's so weird," I said, "I thought I had given myself enough time."

With that, he became very agitated and I can sincerely report that he *lost it*. "Oh, everyone says that! Everyone says they gave themselves enough time, but as soon as I write this ticket, there is a carbon copy that goes right to my supervisor and I have to issue it!" He continued ranting about how everyone blames him when they don't get back in time. He really went for it. As I listened, I felt that he was giving me his career's worth of tyranny, all the years of people who had viciously attacked him verbally, or otherwise. I saw in his face the tight layers of cruelty he had experienced. I truly felt that he let out every drop of anguish.

The patrons in the restaurant were all watching me. I actually felt my heart open as the pressure of that moment rose. I felt a compassion for all the pain he was expressing. I'm not saying he was my new best buddy, but I truly felt for him. He stopped speaking; he would not look at me. There was a pregnant pause.

I nodded and said, "I understand." I felt him during his rant; I understood his pain. I felt gratitude that he had let it all rip. He was so human. An ugly human for sure in that moment—and so human. A real load had lifted from him and it was palpable. I felt an energy around us that was light and expanding. (Angels sang, once again, and a choir somewhere.) My words shocked him. He was visibly startled. He didn't say anything. He looked up at me, and then down as he hurriedly walked to his car. He opened his car door and was getting in. Suddenly, I realized I didn't have a ticket in my hand! It was still on his pad. I said "thank you!"

Before he got into his car, he looked down and waved his pad in the air as if to say "forget about it." I felt a lightness that was unequivocal to any experience I had had in years. The world, meaning my physical environment and my body in it, felt alive and at a higher vibration. I felt amazing.

When I had this experience, I felt no animosity, only surprise. I was naïve. There was only trust in my being. I was not thinking about what *he* did. I could have looked over his shoulder at the parking meter and seen that there were four minutes left and taken his badge number and reported him, or told him to look at the meter to defend my position. It's simply not possible to feel defensive when you feel that alive.

It is a common scene in downtown Toronto to see parking-enforcement officers being verbally attacked. I couldn't feel any position because I only felt the unified field of connection, or what can be described as "trust." What is beautiful about operating this way is that no one gets hurt, and if they are willing, each person can experience the highest outcome. When that happens, the play-ing field in unified. Energetic dynamics in relationships that are not healthy and don't support a true connection actually cancel out. It is nothing less than extremely cool.

After that, the energizing feeling of the unified field lasted for about half an hour. I don't know what he felt! He was probably thinking, "What the hell was that? Why didn't she defend herself?"

No matter what is happening, you can't have any sense that anything is happening *to* you. When you feel a healthy sense of yourself, you don't feel defensive. Even if you experience what looks like separation in the form of a parking ticket, you can't separate. With the officer, I couldn't separate from his consciousness. The empathy I felt for his frustration fused a connection. This connection fed a need. The officer vented and released his pent-up frustration, and the outcome for me was that I *had* paid for parking.

This would be unfathomable to the thinking ego-mind. If we resort to thinking, we are going to want the right outcome for us. We create an "us" and a "them." When we feel separate, we feel the need to protect ourselves. We create the need for a particular outcome.

In non-duality, it never occurs to us to have a preferred out-come. If you get a ticket, you get a ticket, and something arises from that. Something is always arising in non-duality or joy. We can't feel, "I won because I didn't get the ticket." The outcome is myste-rious. *Please know that this is really truly not positive thinking.*

Positive thinking requires positive thoughts. Joy does not *think*. Joy directly experiences what is occurring without doing battle with it.

There are ways that you see and experience life that help you feel like who you are. That is when you are living the healthy ego. The healthy ego cannot feel attacked. Your clear mind recognizes injustices and is interested in listening deeply, communicating, and creating the highest outcome. The healthy ego is curious about what is happening. This curious, open mind is more awake. Potential connections foster resolutions.

Keeping Custody of Your Joy

Two characters on this planet who are in constant joy at this time are (1) the spiritual author Eckhart Tolle, and (2) the surfer dude turtle, Crush in the children's movie *Finding Nemo*. A runner up would be Dory, also from *Finding Nemo*. Dory is a cute fish with an Ellen DeGeneres voice who is curious and has no boundaries. She just swims up to you and wants to play tag. Dear Dory's only challenge is that she has short-term memory loss. She doesn't quite stay in joy as she gets nervous to the point of corrupting it. Still, she comes back to joy real fast—not being able to hold her thoughts helps.

Our task as humans learning to live joyfully is to allow all our feelings to show us how to be who we are. And forget poverty-consciousness, fear-based, limiting thoughts. Since I first experienced constant joy, I sometimes feel as though no one gets how amazing we are. Does anybody else feel this way? I can feel so alive that I turn into a smiling idiot, and I'm not so sure how to go to the variety store in a normal fashion like all the other struggling souls. At exactly the same time, just knowing the struggle is an inside job shows me how very connected we are in this painful inner terrain we create.

When I was in Thailand, we went scuba diving in the most beatific outcropping of coral. I quickly discovered that you cannot smile largely when under water, regardless of how awe-inspiring the oceanic display of colour is! The more I lifted the corners of my mouth, smiling with fantastic delight, the more the water seeped into my face mask. "Sarah has to see this!" I thought. I felt as though my heart was going to burst. I soon came to realize that it's very hard to feel so much joy, beauty, awe, amazement, and connection without sharing it. It's heart-wrenching not to connect and share beauty each day. Joy expands our experience of life and helps us develop connections wherever we go.

After realizing that joy can be constant, I felt displaced. I didn't know how to feel so alive and free *and* be here in life. Living in joy constantly opens you up. I wasn't sure if living in a closed society was dangerous. Where do I go with this openness? Does anybody want a hug?

Joy dilates your senses, and there is no turning back. By giving joy its rightful place in life—by honouring that living in joy may be a sacred continuum that can feel isolating at times—I have learned to hone its aspects. I have learned to respect the fact that I cannot view any circumstance as bad or good. A delicate antenna cues me to leave a conversation when talk gets uncomfortably corrosive.

Living this freely means I talk about what I am discovering rather than what a person did or who won the World Cup. Germany won the World Cup last week. I heard that. Do I care? I care about what it felt like for the person who was telling me. That's where the juice is. That's where I get a piece of them and learn what makes their world splendid.

A clear mind needs space. I spend more time in nature, silence, listening, and breathing. I respect my introvert. I can't report how the stock market is doing or what President Trump said today.

(Thank you, Jesus.) At times I feel like the ditz at the party. Yet I have come to see that by living from a place of joy, my mind doesn't spend time on ho-hum data that are not meaningful.

I don't even have a vested interest in the activities I choose. This means it's not *important* that I practise yoga every day; it's that I chose to. This leaves lots of room to practise how I need to. I'll do yoga at the airport, bum high in the air, before I'm high in the air. (This is so good for your circulation before your flight, it's ridiculous!)

When you get to a point in your life, day, or this moment when you feel as though you *can't* do something (and this can be any aspiration, flossing counts), then know that what you are feeling and its accompanying thought are *false*. There is no life in that thought. Feel who you are. Who are you? You are the soul holding this book realizing that you have that question—and you are opening to *all* of life with that curiosity. Head outside, get on your skateboard, head for the ramp, and maybe you'll get to the other side. Who knows? And by the way, aren't those guys *good*?

The end.

Not of joy.

APPENDICES

*"The web of life both cradles us and
calls to us to weave it further."*

~ JOANNA MACY, AMERICAN
ENVIRONMENTAL ACTIVIST, AUTHOR,
AND SCHOLAR OF BUDDHISM

The Qualities of Joy

Speed Date each of the following qualities to evoke your sense of self which is constant joy.

1. It isn't possible to feel alone.
2. I don't follow a belief system or religion.
3. I don't lose energy or feel any different when I'm around negative people.
4. I am with "what is."
5. Nothing is a problem.
6. My mind isn't wired to struggle; it's naturally peaceful.
7. Loving thoughts replace worrying.
8. I have no opinions about what is happening.
9. I am not optimistic; I don't use mental gymnastics to be positive.
10. True discipline is only structural; it doesn't define how I stick with my choice.

11. I exercise even when I don't feel like it.

12. I am clear and truthful with my words.

13. I am my own inspiration.

14. I can find clarity in the unknown.

15. Each experience in life expands and broadens me.

16. My sense of self-direction doesn't separate me from others. I know I can be unique and I'm *not* selfish.

17. I don't apologize or wait to see if it's okay to do what I need.

18. If I have a disagreement with someone it doesn't build into a conflict.

19. I experience only healthy ego.

20. I have no expectations.

21. I am in flux.

22. I trust.

23. I feel each feeling.

24. I welcome and milk fearful thoughts.

25. I have a keen sense for what to do.

26. I am intrigued when I feel discouraged.

27. When emotionally corrupted, I reach out or do what I need to do.

28. I experience life directly and act according to what is true for me.

29. I continuously integrate my experiences into my life. (Because I do this as I go along, this direct experience of life means I often need less time to process what has happened.)

30. I am nourished by and feast on life. The opposite of being a foodie.

Breathing 101

Learning how to breathe isn't so much about learning how to do something right, it's about getting back in touch with the natural rhythms of your body. Although your breathing is controlled by your nervous system and occurs automatically, you don't want to leave this mechanism of the body to chance. Ineffective breathing reduces your capacity to live joyfully. Ineffective breathing reduces your lung capacity, which means you would inhale less air with each breath, which would mean that you would have to breathe faster, and this revs up your nervous system, which affects your heart rate, blood pressure, and whether you will floss.

By learning to breathe you get familiar with what your body feels like to be relaxed and peaceful, which is actually your natural state. This is a reassuring message; it shows you that you can operate from a more centred and creative state of mind. The following breathing exercise can help you increase your concentration, return to joy, and release the grip of emotional angst.

Sit and Breathe

- Sit as tall and comfortably as you can on a sturdy chair with your feet flat on the floor. (Be careful not to tuck your pelvis under you; sit up on your sitz bones.)
- Lift your shoulders and the let them gently roll back and down.
- Feel as though you are sinking into yourself like flour folded into batter. (Sorry if you were hungry when you started.)
- Imagine a string lifting you from your sitz bones and up through the top of your head (your chin is slightly tilted down).
- Feel your ribs separate as you lift your spine.
- Keep your mouth gently closed and relax the base of your tongue in your mouth.
- Notice your breathing without changing it.
- Feel your face relax.
- As your jaw relaxes, feel a space open between your upper and lower teeth.
- Notice the feeling of your breath coming in and out through your nose. Feel the warmth of it as you inhale. Notice if there is a sensation when you exhale.
- Continue breathing and noticing for as long as you can or wish; three minutes is an excellent minimum length of time.

Dealing with Joy Corruptors

When you stop feeling joy, look up the feeling that is disturbing you in the first column, and then go to the second column to learn what you can do to return to who you are, which is joy. This column also gives you the page number in the text where the feeling is discussed. The third column will validate why you were feeling this way.

When you feel ...	Do the following ...	Reasons for the feeling
Doubt	Feel proud that you can feel disrupted by doubt. Doubt shows you that you don't know how to continue doing something, so be interested in figuring out how to keep going. Look at doubt as a test: Will you let it distract you? Do you know what is important to you? (See page 50.)	Doubt shows you that you are growing. It is a tipping point in your personal evolution. Doubt is fear. The fear in doubt messes with your mind and tries to convince you that you don't have the right to do what is important to you.

Confusion	Feel good about being confused. Confusion reveals that you *want* to get clear. Pause and be okay with the fact that you may not know *right now* what to do. Remember why you are doing what you're doing or why you started. Reawaken what it feels like to be inspired by your own vision. (See page 33.)	Confusion shows you that you are willing to be open to all that you can learn.
You don't know how to trust yourself	Connect with others who have done what you're doing. Reach out as soon as you can and create support in your life. Keep voicing your concerns, fears, doubts, and scaredy-cat moments until they become interesting. Reach out to someone in your life with whom you can air your frustrations with abandoned expression and be truly heard without interruption until you feel completely empty. If you don't have someone in your life who is capable of doing this, hire someone. (Kidding, mostly.) Instead, direct and command the person who *is* right there in your life and is available to only listen without interrupting. Tell this person that you need a friend to support you so you can grasp what you are feeling. (See page 55.)	Recognize that not feeling trust in yourself means you feel separate. You need to feel that someone is supporting you.

Ugly, Unworthy, Not good enough	Feel compassion for yourself. Gently affirm what is important to you. Feel what you want to be in your life right now, whatever the aspiration is. Name the change you want to be. For example, if you feel you should lose weight, access how feeling alive and fit would feel for you. You are not allowed to spend any time feeling unworthy. Unworthy feelings cut you off from life and others (same thing). You cannot feel joy, or like yourself, if you don't feel that you're enough. Do what you need to do to feel like *you*. (See page 91.)	You are finding a reason to slow yourself down. (Then we can deflect self-responsibility and have a "reason" why we aren't successful.) You feel ugly when you compare yourself to others. Realize that you feel ugly because you want to have a reason why you can't do what you are setting out to do. For example, maybe you want to lose weight, and you see someone who is fit. You don't feel good because you wish you didn't have the extra weight *right now*. Feeling ugly gives you an excuse to offset or ignore your aspiration (weight-loss goal). You delay when you feel ugly. You become discouraged. Feeling ugly is a form of doubt.
As though you are wrong	Recognize that you don't know how to know what is true for you. Stand strong and feel alone in what you know is true. "Alone" is not separate. Its true essence is "all one." We are all one—connected— when we are alone.	You don't know what is true for you. You may feel that you are being "called out" on what you know and uncertain how to stand in your truth. Good! Excellent! This is a test of your evolution.

As though you are wrong (cont'd)	We stand in our unique contribution in the world and this connects us to our intelligence, which knows what is true for us by being all that we are. (See page 27.)	
As though you need to settle down or get real	Clasp your hands behind your head, press elbows back—far if that feels good, breathe in deeply, lift your chin, look up; take three deep breaths. Take your arms from behind your head. Shake your hands vigorously for five seconds as though shaking off water. Feel the reason you are doing what you are doing, saying what you're saying, or acting the way you are. Own it. (See page 27.)	You are being requested by life and the circumstances you are in to be true to yourself. This is a test in your evolution. Your circumstances are asking you to keep alive what you know.
Selfish, Guilty	Access your courage: You do *not* need to explain why you are doing what you're doing. Keep the reason you are doing what you're doing alive. Just start what you want to do and then do what you need to do to keep going. Enlist support or do something for yourself that feels fabulous. (See page 71.)	You may feel selfish or guilty if you think you're "not allowed" to do something, such as make a major change in your life. Guilt can be a signal that you have done something for yourself.

Angry	Use Nonviolent Communication (NVC.org) to express what you need to say. If the other person or group isn't listening, keep your truth—what you know—germinating inside you. Keep alive what you know no matter what! This is absolutely necessary. Let no one or no thing deny you your truth. To do this, find a way to feel supported in what you know. Take time to care for yourself in this new, angry feeling that could be shutting you down. Stay open to the growth this uncomfortable feeling is offering you. Also, listen to Rumi: *"Don't think the garden loses its ecstasy in winter. It's quiet, but the roots are down there riotous."* (See page 11.)	There are two kinds of anger: (1) Unhealthy anger, and (2) Useful anger. Unhealthy anger is a deflection. It blames people and circumstances for what (in your mind) is happening to "you." Unhealthy anger creates excuses. Unhealthy anger is also a cover-up for anxiety. You don't know how to have a strong sense of Self that has healthy boundaries. You are afraid you will harm your connection with the person you are angry with as you don't know how to feel what you need. Useful anger has a lot of emotional hutzpah that gives you focus and bravery. Useful anger allows you to cut through what you don't believe in and take action. Useful anger allows you to stay on track and remove obstacles.
Pity for yourself (See "Ugly")	See page 91.	

Lack of courage, fear	Take action or be still. Stand in this moment of feeling a lack of courage and fearful. There is life in being in the immobilizing fear. There is a strong propelling force when you stand in fear and let the stymying, shaky feeling show you how much you want to do what you are trying to do. The fearful feeling is showing you how important it is to you. Just start. You must. Start now. (See page 55.)	Courage leaves your building when you let all the reasons "why I can't" take over your mind.
Anxiety	Closeness will help alleviate anxiety. Reach out to someone to express yourself and feel touched, held, supported, and nurtured in the way you need to be. If you don't have the support you need in your life, then set out to create it. Also express your anxiety, write it out, move it out, dance it, or do artwork. (See page 106.)	Anxiety is a condition of persistent and uncontrollable nervousness, stress, and worry that is triggered by anticipation of future events, memories of past events, or ruminations over day-to-day events—trivial and major—with disproportionate fears of catastrophic consequences. Anxiety reveals that you feel scared. You don't know what to do or how to feel this unsure.

Tired	Do Laughter Yoga (see the resources section). Get outside, breathe deeply, do some gentle or vigorous exercise. Share what you are feeling with someone who can listen deeply and mirror back to you what they see you are feeling without judging you. (See page 58.)	You feel depleted, when you don't know how to go on or let go enough to sleep fully; this weary depletion happens when you are discouraged or feel overwhelmed.
Uninspired and you're going to skip exercising	How your body feels is more important than any other feeling. A freer body is able to feel more joy and adapt better to stress. Schedule your exercise time as you would for your office hours so you do it no matter what. If you know you won't stick with this on your own, set up a time to exercise with a buddy. Be realistic about whether you will exercise and identify the excuses you know you may make, and then set up a plan to address the excuse. For example, if you know you may skip exercising because you feel tired, make an agreement with someone to commit to meeting to exercise together. (See page 58.)	You don't know how to value yourself. You don't know how to begin. You're afraid that you won't do it again after today, like last time. So, you think, "Why start?"

List of Needs

The following list of needs, courtesy of the Center for Nonviolent Communication,[1] is neither exhaustive nor definitive. It is meant as a starting place to support anyone who wishes to engage in a process of deepening self-discovery and to facilitate greater understanding and connection between people.

CONNECTION
acceptance
affection
appreciation
belonging
cooperation
communication
closeness
community
companionship
compassion
consideration
consistency
empathy
inclusion
intimacy
love
mutuality
nurturing
respect/
   self-respect
safety
security

CONNECTION continued
stability
support
to know and be
   known
to see and be seen
to understand and
   be understood
trust
warmth

PHYSICAL WELL-BEING
air
food
movement/exercise
rest/sleep
sexual expression
safety
shelter
touch
water

HONESTY
authenticity
integrity
presence

PLAY
joy
humor

PEACE
beauty
communion
ease
equality
harmony
inspiration
order

AUTONOMY
choice
freedom
independence
space
spontaneity

MEANING
awareness
celebration of
   life
challenge
clarity
competence
consciousness
contribution
creativity
discovery
efficacy
effectiveness
growth
hope
learning
mourning
participation
purpose
self-expression
stimulation
to matter
understanding

[1]Center for Nonviolent Communication (CNVC), "Needs Inventory," © 2005 by Center for Nonviolent Communication, Website: www.cnvc.org, Email: envc@cnvc.org, Phone: +1.505-244-4041.

RESOURCES

Books

Alexander, Rolf. *The Healing Power of the Mind: Practical Techniques for Health and Empowerment.* Rochester, VT: Healing Arts Press, 1989.

Alexander, Eben. *Proof of Heaven: A Neurosurgeon's Journey into the Afterlife.* New York: Simon & Schuster, 2012.

Amen, Daniel G. *Change Your Brain Change Your Life: The Breakthrough Program for Conquering Anxiety, Depression, Obsessiveness, Anger, and Impulsiveness.* New York: Three Rivers Press, 1998.

Aurobindo, Sri. *Bases of Yoga.* Twin Lakes, WI: Lotus Press, 1985.

_____. *Essays on the Gita.* Twin Lakes, WI: Lotus Light Publications, 1995.

_____. *The Integral Yoga: Sri Aurobindo's Teaching and Method of Practice.* Twin Lakes, WI: Lotus Press, 1993.

_____. *The Life Divine,* 2nd ed. Twin Lakes, WI: Lotus Press, 1990.

Bailey, Elisabeth. *The Sound of a Wild Snail Eating: A True Story.* New York: Workman Publishing, 2010.

Barks, Coleman, trans. *The Essential Rumi.* New York: HarperCollins Publishers, 1995.

Beck, Martha. *Expecting Adam: A True Story of Birth, Rebirth, and Everyday Magic.* New York: Three Rivers Press, 2011.

_____. *The Joy Diet: 10 Daily Practices for a Happier Life.* New York: Crown Publishers, 2003.

Brennan, Barbara Ann. *Light Emerging: The Journey of Personal Healing.* New York: Bantam New Age Books, 1993.

Brezsny, Rob. *Pronoia Is the Antidote for Paranoia: How the Whole World Is Conspiring to Shower You with Blessings.* Berkeley, CA: North Atlantic Books, 2009.

Brown, Brené. *I Thought It Was Just Me (but it isn't): Making the Journey from "What Will People Think?" to "I am Enough"*. New York: Gotham Books, 2007.

Bushrui, Suheil, ed. *The Essential Gibran*. Oxford, UK: Oneworld Publications, 2006.

Chödrön, Pema. *Practicing Peace in Times of War*. Boulder, CO: Shambhala Publications, 2007.

Degler, Teri. *The Divine Feminine Fire: Creativity and Your Yearning to Express Your Self*. Brooklyn, NY: Dreamriver Press, 2009.

_____. *Fiery Muse: Creativity and the Spiritual Quest*. Toronto, ON: Random House, 1996.

Doidge, Norman. *The Brain That Changes Itself: Stories of Personal Triumph from the Frontiers of Brain Science*. New York: Penguin Books, 2007.

_____. *The Brain's Way of Healing: Remarkable Discoveries and Recoveries from the Frontiers of Neuroplasticity*. New York: Viking, 2015.

Dupont, Caroline Marie. *Enlightened Eating: Nourishment for Body and Soul*. Summertown, TN: Book Publishing Company, 2007.

Feuerstein, Georg. *Tantra: The Path of Ecstasy*. Boston, MA: Shambala, 1998.

_____. *Yoga: The Technology of Ecstasy*. Los Angeles: TarcherPerigee, 1989.

_____. *The Yoga-Sutra of Patañjali: A New Translation and Commentary*. Rochester, VT: Inner Traditions Bear & Company, 1992.

Fox, Matthew. *The Coming of the Cosmic Christ*. New York: HarperCollins, 1988.

_____. *Creativity: Where the Divine and the Human Meet*. New York: Jeremy P. Tarcher/Penguin, 2004.

Fraser, Sylvia. *The Rope in the Water: A Pilgrimage to India*. Markham, ON: Thomas Allen & Son, 2001.

Friends of Peace Pilgrim, eds. *Peace Pilgrim: Her Life and Work in Her Own Words*. Hemet, CA: Ocean Tree Books, 1998.

Gannnon, Sharon, and David Life. *Jivamukti Yoga: Practices for Liberating Body and Soul*. New York: Ballantine Books. 2002.

Gibran, Kahlil. *The Prophet*. New York: Alfred A. Knopf, 1973.

Gordon, Mary. *Roots of Empathy: Changing the World, Child by Child*. Toronto, ON: Thomas Allen Publishers, 2007.

Hardy, Janet W., and Dossie Easton. *The Ethical Slut: A Practical Guide to Polyamory, Open Relationships, and Other Freedoms in Sex and Love.* Berkeley, CA: Ten Speed Press, 2017.

Hawkins, David R. *The Eye of the I: From Which Nothing Is Hidden.* Carlsbad, CA: Hay House Publishing, 2001.

_____. *Power vs. Force: The Hidden Determinants of Human Behavior.* Carlsbad, CA: Hay House Publishing, 2012.

Housden, Roger. *Ten Poems to Change Your Life.* New York: Harmony Books, 2001.

Jois, Sri K. Pattabhi. *Yoga Mala: The Original Teachings of Ashtanga Yoga Master Sri. K. Pattabhi Jois.* New York: North Point Press, 2010.

Krishnamurti, Jiddu. *The Awakening of Intelligence.* New York: Harper-One, 1987.

_____. *Education and the Significance of Life.* New York: HarperCollins, 1981.

_____. *On Fear.* New York: HarperOne, 1994.

_____. *On Love and Loneliness.* New York: HarperOne, 1994.

Kraftsow, Gary. *Yoga for Wellness: Healing with the Timeless Teachings of Viniyoga.* New York: Penguin Compass, 1999.

Lipton, Bruce H. *The Biology of Belief: Unleashing the Power of Consciousness, Matter & Miracles.* Carlsbad, CA: Hay House Publishing, 2016.

Lussier, Reine-Claire, and Mario Gaal, *Ojja 2: Gaiayoga: Teachings for Our Souls.* Québec, QC: Éditions Gaiayoga, 2006.

Lussier, Reine-Claire, and Anna Takahashi, *The Yoga of Vowels.* Québec, QC: Éditions Gaiayoga, 2005.

Marx Hubbard, Barbara. *Emergence: The Shift from Ego to Essence.* Newburyport, MA: Hampton Roads Publishing, 2012.

_____. *The Hunger of Eve: One Woman's Odyssey Toward The Future.* Eastbound, WA: Sweet Forever Publishing, 1989.

Malone, Thomas Patrick. *The Art of Intimacy.* New York: Simon & Schuster, 1987.

Macy, Joanna. *World as Lover, World as Self: A Guide to Living Fully in Turbulent Times.* Berkeley, CA: Parallax Press, 2007.

Macy, Joanna, and Chris Johnstone. *Active Hope: How to Face the Mess We're in without Going Crazy.* Novato, CA: New World Library, 2012.

Mahesh, Maharishi Yogi. *Science of Being and Art of Living: Transcendental Meditation*. New York: Penguin Books, 2001.

Maté, Gabor. *When the Body Says No: The Cost of Hidden Stress*. Toronto, ON: Vintage Canada, 2004.

May, Rollo. *The Courage to Create*. New York: W.W. Norton & Company, 1975.

Murphy, Michael. *The Future of the Body: Explorations into the Further Evolution of Human Nature*. New York: Penguin Putnam, 1992.

Northrup, Christiane. *Mother-Daughter Wisdom: Understanding the Crucial Link between Mothers, Daughters, and Health*. New York: Bantam Books, 2006.

———. *Women's Bodies, Women's Wisdom: Creating Physical and Emotional Health and Healing*. New York: Bantam Books, 2010.

O'Donohue, John. *Divine Beauty: The Invisible Embrace*. London, UK: Bantam Press, 2003.

Oriah. *The Dance: Moving to the Deep Rhythms of Your Life*. New York: HarperOne, 2009.

———. *The Invitation*. New York: HarperOne, 2006.

Palmer, Amanda. *The Art of Asking: How I Learned to Stop Worrying and Let People Help*. New York: Grand Central Publishing, 2014.

Pearce, Joseph Chilton. *The Biology of Transcendence: A Blueprint of the Human Spirit*. Rochester, VT: Park Street Press, 2004.

———. *The Crack in the Cosmic Egg: Challenging Constructs of Mind and Reality*. New York: Crown Publishers, 1971.

Pink, Daniel H. *A Whole New Mind: Why Right-Brainers Will Rule the Future*. New York: Riverhead Books, 2006.

Roche, Lorin. *The Radiance Sutras: 112 Gateways to the Yoga of Wonder & Delight*. Boulder, CO: Sounds True, 2014.

Rosenberg, Marshall B. *Nonviolent Communication: A Language of Life: Life-Changing Tools for Healthy Relationships*. Encinitas, CA: PuddleDancer Press, 2015.

Roth Gabrielle. *Sweat Your Prayers: The Five Rhythms of the Soul—Movement as Spiritual Practice*. New York: Jeremy P. Tarcher/Putnam, 1998.

Roth, Gabrielle, and John Louden. *Maps to Ecstasy: A Healing Journey for the Untamed Spirit*. Novato, CA: New World Library, 1998.

Roth, Geneen. *Women Food and God: An Unexpected Path to Almost Everything.* New York: Scribner, 2011.

Ruiz, Don Miguel. *The Four Agreements: A Practical Guide to Personal Freedom.* San Rafael, CA: Amber-Allen Publishing, 1997.

_____. *The Mastery of Love: A Practical Guide to the Art of Relationship.* San Rafael, CA: Amber-Allen Publishing, 1999.

Salzberg, Sharon. *The Force of Kindness: Change Your Life with Love & Compassion.* Boulder, CO: Sounds True, 2010.

Saraswati, Swami Satyananda. *Asana Pranayama Mudra Bandha.* Bengaluru, India: Nesma Books India, 2008.

Satprem. *The Mind of the Cells.* New York: Institute for Evolutionary Research, 1982.

_____. *Sri Aurobindo or the Adventure of Consciousness.* New Delhi, India: The Mother's Institute of Research, 2000.

Scaravelli, Vanda. *Awakening of the Spine: Yoga for Health, Vitality and Energy.* New York: Harper One, 2015.

Schiffmann, Eric. *Yoga: The Spirit and Practice of Moving into Stillness.* New York: Pocket Books, 1996.

Shepherd, Philip. *New Self, New World: Recovering Our Senses in the Twenty-First Century.* Berkeley, CA: North Atlantic Books, 2010.

Singer, Michael A. *The Untethered Soul: The Journey Beyond Yourself.* Oakland, CA: New Harbinger Publications, 2007.

Starhawk. *Dreaming the Dark: Magic, Sex and Politics.* Boston, MA: Beacon Press, 1982.

Tolle, Eckhart. *A New Earth: Awakening to Your Life's Purpose.* New York: Penguin Books, 2016.

Trungpa, Chögyam. *Shambhala: The Sacred Path of the Warrior.* Boston, MA: Shambhala Publications, 2007.

_____. *The Myth of Freedom and the Way of Meditation.* Boston, MA: Shambhala Publications, 2007.

Vasil, Adria. *Ecoholic Body: Your Ultimate Earth-Friendly Guide to Living Healthy & Looking Good.* Toronto, ON: Vintage Canada, 2012.

Venable Raine, Nancy. *After Silence: Rape & My Journey Back.* New York: Three Rivers Press. 1998.

Weed, Susun S. *Menopausal Years: The Wise Woman Way: Alternative*

Approaches for Women 30–90. New York: Ash Tree Publishing, 1992.

Wilber, Ken. *No Boundary: Eastern and Western Approaches to Personal Growth*. Boston, MA: Shambhala Publications, 2001.

William, Anthony. *Life-Changing Foods: Save Yourself and the Ones You Love with the Hidden Healing Powers of Fruits & Vegetables*. Carlsbad, CA: Hay House Publishing, 2016.

Zukav, Gary. *The Seat of the Soul*. New York: Simon & Schuster, 1989.

Children's Books

Boritzer, Etan, and Robbie Marantz. *What is God?* Richmond Hill, ON: Firefly Books, 1990.

Hicks, Jerry, and Esther W. Hicks. *Sara and the Foreverness of Friends of a Feather*. San Antonia, TX: Abraham-Hicks Publications, 2000.

Munsch, Robert, and Michael Martchenko. *The Paper Bag Princess*. Toronto, ON: Annick Press, 2002.

Silverstein, Shel. *The Giving Tree*. New York: HarperCollins, 2014.

Striker, Susan. *The Anti-Coloring Book: Creative Activities for Ages 6 and Up*. New York: Henry Holt and Company, 2001.

Movies and YouTube Videos

Captain Fantastic (Drama/Comedy). Director: Matt Ross. Starring Viggo Mortensen. 2016.

> Ben and his wife, Leslie, and their six children live deep in the wilderness of Washington State. Isolated from society, Ben and Leslie devote their existence to raising their kids, educating them to think critically, training them to be physically fit, guiding them in the wild without technology, and demonstrating the beauty of co-existing with nature. When Leslie dies suddenly, Ben must take his intelligent offspring into the outside world for the first time. I show this movie to my teen yoga class to promote discussion and bravery.

Inner Worlds, Outer Worlds (Documentary). Producer/Director: Daniel Schmidt. Narrator: Patrick Sweeney. 2012.

Canadian Daniel Schmidt, the creator of this documentary, is also a musician and meditation teacher. The film explores the nature of reality and seeks to bridge the gap between the inner world of our conscious experience and the outer world with which we interact and yet have little control over.

Miss Representation (Documentary). Director: Jennifer Siebel Newson. Screenplay: Jennifer Siebel Newsom, Jessica Congdon, Claire Dietrich, and Jenny Raskin. Featuring: Jennifer Siebel Newsom, Geena Davis, and Gloria Steinem. 2011.

This documentary exposes how mainstream media and culture depict women, demonstrating why they feel the way they do about their bodies and their relationships with men. I show this documentary to my teen yoga class to help them see the influences they may not realize they are buying into.

Take This Waltz (Drama). Director: Sarah Polley. Screenplay: Sarah Polley. Starring Michelle Williams, Seth Rogen, and Luke Kirby. 2012.

This movie explores the concept of marriage, relationships, and intimate needs. The characters help us relate to our own questions and perhaps suppressed needs.

The Princess Bride (Fantasy/Romance). Director: Rob Reiner, Screenplay: William Goldman. Starring Cary Elwes and Robin Wright. 1987.

Based on William Goldman's novel of the same name, this is a fairy-tale adventure about a fantastically loving young woman and her one true love. It is filled with life lessons, and I recommend it for children of all ages, and especially crusty older adults.

Unity: The Interconnectedness of Life on Earth, The Orchard (Documentary). Director: Shaun Monson. Narrators: 100 celebrities, including Ben Kingsley, Ellen DeGeneres, Joaquin Phoenix, and Helen Mirren.

This compassionate, powerful, and inspiring film is about being kind to each other, ourselves, and all the beings on this beautiful planet.

"Famous violinist, Joshua Bell, plays in a subway station." YouTube video, 2007, https://www.youtube.com/watch?v=ULbxxP4mSNI.

This two-and-a-half-minute YouTube video begins with the following introduction: "A man sat at a metro station in Washington DC and started to play the violin; it was a cold January morning. He played six Bach pieces for about 45 minutes." The violinist was Joshua Bell, "one of the best musicians in the world." Only young children, one under three years old, stopped to listen, almost everyone else hurried to work. This slice of life in a metro station shows the amount of time people have to stop and be enchanted.

Selected Websites

Celeste Shirley, Celesteshirley.com. Visit my website for many videos related to this book, including yoga exercises for anxiety and how to feel difficult emotions and stay in joy.

The Center for Nonviolent Communication, www.cnvc.org. Marshall Rosenberg began this four-step communication model to help individuals speak from the heart. It is useful in any situation where there are disagreements. I even used his technique while on my bike and being bullied by an angry driver.

Gaia, www.gaia.com. This site is a resource for inspirational and thought-provoking films, documentaries, and video interviews on yoga and exercise, truth seeking, and consciousness raising (transformation). You can stream these programs on the screen of your choice. When I want to experience entirely new classes in dance, yoga, or pilates, or I want to improve my handstand or core strength, I go here.

HeartMath Institute, www.heartmath.org. The HeartMath Institute provides scientifically based tools to help individuals, families, groups, and organizations bridge the connection between their hearts and minds to enhance their life experiences and deepen their connection with the hearts of others.

The Institute for Noetic Sciences (IONS), noetic.org. The goal stated of the Institute of Noetic Sciences is "to create a shift in consciousness worldwide—where people recognize that we are all part of an inter-connected whole and are inspired to take action to help humanity and the planet thrive."[1] You can watch a great video on YouTube that outlines what they are about: https://www.youtube.com/watch?time_continue=121&v=1lP2UNszIKc.

Laughter Yoga International. https://laughteryoga.org. Laughter Yoga was developed by a medical doctor from India, Dr. Madan Kataria, the "Laughter Yoga Guru," and it has spread worldwide. This site will help you find trainers, workshops, and laughter clubs in your area, and it is full of Laughter Yoga "exercises." I became a certified teacher of Laughter Yoga after training with Dr. Kataria. I have found that the effects of "laughing for no reason" are as powerful as meditation, and I recommend it highly. Laughter yoga oxygenates the body and brain and it has been scientifically proven to lower the level of stress hormones and reduce blood pressure.

Roots of Empathy. http://rootsofempathy.org. Roots of Empathy is an international organization that offers empathy-based programs for children from kindergarten to grade eight. Its aim is to break the intergenerational cycle of violence and poor parenting by building the capacity in the next generation for responsive parenting through raising levels of empathy, which will result in more caring relation-ships and reduced levels of bullying and aggression and promote children's positive social behaviours.

TED Talks: Jill Bolte Taylor; TED2008: "My Stroke of Insight," https://www.ted.com/talks/jill_bolte_taylor_s_powerful_stroke_of_insight.

TED Talks: Amanda Palmer, TED2013: "The Art of Asking," https://www.ted.com/talks/amanda_palmer_the_art_of_asking.

[1]Institute of Noetic Sciences. "IONS Overview: Our Goal" (2018), http://noetic.org/about/overview.